# SHAMANS THROUGH TIME

# SHAMANS
## Through Time

### 500 YEARS ON THE PATH
### TO KNOWLEDGE

*Edited by*

## Jeremy Narby and Francis Huxley

JEREMY P. TARCHER/PUTNAM

*a member of Penguin Putnam Inc.*

NEW YORK

Most Tarcher/Putnam books are available at special quantity discounts for bulk purchases for sales promotions, premiums, fund-raising, and educational needs. Special books or book excerpts also can be created to fit specific needs. For details, write Putnam Special Markets, 375 Hudson Street, New York, NY 10014.

Jeremy P. Tarcher/Putnam
a member of
Penguin Putnam Inc.
375 Hudson Street
New York, NY 10014
www.penguinputnam.com

Library of Congress Cataloging-in-Publication Data

   Shamans through time / edited by Jeremy Narby and Francis Huxley.
      p.   cm.
   Includes bibliographical references and index.
   ISBN 1-58542-091-3
   1. Shamanism.   I. Narby, Jeremy.   II. Huxley, Francis.
   BL2370.S5 S526     2001                00-054538
   291.1'44—dc21

Printed in the United States of America

10  9  8  7  6  5  4  3  2  1

This book is printed on acid-free paper.☉

*Book design by Jennifer Ann Daddio*

# Contents

Note to Readers    *xi*

Introduction: Five Hundred Years of Shamans and Shamanism
*Jeremy Narby and Francis Huxley*    *1*

## PART ONE
## The Christian View: "Ministers of the Devil"

1. "Devil Worship: Consuming Tobacco to Receive Messages
from Nature" (1535)    *Gonzalo Fernandez de Oviedo*    *11*

2. "Ministers of the Devil Who Learn About the Secrets
of Nature" (1557)    *André Thévet*    *13*

3. "Evoking the Devil: Fasting with Tobacco to Learn How
to Cure" (1664)    *Antoine Biet*    *16*

4. The Shaman: "A Villain of a Magician Who Calls Demons"
(1672)    *Avvakum Petrovich*    *18*

PART TWO

## The Humanist View Becomes Rationalist:
## From "Esteemed Jugglers" to "Impostors"

5. "The Savages Esteem Their Jugglers"
   (1724)   *Joseph François Lafitau*                                        23

6. "Shamans Deserve Perpetual Labor for Their Hocus-Pocus"
   (1751)   *Johann Georg Gmelin*                                            27

7. "Blinded by Superstition"
   (1755)   *Stepan Petrovich Krasheninnikov*                                29

8. "Shamans Are Impostors Who Claim They Consult
   the Devil—And Who Are Sometimes Close
   to the Mark" (1765)   *Denis Diderot and colleagues*                      32

9. Misled Impostors and the Power of Imagination
   (1785)   *Johann Gottfried Herder*                                        36


PART THREE

## Enter Anthropologists

10. Animism Is the Belief in Spiritual Beings
    (1871)   *Edward B. Tylor*                                               41

11. A White Man Goes to a *Peaiman*
    (1883)   *Everard F. Im Thurn*                                           43

12. The *Angakoq* Uses a Peculiar Language and
    Defines Taboos (1887)   *Franz Boas*                                     47

13. The-Man-Who-Fell-from-Heaven Shamanizes
    Despite Persecution (1896)   *Wenceslas Sieroshevski*                    49

14. *Shamanism* Is a Dangerously Vague Word
    (1903)   *Arnold Van Gennep*                                            51

15. "Doomed to Inspiration" (1904)   *Waldemar Bogoras*                     53

16. Ventriloquist and Trickster Performances for Healing
    and Divination (1908)   *Vladimir Ilich Jochelson*                    *58*

17. "A Motley Class of Persons" (1908)   *Roland B. Dixon*               *64*

18. Seeking Contact with Spirits Is Not Necessarily
    Shamanism (1910)   *Franz Boas*                                        *69*

19. "The Shaman Practices on the Verge of Insanity"
    (1914)   *Marie Antoinette Czaplicka*                                 *72*


PART FOUR

## The Understanding Deepens

20. Near-Death Experience
    (1929)   *Ivalo and Knud Rasmussen*                                   *79*

21. Seeking Knowledge in the Solitude of Nature
    (1930)   *Igjugârjuk and Knud Rasmussen*                              *81*

22. Summoning the Spirits for the First Time
    (1932)   *Black Elk and John G. Neihardt*                             *84*

23. The Shaman's Assistant (1935)   *Sergei M. Shirokogoroff*            *90*

24. Shamans Charm Game (1938)   *Willard Z. Park*                        *94*

25. Climbing the Twisted Ladder to Initiation
    (1944)   *Alfred Métraux*                                             *97*

26. Aboriginal Doctors Are Outstanding People
    (1945)   *Adolphus Peter Elkin*                                      *103*

27. Shamans as Psychoanalysts (1949)   *Claude Lévi-Strauss*            *108*

28. Using Invisible Substances for Good and Evil
    (1949)   *Alfred Métraux*                                            *112*

29. The Shamanin Performs a Public Service with
    Grace and Energy (1955)   *Verrier Elwin*                            *115*

30. "The Shaman Is Mentally Deranged"
    (1956)   *George Devereux*                                           *119*

31. Clever Cords and Clever Men (1957)   *Ronald Rose*   *121*

32. Singing Multifaceted Songs (1958)   *Vilmos Diószegi*   *128*

33. !Kung Medicine Dance (1962)   *Lorna Marshall*   *131*

PART FIVE

## The Observers Take Part

34. Smoking Huge Cigars (1956)   *Francis Huxley*   *137*

35. "I Was a Disembodied Eye Poised in Space"
    (1957)   *R. Gordon Wasson*   *141*

36. Fear, Clarity, Knowledge, and Power
    (1968)   *Carlos Castaneda*   *148*

37. "I Found Myself Impaled on the Axis Mundi"
    (1974)   *Barbara Myerhoff*   *154*

38. A Shaman Loses Her Elevation by Interacting with Observers
    (1977)   *Maria Sabina and Alvaro Estrada*   *166*

39. "I Felt Like Socrates Accepting the Hemlock"
    (1980)   *Michael Harner*   *169*

40. Experiencing the Shaman's Symphony to Understand It
    (1987)   *Holger Kalweit*   *178*

PART SIX

## Gathering Evidence on a Multifaceted Phenomenon

41. A Washo Shaman's Helpers (1967)   *Don Handelman*   *187*

42. Magic Darts, Bewitching Shamans, and Curing Shamans
    (1968)   *Michael Harner*   *195*

43. "Remarkably Good Theater" (1973)   *John T. Hitchcock*   *200*

44. Two Kinds of Japanese Shamans: The Medium and the Ascetic
    (1975)   *Carmen Blacker*   *207*

45. Music Alone Can Alter a Shaman's Consciousness, Which
    Itself Can Destroy Tape Recorders (1975)   *Dale A. Olsen*        *212*

46. Shamans Are Intellectuals, Translators, and Shrewd Dealers
    (1975)   *Gerardo Reichel-Dolmatoff*                              *216*

47. Shamans, Caves, and the Master of Animals
    (1979)   *Walter Burkert*                                         *223*

48. "Plant Teachers" (1984)   *Luis Eduardo Luna*                     *227*

49. A Shaman Endures the Temptation of Sorcery
    (and Publishes a Book) (1990)   *Fernando Payaguaje*              *230*

50. Interview with a Killing Shaman
    (1992)   *Ashok and Peter Skafte*                                 *234*

51. Invisible Projectiles in Africa
    (1994)   *Malidoma Patrice Somé*                                  *238*

PART SEVEN

# Global Knowledge and Indigenous Knowledge
# Come Together and Remain Apart

52. Science and Magic, Two Roads to Knowledge
    (1962)   *Claude Lévi-Strauss*                                    *245*

53. Shamans, "Spirits," and Mental Imagery
    (1987)   *Richard Noll*                                           *248*

54. Dark Side of the Shaman (1989)   *Michael F. Brown*               *251*

55. Shamans Explore the Human Mind
    (1990)   *Roger Walsh*                                            *257*

56. Training to See What the Natives See
    (1992)   *Edith Turner*                                           *260*

57. "Twisted Language," a Technique for Knowing
    (1993)   *Graham Townsley*                                        *263*

58. Magic Darts as Viruses (1993)   *Jean-Pierre Chaumeil*            *272*

59. Bubble, Bubble, Toil and Trouble: Tourists and
    Pseudo-Shamans (1994)   *Marlene Dobkin de Rios*                277

60. Shamans and Ethics in a Global World
    (1995)   *Eleanor Ott*                                          280

61. Shamans as Botanical Researchers (1995)   *Wade Davis*          286

62. Shamanism and the Rigged Marketplace
    (1995)   *Piers Vitebsky*                                       291

63. An Ethnobotanist Dreams of Scientists and Shamans
    Collaborating (1998)   *Glenn H. Shepard*                       298

64. Shamans and Scientists (2000)   *Jeremy Narby*                  301


Envoi                                                              306

References and Permissions                                        307

Notes on the Editors' Commentaries and Further Reading            316

Topical Index                                                     318

Acknowledgments                                                   322

About the Editors                                                 323

# Note to Readers

This book will take you on a journey through time in which you will find eyewitness reports of shamans by priests, explorers, adventurers, natural historians, and political dissidents. You will see how the field of anthropology grew out of this past and led to an even deeper quest for knowledge, first from a distance, and then in a more intimate way, when researchers began taking part in shamanic sessions.

The editors translated many of the early texts, as well as several later ones. References to these translations are noted in the back of the book.

# Introduction:
# Five Hundred Years of
# Shamans and Shamanism

## JEREMY NARBY AND FRANCIS HUXLEY

Five centuries ago, when Europeans began to explore the Americas, they came across people in many communities who claimed to communicate with spirits in order to learn about life and healing. Some of these people would fast until they looked like skeletons; others would drink tobacco juice through funnels or wear collars filled with stinging ants. After witnessing such acts, the Europeans often expressed profound distaste when they wrote about them. In 1557, for example, French priest André Thévet visited Brazil and described the people who behaved in this way as "ministers of the Devil." Thévet questioned these people's quest to learn what he considered to be forbidden knowledge: "What need is there to research with too much curiosity into the secrets of nature and other things, knowledge of which Our Lord has reserved for Himself? Such curiosities indicate an imperfect judgement, ignorance, and a lack of faith and good religion."

In the seventeenth century, Russians began colonizing Siberia, and they, too, found individuals who claimed to communicate with spirits. Among the Tungus-speaking people of Eastern Siberia, such individuals were called *saman* or *shaman*. These *shaman* played drums, sang, and put on ventriloquist and trickster performances, imitating animal sounds in the dark or pretending to stab themselves with knives.

1

They claimed they could heal people, or harm them, influence the weather or the availability of game, and foresee the future. Priest Avvakum Petrovich, who provided the first written account of a Siberian *shaman*, described him as "a villain of a magician who calls the demons."

As European observers spread out into the world, they came upon many different people who said they communicated with spirits to learn about life and healing. These people were designated by many names in many languages, such as *pagé, piayé, angakkut, arendiouannens,* and *shaman.* The observers, who came from countries such as Spain, England, France, Russia, and Germany, referred to them in their respective languages as jugglers, sorcerers, wizards and conjurers, and other, often derogatory, terms.

By the eighteenth century, in the period known as the "Enlightenment," Europeans began observing the world with a different gaze. The German philosopher Immanuel Kant declared the motto of the Enlightenment to be "Dare to Know!" Yet, early rationalist observers generally dismissed shamans. They no longer feared knowledge, but shamans still troubled them with their odd behavior. In their view, shamanic performances and tricks had little to do with true knowledge.

These observers were budding scientists. They aspired to a measured and "objective" gaze. Their goal was to understand the world through reason. When they came upon shamans, they tended to view them as impostors who deserved debunking. For example, when German professor Johann Gmelin witnessed a performance in Siberia by a Tungus shaman and his assistants, he concluded that they deserved perpetual labor in the silver mines for their "hocus-pocus."

The nineteenth century gave birth to the academic study of human beings. This new discipline, called social anthropology or ethnology, got off to a poor start. The first anthropologists believed that indigenous people were "savages" and "primitives" and belonged to "inferior societies." Unfortunately, these early anthropologists did not provide many useful reports on shamans at a time when western civilization ran roughshod over indigenous societies and shamanism was rapidly changing.

Toward the end of the nineteenth century, however, some anthropologists realized that there was no fundamental difference between themselves and the people they were observing. For example, German-American Franz Boas wrote in 1887: "The Eskimo is a man as we are; his feelings, his virtues, and his shortcomings are based in human nature, like ours."

At the beginning of the twentieth century, anthropologists started taking their biases into consideration. This improved their observation skills and led them to write an unprecedented number of detailed reports on shamans. They also started giving shamans the opportunity to speak for themselves. Danish anthropologist Knud Rasmussen, for example, took down word-for-word accounts of the Inuit and published them in the 1920's. One shaman called Igjugârjuk told Rasmussen: "True wisdom is only to be found far away from people, out in the great solitude, and it is not found in play but only through suffering. Solitude and suffering open the human mind, and therefore a shaman must seek his wisdom there." Through such texts it became possible to learn about these practitioners in a new empathetic way.

In Rasmussen's time, not all anthropologists were so open-minded. Some viewed shamans as mentally ill—given that they had hallucinations they took seriously, claimed to communicate with spirits, and spoke with voices not their own. For decades, anthropologists debated the mental health of shamans. In his fine dialectical style, French anthropologist Claude Lévi-Strauss turned this debate on its head. He argued that shamans were more like psychoanalysts than psychopaths. Other observers confirmed that shamans were often among the healthiest individuals in their communities and were usually considered doctors by their peers.

By the middle of the twentieth century, anthropologists had reported in detail on shamans in places as remote from one another as Australia, the Arctic, and the Amazon. Locally these practitioners were called by different names, but these terms all seemed to be synonymous with the Siberian *shaman*. In light of this similarity, Swiss anthropologist Alfred Métraux used the term to describe the Amazonian *piai* he was studying. According to Métraux, the shaman's functions include curing illnesses, charming game, interpreting signs or omens, influencing the weather, and predicting the future. The shaman can also cause harm, he said.

But beneath this bewildering array of skills and functions, Métraux saw an underlying unity. In 1944 he defined the shaman as "any individual who maintains by profession and in the interest of the community an intermittent commerce with spirits, or who is possessed by them." This remains the simplest definition for what is often a confusing subject.

In 1951, Romanian historian of religions Mircea Eliade finished his landmark book *Shamanism: Archaic Techniques of Ecstasy*, which documented the striking correspondences in shamanic practices, worldviews, and symbolic behaviors in hundreds of societies around the world. Eliade's work showed that shamanic practices and conceptions were ancient and profoundly human, and therefore worthy of broad interest.

Eliade also put his finger on why the shaman would become such an attractive figure in the second half of the twentieth century, in an era when people were experiencing dissatisfaction with traditional religion. Shamanism is "the religious experience par excellence," wrote Eliade. "The shaman, and he alone, is the great master of ecstasy." Eliade presaged the explosion of interest in shamanism that would reach its peak in the New Age movement.

Researchers were also developing a method of observation that would change the face of anthropological studies. Called "participant observation," it involved living with people and taking part in their activities while attempting to observe them with detachment. This led anthropologists to take an active part in shamanic sessions in view of understanding them.

In the 1950's, other scientists and writers were discovering the power of hallucinogens such as LSD and mescaline. They found that these substances could radically modify a person's awareness of the world. This indicated that hallucinogens worked by modifying brain chemistry, rather than by superstition and suggestion.

When western observers began participating in shamanic sessions involving hallucinogenic plants, they found, to their astonishment, that they could have experiences similar to those described by shamans. One report in particular gained widespread attention. In Mexico, American banker Gordon Wasson ate psilocybin mushrooms in a session conducted by Mazatec shaman Maria Sabina. In a long article in *Life* magazine in 1957, he described flying out of his body. Up to this point, most accounts of shamanism had appeared in obscure academic journals. But hundreds of thousands of people read Wasson's account, and many followed his example, ultimately causing serious trouble for Maria Sabina.

In the 1960's, hallucinogens were used by many young people throughout the world. Onto this stage came Carlos Castaneda, an anthropology student who claimed to have studied with a Yaqui Indian in Arizona and Mexico by becoming a "sorcerer's apprentice." Castaneda took participant observation one step further. He brought back reports of an outlandish but coherent world, a "separate reality," to which he had journeyed under the influence of hallucinogenic plants. Castaneda published a firsthand account of his apprenticeship in 1968, entitled *The Teachings of Don Juan: A Yaqui Way of Knowledge*. The book and its sequels became worldwide bestsellers.

Castaneda called his teacher a sorcerer, which in Latin means diviner. The English term has come to acquire a negative meaning and refers to people who "use power gained from the assistance or control of evil spirits, especially for divination," according to *The Oxford English Dictionary*. Castaneda did not describe his teacher as a healer but as a man of knowledge with an interest in power. This, combined with descriptions of techniques readers could try themselves, caught the fancy of millions of people. Searching for a "power spot," using peripheral vision to see, or ingesting psilocybin mushrooms gave readers the exhilarating impression that they, too, could be apprentice sorcerers and experience shamanism firsthand.

Soon, however, critics began voicing doubts about the authenticity of Castaneda's writings. It seems he did make up parts of his accounts, but they appear to be based on real experience and research. Above all, they were easy and enjoyable to read. Using literary devices, Castaneda played shaman-style tricks on his readers, astounding people by sleight of hand to free their minds from their preconceptions about reality.

In the wake of Castaneda's books, millions of people became interested in shamans in a hands-on way. There was a great flowering of neo-shamanism in the New Age movement, concentrated in the United States but increasingly spreading around the world. These neo-shamans have barely been studied.

Researchers in the last three decades of the twentieth century produced more texts on shamans than in any previous period in history, and shamans themselves became involved in producing their own texts. Mazatec shaman Maria Sabina's oral autobiography, for example, has been translated into several languages.

By looking at the fine grain of shamanism, anthropologists have found a rich and internally coherent way of understanding the world. In recent years they have come to see shamanism as "an ensemble of techniques for knowing," as British anthropologist Graham Townsley says. Researchers currently see shamans not just as healers but as sophisticated producers of meaning. Thus they have started putting shamans on the same intellectual footing as themselves.

There is still much research to be done. While scientists have tapped shamans for their knowledge about healing plants to make pharmaceuticals, researchers have yet to study the efficacy of shamanic healing nor have they explored how shamans understand nature and the world. Shamans appear to be early explorers of the human mind; yet, their systems of psychology have barely been studied. In light of what is now known about mind/body healing, shamans need no longer be viewed as charlatans for tricking people into getting well or as impostors for using sleight of hand and ventriloquism. They may be more like mind doctors.

The recent willingness of scientists to take shamans seriously indicates that a dialogue between these two worldviews may be possible. But it will not be easy. Shamanism is grounded in self and subjectivity, while science has a method that seeks to rise above the researcher's subjective self. In many ways shamanism is an autology, or the study of self, while science is a heterology, the study of others.

Some psychologists and doctors now see shamanism as a way of harnessing the power of mental imagery. But it is more than that: It is about knowledge, healing, and power—and it is ambiguous by nature. Apprentice shamans often experience a strong desire to abuse their newly acquired power and to harm people, as Secoya shaman Fernando Payaguaje points out in his own book. And others have succumbed to the dark side of sorcery. As American anthropologist Michael Brown writes: "Shamanism affirms life but also spawns violence and death."

We have come full circle, back to the reports by sixteenth-century observers, who saw shamans as agents of evil. A one-sided view, but not entirely misguided.

Looking back, it does not seem wrong to say that shamans are jugglers, in the sense that they can handle several things at the same time, incorporating new elements into their act. For example, in the Amazon today, shamans are alive and well and living in forests and towns, speaking Spanish and Portuguese as well as indigenous languages, and going back and forth between mestizo and indigenous societies.

Shamans have always specialized in going between worlds, and nothing suggests that they are less equipped than others to deal with the changing world we find ourselves in. Shamanism is resilient and "chameleon-like," as British anthropologist Piers Vitebsky says. It can take on cunning new disguises.

Shamans and their observers have been doing a strange dance for centuries. Although many observers have begun to take them seriously, there still appears to be a "force field" that keeps shamans apart, as American anthropologist Edith Turner once said. It involves a conflict of beliefs about the fundamental nature of reality. Many observers, especially those trained as scientists, are philosophical materialists. They believe that everything that exists is either made up of physical matter or dependent on matter for its existence. Shamans do not. They believe in spirits.

Even after five hundred years of reports on shamanism, its core remains a mystery. One thing that has changed over the last five centuries, however, is the gaze of the observers. It has opened up. And understanding is starting to flower.

# PART ONE

# The Christian View: "Ministers of the Devil"

Judging texts written in the sixteenth and seventeenth centuries is tricky. If authors did not clearly disavow the Devil in their writings, they could incur accusations of heresy and risk capital punishment, or their writings could be banned. Spanish navigator and natural historian Gonzalo Fernández de Oviedo was a perceptive and open-minded observer for his time, but he called indigenous tobacco use "Devil worship." Did he really believe what he wrote? Hard to know. Perhaps Oviedo only used those words because he felt he had to.

This was a difficult period for people who claimed to communicate with spirits. A witch-craze engulfed Europe. Church and lay authorities, Catholic and Protestant alike, tortured and executed tens of thousands of "witches," most of whom were women. In Central and South America, colonial and church authorities put to death thousands of people, accusing them of witchcraft.

A passage in the Bible says: "You shall not permit a *kashaph* to live" (Exodus 22:18). In Hebrew, the word means magician, diviner, sorcerer, or one with a familiar spirit. Biblical translations from this period translated *kashaph* as "witch," and so provided "divine" sanction to execute them.

Exactly what "witches" did remains unclear. Most historical evidence consists of confessions extracted under torture. Witches confessed that they had flown to sabbaths on animals or brooms after rubbing an ointment on their bodies. They confessed that they had made a pact with the Devil, repudiated Christianity, desecrated the eucharist and crucifix, participated in orgies, sacrificed children, and practiced cannibalism. European "witchcraft" seems to have been a strange mix of pagan magic, sorcery, and Christian thought.

In those days Europeans believed that spirits with which one could communicate were necessarily evil. As historian Jeffrey Russel explains in his book *A History of Witchcraft: Sorcerers, Heretics, and Pagans*:

> Apocalyptic Judaism perceived the spirits as evil demons in league with one another under the generalship of the Devil, the principle of evil. It followed from this belief that a sorcerer who invokes spirits is calling upon the servants of Satan. Christianity made the argument air-tight. Good spirits such as angels and saints could not be compelled, Christians argued, but only supplicated. The only spirits that could be compelled were evil spirits. A sorcerer compelled spirits; therefore, the spirits he called upon were evil. Further, the power of the Devil is so overwhelming that anyone foolishly attempting to control his servants will find himself instead controlled by them. The sorcerer becomes the servant of the demons and a subject of Satan.

These beliefs led Europeans to view shamans with distaste, and since most Europeans who wrote about shamans during this period were clergymen, their biases were often severe.

# 1.

# "Devil Worship: Consuming Tobacco to Receive Messages from Nature"

GONZALO FERNÁNDEZ DE OVIEDO

(1535)

*In the early sixteenth century, Spanish navigator and natural historian Gonzalo Fernández de Oviedo described old men using tobacco to communicate with spirits among the indigenous inhabitants of Hispaniola (the island currently comprising Haiti and the Dominican Republic). Oviedo, who wrote in Spanish, did not use the word shaman, which would come from Russia later. By the time Oviedo published his book in 1535, the island's indigenous inhabitants had mostly been exterminated. This explains why Oviedo referred to them in the past tense.*

Among other vices, the Indians of this island had a very evil one which consists of taking a smoke they call *tabaco*, in order to get out of their minds. . . . They consume it in the following way: the caciques and chiefs had little hollow canes . . . of the thickness of the little finger, and these canes had two tubes joined into one. . . . And they put the two tubes into the nostrils and the other one into the smoke and herbs that were burning and smouldering . . . and they took the emanation and smoke, one, two, three, or more times, as often as they could stand it, until they were out of their minds, lying on the ground drunk or overpowered by a deep and heavy sleep. . . .

The Indians consider this herb very precious and cultivate it for the above-mentioned effect in their gardens and fields; the taking of this herb and smoke was to them not only a healthy practice but a very sacred thing. And this is how the cacique or chief falls to the earth, and his wives (who are numerous) take him, and carry him to his hammock. . . .

It is not astonishing that the Indians are stuck in the errors I have mentioned, and that they make other errors such as they do not know Almighty God and they worship the Devil in diverse forms and images, as is the custom among these peoples in the Indies; because, as I have said, they paint, engrave, or carve a demon they call *cemí* in many objects and places, in wood or clay, and also in other materials, as ugly and frightful as the Catholics represent him at the feet of Saint Michael or Saint Bartholomew, but not bound in chains, but revered: sometimes as if sitting in judgment, sometimes standing, in different ways. These infernal images they had in their houses in specially assigned and dark places and spots that were reserved for their worship; and there they entered to pray and to ask for whatever they desired, be it rain for their fields and farms, or bountiful harvests, or victory over their enemies; and there, finally, they prayed to him and had recourse to him in all their needs, to find a remedy for them. And inside there was an old Indian who answered them according to their expectations or in accordance with a consultation addressed to him whose evil image was standing there; and it is to be thought that the Devil entered into him and spoke through him as through his minister; and as he is an old astrologer, he told them the day on which it would rain, and other messages from Nature. The Indians greatly revered these old men and held them in high esteem as their priests and prelates; and they were the ones who most commonly consumed tobacco and the smoke mentioned above, and when they woke up they advised if war should be declared or postponed; and they did not undertake or carry out anything that might be of importance without considering the Devil's opinion in this way.

# 2

# "Ministers of the Devil Who Learn About the Secrets of Nature"

ANDRÉ THÉVET

(1557)

*In the middle of the sixteenth century, French Franciscan priest André Thévet spent several months in Brazil, living in the first European colony in Rio de Janeiro. He gathered information about the area's indigenous inhabitants, who were Tupinamba. He subsequently published a book called* The Singularities of Antarctic France, *in which he described the activities of certain natives called* pagé *who abstained from sex and isolated themselves to communicate with spirits. Although Thévet disapproved of their practices, he was the first person to introduce tobacco to France. Thévet noticed that the* pagé *learned the secrets of nature but considered this forbidden knowledge.*

These people—being thus removed from the truth, beyond the persecutions they receive from the evil spirit and the errors of their dreams—are so outside of reason that they adore the Devil by means of his ministers, called *pagé*. These *pagé* or *Caribs*, are people of evil custom who have given themselves over to serve the Devil to deceive their neighbors. Like impostors, they usually do not reside anywhere, so as to disguise their nastiness and be honored by others; they are vagabonds, who wander here and there through the woods and other places, and who rarely return among other people and only at certain hours, making them believe that they have communicated with the spirits about public matters, and that one must do thus or thus, lest this or that occur; they are then received and caressed with honor, and are fed and looked after without doing anything else. . . .

Sometimes, if it happens that these *pagé* do not tell the truth and that things turn out differently than forecast, people have no difficulty in putting them to death, as unworthy of the title and dignity of *pagé*. Each village, whether large or small, feeds one or two of these venerables. And when it is a question of knowing something important, they use certain ceremonies and diabolical invocations, which are accomplished in the following way. First they construct a new hut, in which no man has ever lived, and set up a white and clean bed in their style; they take a large quantity of supplies to the hut, such as *cahoiun*, which is their usual drink, made by a young virgin girl of ten or twelve years, along with flour made from the roots, which they use instead of bread. With all things prepared in this fashion, the people lead the gentle prophet to the hut, where he will remain alone, after a young girl has washed him. But one must note that before this mystery, he must abstain from his wife for nine days. Being alone in there, and with the people retired at a distance, he lies flat out on this bed and starts to invoke the evil spirit for an hour or more, doing I do not know what customary ceremonies; to the point that by the end of his invocations, the spirit comes to him whistling, as they say, and piping. The others told me that this evil spirit never appears in the presence of all the people, so that they never see him, but only hear some noise and howling. . . .

Mainly they undertake no enterprise without the answer of their prophet. When the mystery is accomplished, the prophet comes out, and is immediately surrounded by the people. He makes a speech in which he tells all that he heard. And God knows the caresses and presents that each person gives him. The Americans are not the first to practice abusive magic; before them, it was familiar to several nations, back to the time of Our Lord, who erased and abolished the power that Satan exercised over human kind. It is therefore not without reason that it is forbidden by the Scriptures.

Of this magic we find two main kinds, one by which one communicates with evil spirits, the other which gives intelligence about the most secret things of nature. It is true that one is more vicious than the other, but both are full of curiosity. When we have all the things we need and when we understand as much as God enables us to, what need is there to research with too much curiosity into the secrets of nature and other things, knowledge of which Our Lord has reserved for Himself? Such curiosities indicate an imperfect judgment, ignorance, and a lack of faith and good religion. Even more abused are the simple people who believe such impostures. I cannot cease to wonder how it is that in a land of law and police, one allows to proliferate like filth a bunch of old witches who put herbs on their arms, hang written words around their necks, and many mysteries, in ceremonies to cure fevers and other things, which are only true idolatry, and worthy of great punishment.

# 3.

# "Evoking the Devil: Fasting with Tobacco to Learn How to Cure"

ANTOINE BIET

(1664)

*In 1652, French priest Antoine Biet accompanied an expedition to South America. In what is now called French Guyana, Biet observed the customs and practices of the area's indigenous inhabitants, who were Caribs. Biet observed that the local doctors, known as* piayés, *endured a rigorous training to learn their profession. The ordeal included fasting until they fainted, being bitten by large black ants, and drinking large quantities of tobacco juice. The bite of these ants causes extreme pain and lasts for weeks. Those who survive a massive dose of ant toxin come back to normal life much fortified.*

He who aspires to be a *piayé* is first put in an ancient's home. He stays there a very long time, to receive instruction and to make, as it were, his novitiate, sometimes serving his master for the period of ten years. The ancient *piayé* observes him to see whether he has in him the qualities necessary for a *piayé*. He is not elevated to this dignity until the age of twenty-five or thirty years.

When the time has come that they are to put him to the tests, first they make him fast as strictly as the chief and even more so, because, for a year, he eats only boiled millet and a very little cassava. On this fare, he becomes so thin that he seems a skeleton with nothing but skin stretched over his bones and becomes almost without strength. The old *piayés* assemble after this long fast, shut themselves up into a hut, and teach the aspirant the way to call up the demon or to consult him. In place of whipping the aspiring captain [as certain Christian monastics do], they make him dance until he is so exhausted because of the weakness caused by his fasting that he falls fainting and swooning to the ground. To revive him they put on him girdles and collars of those great black ants whose bites cause so much pain. They open his mouth by force and put in it a sort of funnel into which they pour a great vessel full of juice drawn from tobacco. This strange medicine causes him to have vertigo and vomit blood. Its effects last several days.

After such violent remedies, and such rigorous fasts, he is made a *piayé* and has the power of curing illnesses and evoking the Devil. But, to do so properly, he is ordered a fast of three years duration. The first year he eats millet and bread, the second, crabs with his bread and the third, some little birds. They keep these fasts so exactly that, although the others drink and make good cheer in their feasts and assemblies, they no longer drink a draught, since they believe that, if they broke this fast, they would have no power over illnesses or over the devils to evoke them.

These poor infidels are in such blindness! See what they suffer in this life for a vain honor; they are true penitents of the Demon, who starts to make them feel the torments of Hell, while they are still alive. These miserable doctors are obliged to abstain from time to time from certain things and to drink that rude potion of tobacco. Sometimes they drink as much of it as a great drunkard can take wine. Doubtless their stomachs grow accustomed to this sort of drink since they can tolerate it.

# 4.

# The Shaman: "A Villain of a Magician Who Calls Demons"

## AVVAKUM PETROVICH

## (1672)

*The first person to use the word* shaman *in a published text was Avvakum Petrovich, a leader of the conservative clergy in Russia in the second half of the seventeenth century. Avvakum's description of a Tungus shaman appeared in his autobiography, which is considered to be one of the first major works in Russian literature. In the summer of 1661, the czar deported Avvakum to Siberia. The head of the expedition, a man called Paskov, decided to consult a local shaman. Avvakum's mixture of prayers and paranoia blurs the lines between priest and shaman.*

As he was about to send his son Jeremy to wage war against the Mongol kingdom—along with seventy-two cossacks and twenty natives— Paskov obliged a native to do the shaman, that is to say the diviner: will the expedition be successful, and will they return victorious? That evening, this villain of a magician brought a living ram over near my hut and started to practice his magic on it: Having turned it over, he wrung its neck and cast off its head. Then he started to jump and dance and call the demons; finally, making piercing screams, he threw himself on the ground and foam came out of his mouth. The demons pressed him, and he asked them: "Will the expedition be successful?" And the demons replied: "You will return with a great victory and great wealth." This made the governors [Paskov and his son] happy, and everybody declared joyfully: "We will come back rich!"

Oh! what bitterness for my soul, which has yet to sweeten! I was a bad pastor, and had lost my flock and in my grief I forgot what the Gospel says. . . . I cried out and proclaimed to the Lord: "Listen to me, my God! Listen to me, clear king of heaven! Listen to me, may not one of them return! Dig a tomb for them there! Send them evil, Lord, send it to them! And lead them to their loss, so that the diabolical prophesy not be accomplished!" And many other similar words. In secret I also addressed the same prayer to God.

They told Paskov the wishes I was making, and he was content to cover me with insults.

He dispatched his son with the troops. They left at night, when the stars were out. At that moment I took pity on them: My soul saw that they would be massacred, and that I was the one calling death on them! Some of them came to say good-bye to me, and I told them: "You will die!" No sooner had they set off than their horses started to neigh, and here, the cows lowed, the ewes and goats bleated, and the dogs howled, and the natives, like the dogs, also howled. Dread fell on everybody. Jeremy sent me a message and implored: Master, my father, pray for me! . . .

So they were far away, gone off to war. Jeremy inspired pity in me: I pressed the Lord to spare him. We were waiting for their return: They did not arrive according to the agreed time. Paskov did not allow me to approach him. One day, he installed a small chamber and lit a great fire. He wanted to put me to the question. I was familiar with his tricks: It was difficult to survive that kind of fire. . . . And here two torturers came running toward me. Marvelous is the work of the Lord, unfathomable are the plans of the Almighty! Just then, a wounded Jeremy, with another cavalryman, went by on the path in front of my chamber. He hailed the torturers, and took them away with him. Paskov left the chamber, and went out to meet his son, like a man drunk with pain. And Jeremy, having exchanged greetings with his father, told him everything in detail: how the whole troop was massacred without any survivors, how he was wounded by the Mongols and how a native helped him to escape through deserted places, how he crossed rocky mountains and wandered seven days through the forest without food—he ate a squirrel!—and how a man who looked like me appeared to him in a dream, blessed him, and told him which way to go: This gave him a start, made him joyful, and he found the right path. As he was telling this to his father, I arrived to greet them. Paskov laid his eyes on me—like a polar bear, he would eat me alive, but the Lord will not give me over to him!—sighed, and said: "There is your work! How many men did you send to death!" But Jeremy said: "Master, my father, return to your cabin! Be quiet, for the love of Christ!" And I left them.

# The Humanist View Becomes Rationalist: From "Esteemed Jugglers" to "Impostors"

In the 1700's, when observers from the Enlightenment came upon *pagé, angakkut,* or *shaman,* they tended to see impostors. This was a relatively progressive view in those days. Previous observers had mainly perceived such people as "agents of the Devil"—a serious charge in times of witch-hunting. By judging shamans as impostors, Enlightenment observers implied that shamans did not really communicate with the Devil. This took away the witch-hunters' justification for executing people.

Despite this progressive move, from condemnation to mere debunking, most eighteenth-century observers had difficulty understanding shamans. The Russian imperial government sent numerous scientific observers to explore Siberia; a scientist like Stepan Krasheninnikov wrote that he found shamanic notions "absurd and ridiculous." Nevertheless he reported on them extensively.

In her excellent book *Shamanism and the Eighteenth Century,* Gloria Flaherty comments on this ambiguity:

> The eighteenth century was too deeply involved with the occult to have us continue to associate it exclusively with rationalism, humanism, scientific determinism, and classicism. Manifestations of irrationalism, supernaturalism, organicism, and romanticism appeared uninterruptedly throughout. It was precisely the tension between those who limited themselves to enlightenment of a purely rational sort and those who included serious consideration of what was derogatorily called the night-side of nature that informed the very way in which Western European knowledge was advanced. That relentless tension helped revolutionize human thought, and affected the shape the world was to take.

Denis Diderot, one of the key figures of the Enlightenment, expressed an ambiguous view of shamans. As a professed atheist (who had benefited from a Jesuit education), Diderot saw shamans as "impostors" and "jugglers," but he also thought "the supernatural occasionally enters into their operation," and "they are sometimes quite close to the mark."

Many early rationalist observers did not suspect that shamans were doing anything other than deceiving their fellows with song and dance, tricks, and sleight of hand. But some, like Johann Herder, realized that the activities of shamans had to do with the power of the imagination and of the human mind. Two centuries later, other investigators would pick up where Herder left off.

# 5

# "The Savages Esteem Their Jugglers"

## JOSEPH FRANÇOIS LAFITAU

### (1724)

*Among early observers, French Jesuit missionary Joseph François Lafi-tau stands out as an exemplar of open-mindedness. In the early eigh-teenth century, he spent five years living among the Iroquois and Huron near Montreal. Then he reported that they distinguished between those who communicated with spirits for the good of the community and those who did the same to harm people. He argued that the Devil played no part in the work of the former. He used their native names, but he also called them "jugglers," a word synonymous with magicians in Europe. Nevertheless, he acknowledged that there was something more to their practices than just trickery. Lafitau was an enlightened precursor of modern anthropology. In those days, Jesuits were the most illustrious educators in Europe; even people who were lukewarm to religion sent their children to Jesuit schools.*

In all the times of paganism, the diviners have been regarded as sages who had the knowledge of things divine and human, knew the efficacy of plants, stones, metals, all the occult virtues, and all the secrets of na-ture. Not only did they sound the depths of hearts but they foresaw the future. They read in the stars, in the books of the destinies and car-ried on with the gods an intimate commerce of which the rest of mankind was unworthy. Their seeming austerity of life and conventionality and the fact that they were above criticism and censure rendered them respectable to all who came to consult them as oracles and spokespeople of the divinity.

The *Arendiouannens* or *Agotsinnachens*, who are the [Huron and Iroquois] successors of these diviners, are also extraordinary people rendered so important by their status as to be consulted in all things as sources of truth. Not only do they explain dreams and expose the secret desires of the soul, but there is nothing outside the scope of their knowledge. Predictions of the future, the success of a war or of a journey, the secret causes of a malady, bringing good luck to a hunting or fishing party, finding stolen objects, casting spells and curses—in short, everything that concerns divination—is absolutely within their jurisdiction. Such questions must be entrusted to them so they can discover the source of the evil, conjure it, turn it aside, and apply a suitable remedy to it. Thus they do not deny themselves anything in showing off their trade.

They have another species of extraordinary people whom they call *Agotkon* or spirits. These are the ones who cast spells or curses. There is a great number of them of both sexes. The women especially are suspected of playing a part in this little business. Since they have no aim except to cause harm, they are regarded with horror and forced to hide for their wicked mysteries. They serve to accredit the diviners whose principal occupation is to discover these spells, make known their authors, and bring some remedy for them. . . .

The missionaries of New France have had most to suffer from these diviners, who keep the people in their ancient superstitions and form the greatest obstacle to their conversion. At first, the missionaries examined very carefully whether the Demon had a part in their spells and other superstitious practices; no matter how much trouble they took, however, they could discover nothing on which to base an assured judgment. In this uncertainty, they took the part of condemning their superstitions which are certainly bad and of baptizing only those who would make an open profession of condemning and renouncing them. They believed, however, that they should regard what the people themselves said of their spells and of their divination as ineptitudes and they saw, in their so-called diviners, only charlatans and quite poor doctors who have always since then been called *jugglers* as if their art was nothing but simple charlatanism.

It is not for me to decide this question and I am quite willing to believe that all the magic tricks of these Jugglers have, as their basis, only the natural, not so much because their superstitions are suspect and often contrary to the event, as they claim (for the Demon has always been the father of lies and has thrown men into error by false and ambiguous oracles) as because, in fact, there are scarcely any means of illusions and omens which cannot be imitated by tricks of skill; so that it is almost impossible to distinguish the reality from the deceit.

In spite of all that, there are certain things which have struck me and which I believe deserve particular attention. . . .

The power of doing extraordinary things stems from the same principle in both cases, that is, from communication with the spirits. The esteem of the savages for their jugglers and their extreme antipathy to those who cast spells make me believe that they make some distinction between those who they think communicate with the spirits in such a way that they think that good spirits are the cause of the miracles done by their diviners, and the evil ones, on the contrary, who are the authors of their curses and witchcraft. . . .

The jugglers have some innate quality which takes even more after the divine. One sees them go visibly into that state of ecstasy that binds all the senses and keeps them suspended. The foreign spirit appears to take possession of them in a palpable and sensible manner and to master their organs in a way that acts in them immediately. It casts them into frenzies of enthusiasm and all the convulsive movements of the Sibyl. It speaks from the depths of their chests and causes the fortune-tellers to be considered ventriloquists. It raises them sometimes up into the air or makes them greater than their real stature.

In this state of enthusiasm their spirit seems absorbed in that which possesses them. They are no longer themselves, like those di-

viners of whom Iamblichus speaks, in whom the outside spirit oper-
ated in such a way that not only did they not know themselves but
they had no feeling and did not feel any hurt during that time so that
one could touch them with fire without burning them, pierce them with
blazing spits, then rain axe blows on their shoulders and cut their arms
with razors. Indeed, in these ecstasies, one can see them swallow fire,
walk on burning coals without being hurt, like those mentioned by Vir-
gil, who were inspired by Apollo on Mount Soracte, or those mentioned
by Strabo who divined by the spirit of the goddess Feronia, or the
women of Castabala in Sicily of whom the same author speaks who
were consecrated to Diana Perasia. Furthermore, they stick long pieces
of wood down their gullets, coil living serpents in their breasts, and do a
thousand other tricks that appear to border on the marvelous.

It is while they are performing these marvels that they see things
within themselves or those represented to them outside in an infinite
number of different ways for they have almost the same ways of di-
vining by pyromancy, hydromancy, and other methods as we see in
authors who have treated of magic and divination. The spirit also acts
in them as it did in antiquity by certain signals such as the sound of
bronze cymbals or other musical instruments, certain potions, divin-
ing wands, flour, calculations, and the like. . . .

[The] thing which has struck me is the inward belief of all of them
in the Demon's power over them, in the efficacy of spells and the
power of their jugglers to know and reveal the caster of spells. Is it
very probable that, since their origin they have been bewitched by
these beliefs, they would not have discovered the deceit if it had been
only pure boasting? Since each of these nations is small, fraud is easier to find out, and the fact that the older men, the most important,
knew about it, would have been more than sufficient to destroy such
a pretension. But this belief is so general and deep-rooted that there
is not one nation in all of America which has not its diviners or jugglers, not one which does not fear spells, not one where any refuses to
have recourse to the jugglers, and does not willingly undergo all the
tests of the initiations to be made a juggler himself.

# 6

# "Shamans Deserve Perpetual Labor for Their Hocus-Pocus"

## JOHANN GEORG GMELIN

### (1751)

*German professor of chemistry and botany Johann Georg Gmelin spent ten years exploring Siberia. He subsequently published a four-volume book of travels containing observations about shamans. Gmelin paid for shamanic performances, the better to debunk them. One is left wondering why he felt such violent antipathy toward shamans. Two centuries later Gmelin's wish was fulfilled: Soviet authorities interned Siberian shamans in labor camps, or executed them.*

Prior to my departure I still had an opportunity to watch a Tungus shaman practice his magic. At our request, he visited us the first night, and when we asked him to give us a demonstration of his art, he asked us to wait until the night, which we willingly agreed to do. At 10 P.M. he took us to a distance of one verst [Russian measure of length, about 0.66 mile], and then bade us sit down. He himself stripped naked, then put on his shaman's coat, which was made of leather, and was decked out with all kinds of iron instruments. On each shoulder he had a jagged iron horn, to the consternation of many. . . . Within the circle formed by our people, he kept running to and fro along the fire, and made an infernal racket with the iron bells inside his dress. . . . At last he started leaping and shouting, and soon we heard a chorus that was singing along with him. It was his believers, some of whom he had brought with him. Unnoticed, they had slipped into our circle and were singing along with him, so that the devils might hear them the better. At length, after a lot of hocus-pocus and sweating, he would have had us believe that the devils were there. He asked us what we wanted to know. We put a question to him. He started his conjuring tricks, while two others were assisting him. In the end we were confirmed in our opinion that it was all humbug, and we wished in our hearts that we could take him and his companions to the Urgurian silver mine, so that there they might spend the rest of their days in perpetual labor.

# 7

# "Blinded by Superstition"

## STEPAN PETROVICH KRASHENINNIKOV

### (1755)

*Botanist Stepan Petrovich Krasheninnikov reported to the Russian im-
perial government that the people of Kamchatka (eastern Siberia) had
"absurd beliefs" and that their shamans performed "crude tricks." He
felt these people were blinded by superstition.*

All the beliefs they have about their gods and devils or evil spirits are
disconnected and so absurd and ridiculous that anyone unfamiliar
with these peoples would have a hard time believing that they hold all
these strange ideas as infallible truths; nonetheless, they try their
best to make sense out of everything that exists; they even try to understand the thoughts of fish and birds. Their mistake is that they
never consider whether their ideas are right or wrong. They accept
everything easily, without reflection on it. . . .

It would be superfluous to dwell as long on this tribe [the Koriaks]
as on the Kamchadals, since their way of life is so similar. Generally
speaking, all of these natives are idolaters, are very backward, and
only in their human appearance do they differ from animals; for this
reason we shall give only a brief account of each tribe and will only
give longer descriptions of the way in which they differ from the
Kamchadals. . . .

When their shamans make sacrifices, they beat on little drums which are made in the same way as those of the Iakuts and other pagan natives of this country; but the Koriak shamans wear no special costume as the others do. Among the settled Koriaks there are shamans who are considered doctors and who, these superstitious people believe, can cure illnesses by beating on these little drums. It is a very interesting fact that there is no nation, no matter how wild and barbaric, whose shamans are not cleverer, more adroit and shrewder than the rest of the people.

In 1739 in Lower Kamchatka I saw a famous shaman. He was from a place called Ukinsk, and his name was Karymliach. He was considered a man of great learning and he was much respected, not only by these people but even by our Cossacks because of the amazing things he did. He pierced his abdomen with a knife and drank the blood which gushed out; but he did this so clumsily that one would have to be blinded by superstition as these people are not to see through such a gross deceit. He began by beating on his drum several times while he was kneeling; after that he plunged a knife into his belly, squeezed the supposed wound to make the blood gush out, and, thrusting his hand under his robe, he drew it back filled with blood and licked his fingers. I couldn't keep from laughing for he performed his trick so crudely that he would have had a hard time in our country being accepted by our apprentice thimbleriggers. One could see him slide the knife along his stomach and pretend to stab himself, then squeeze a bladder to make blood come out. After he had finished all this conjuring and magic, he felt he was astonishing us all the more by lifting up his shirt and showing us his belly all smeared with blood. He assured us that this blood (which was seal blood) had actually come from his wound, and that he had just healed it up by his magic. He also told us that evil spirits came to him from various places and appeared to him in different forms, that some came from the sea and others from volcanoes; that there were small ones and big ones; that several had no hands; that some had been completely burned, and others only half burned;

that those who came from the sea seemed richer than the others and that their garments were made of a grass which grows along rivers; he said they came to him in a dream and that when they came to visit him they tormented him so cruelly that he was almost out of his mind in a kind of delirium.

# 8.

# "Shamans Are Impostors Who Claim They Consult the Devil—And Who Are Sometimes Close to the Mark"

DENIS DIDEROT AND COLLEAGUES
(1765)

*French man of letters and philosopher Denis Diderot served as chief editor of the* Encyclopédie, *one of the main works of the Enlightenment. Its underlying philosophy was rationalism. Diderot was an exponent of materialist atheism, but his views on "shamans" and "jugglers" show that his conviction was flexible. Diderot was the first to try to define shamans. He successfully identified many of their facets. He also defined shamans and jugglers separately, because "shamans" came from Russia and "jugglers" was used to describe Americans.*

SHAMANS, noun, masc. plural, is the name that the inhabitants of Siberia give to impostors who perform the functions of priests, jugglers, sorcerers, and doctors. These shamans claim they have an influence on the Devil, whom they consult to know the future, to cure illnesses, and to do tricks that seem supernatural to an ignorant and superstitious people: To do this they use drums which they beat with strength while dancing and spinning with surprising speed; once they have alienated themselves from these contortions and fatigue, they claim that the Devil manifests himself to them, if he is in a good mood.

Sometimes the ceremony ends [when the shaman] pretends to stab himself with a knife, which increases the astonishment and respect of the imbecilic spectators. These contortions are usually preceded by the sacrifice of a dog or a horse, which they eat while drinking quantities of brandy. And the whole comedy ends [when the spectators] give money to the shaman, who does not pride himself on disinterestedness any more than other impostors of the same kind.

JUGGLERS *(Divination)*, magicians or enchanters much renowned among the savage nations of America, and who make up the profession of medicine men among them.

According to Father Charlevoix, the jugglers profess that they only have commerce with what they call *beneficial genies*. They boast that, through these genies, they can know what is happening in the most distant countries, or what must occur in the most distant times; that they discover the source and nature of the most hidden illnesses, and that they have the secret to heal them; that they discern the course of action to take in the most complicated matters; that they can succeed with the most difficult negotiations; that they can make the gods favorable to warriors and hunters; that they can understand the language of birds, etc. . . .

One of their more common preparations to do their tricks consists of locking themselves into steamrooms to make themselves sweat. In this they differ in nothing from the Pythia as the poets represented them. One sees them enter into convulsions and enthusiasms and perform actions which seem beyond human forces. The language they speak in their invocations has nothing in common with any other savage tongue; and it is probable that it consists of only formless sounds, produced on the spot by a heated imagination, and that these charlatans have found a way to make it pass for a divine language; they take on tones of voice, sometimes they raise their voice, then they imitate a small frail voice, quite similar to the voice of our puppets, and people believe that it is the spirit talking to them. They contend that they suffer a lot during these occasions, and there are some who cannot be hired easily to give themselves to the spirit that agitates them, even if one pays them well. People have seen the stakes of these steamhouses bend down to the ground, while the juggler stayed quietly inside, without moving, without touching the stakes, while he was singing and predicting the future. This circumstance and several singular and detailed predictions that people have heard them make quite a long time before the event, which are fully justified by the event, make one think that the supernatural occasionally enters into their operations and that they do not always guess by chance.

Jugglers by profession can only establish a kind of pact with the genies and attain the people's respect if they have previously developed their character through fasts, which they take very far, and during which they do nothing other than beat the drum, scream, yell, sing, and smoke. The presentation then turns into a kind of orgy, with ceremonies that are so extravagant and accompanied by so many furies that one would think the Devil takes possession of people. Strictly speaking, they are not the priests of the nation, because the heads of family perform that function, but they present themselves as interpreters of the gods. To do their tricks, they use the bones and skins of serpents, with which they also make headbands and belts. It is certain that they have the secret for charming serpents or, to speak more exactly, to make them drowsy; they take them alive, handle them, and put them on their breast without harming themselves. It is also up to the jugglers to explain dreams and omens and to press or stall the army's advance during military expeditions, which they always accompany. They persuade the majority of people that they have ecstatic transports, in which the genies reveal the future and hidden things to them. This is how they persuade people of whatever they wish.

But the main occupation of jugglers, or at least the one which they gain most profit from, is Medicine. Although they generally exercise this art with principles based on knowledge of medicinal plants, experience, and conjecture, as one does everywhere, they usually mix in superstition and charlatanism.

For example, on some occasions they say that they will communicate the virtue of healing all kinds of wounds to the roots and plants, and even bring the dead back to life. They immediately set about singing, and one supposes that, during this concert, which they accompany with many grimaces, the medicinal virtue is spread to the drugs. Then the main juggler tests them; he starts by making his lips bleed. The blood that the impostor deftly sucks ceases to flow and people call it a miracle. After this, he takes a dead animal and allows those present to assure themselves that it is lifeless; then, he inserts a small tube under the tail and stirs it around, while blowing herbs into its mouth. Sometimes they pretend to bewitch several savages, who appear to expire; then, by putting a given powder on their lips, they bring them back to life. Often, when there are wounds, the juggler cuts the wound with his teeth and then shows a piece of wood, or something similar, that he had previously placed in his mouth; he makes the sick person believe that he has pulled it from his wound and that it was the charm that caused the danger of his illness.

If the sick person thinks his illness is due to an evil spell, then all attention is given to discovering it, and this is the duty of the juggler. He starts by making himself sweat; and when he is quite tired he screams, struggles, and invokes his genie; he attributes the cause of the illness to the first extraordinary thing that comes to mind. Several drink a special beverage before entering the steamroom; they say it is very important to receiving the celestial impression; and they claim that the presence of spirit manifests itself through an impetuous wind that suddenly picks up, or through a roaring that can be heard under the ground, or through the shaking and rattling of the steamroom. Then, full of his so-called divinity, and resembling more a man possessed by the Devil than a man inspired by heaven, he pronounces with an affirmative tone on the state of the patient and sometimes is quite close to the mark.

# 9.

# Misled Impostors and the Power of Imagination

JOHANN GOTTFRIED HERDER

(1785)

> *German critic, theologian, and philosopher Johann Gottfried Herder mentioned shamans in his work* Outlines of a Philosophy of the History of Man. *He viewed them with more indulgence than most of his contemporaries. He saw that a shaman required a community of believers. He also understood the importance of imagination, for shamans and for human beings in general.*

Usually one sees the Angetots, the magicians, the magi, the shamans, and the priests as the originators of this blindness of the common people, and one thinks that one has explained everything by calling them impostors. In most places, this is the case, naturally; but let us never forget that they belong to the people as well, and that they, too, were misled in the past. They were conceived in and brought up with the imaginary representations of their tribe: Their initiation occurred through fasts, solitude, efforts of imagination, as well as the exhaustion of body and soul; thus, nobody becomes a magician before his spirit appears to him and the deed is accomplished in his soul. He will then go on to perpetuate this deed for others over the course of his entire life through similar and repeated efforts of mind and the exhaustion of the body. The most distant travelers have been astounded in the face of such juggleries, because they have seen successes of the strength of imagination which they hardly believed possible and which they often did not know how to explain. Indeed, among all the forces of the human soul, imagination is perhaps the least explored: Given that it relates to the construction of the entire body, and in particular of the brain and nerves—as numerous and astonishing illnesses demonstrate—it seems therefore not only to be the link for, and the basis of, all the subtle forces of the soul but also the knot of the relationships between mind and body, as well as the budding flower of the entire organization of the senses for the other uses of the forces of thinking.

# PART THREE

# Enter
# Anthropologists

The birth of social anthropology in the second half of the nineteenth century gave human beings the opportunity to study themselves and their differences. In theory, this was a joyous event; in practice, it started with "white men" studying "primitives."

Fortunately, a number of anthropologists went to places like the Canadian Arctic, Siberia, and British Guiana and wrote clear reports about the people living there. These reports showed that all kinds of people became shamans: young and old, men and women, through gift, illness, or dedication. Anthropologist Roland Dixon called shamans "a motley class of persons."

Shamans could also do many things: They healed, hexed,

charmed game, predicted the future, influenced the weather, and interpreted omens. Anthropological reports showed that shamans were different people who did different things. Yet, they all claimed to communicate with spirits in the interest of their community. This gave the phenomenon an underlying coherence.

# 10

# Animism Is the Belief in Spiritual Beings

## EDWARD B. TYLOR

### (1871)

*Englishman Edward B. Tylor, one of the founders of anthropology, proposed the term* animism *to refer to the belief of spiritual beings in nature and in humans. Tylor referred to indigenous people as "lower races" and "savages." But he rose above the prejudices of his time by placing these people on the same continuum as "high modern culture," in which he also saw elements of animism. Animism* remains a useful term to characterize the worldview of shamans.

The first requisite in a systematic study of the religions of the lower races is to lay down a rudimentary definition of religion. By requiring in this definition the belief in a supreme deity or of judgment after death, the adoration of idols or the practice of sacrifice, or other partially-diffused doctrines or rites, no doubt many tribes may be excluded from the category of religious. But such narrow definition has the fault of identifying religion rather with particular developments than with the deeper motive that underlies them. It seems best to fall back at once on this essential source and simply to claim, as a minimum definition of religion, the belief in Spiritual Beings. . . .

I propose here, under the name of Animism, to investigate the deep-lying doctrine of Spiritual Beings, which embodies the very essence of Spiritualistic as opposed to Materialistic philosophy. Animism is not a new technical term, though it is now seldom used. From its special relation to the doctrine of the soul, it will be seen to have a peculiar appropriateness to the view here taken of the mode in which theological ideas have been developed among mankind. . . .

Animism characterizes tribes very low in the scale of humanity, and thence ascends, deeply modified in its transmission, but from first to last preserving an unbroken continuity, into the midst of high modern culture. Doctrines adverse to it, so largely held by individuals or schools, are usually due not to early lowness of civilization but to later changes in the intellectual course, to divergence from, or rejection of, ancestral faiths; such newer developments do not affect the present inquiry as to the fundamental religious condition of mankind. Animism is, in fact, the groundwork of the Philosophy of Religion, from that of savages up to that of civilized men. And although it may at first sight seem to afford but a bare and meagre definition of a minimum of religion, it will be found practically sufficient; for where the root is, the branches will generally be produced.

# 11.

# A White Man Goes
# to a *Peaiman*

### EVERARD F. IM THURN

### (1883)

*Anthropologist Everard F. Im Thurn lived among the Macusi people of British Guiana. He described the activities of indigenous doctors known as* peaiman *and their fights against the evil* kenaima *spirits. Im Thurn described these indigenous doctors as singers, magicians, actors, and ventriloquists. He allowed himself to be entranced by a* peaiman.

On one occasion, when living with Macusi Indians on the savannahs, and suffering from slight headache and fever, a peaiman, with whom I had endeavoured to establish friendly relations, offered to cure me. It was too good an opportunity to be lost, and I accepted. An hour or two after dark I carried my hammock to the house where the man was living, and there re-slung it. According to request, I had brought with me a pocketful of tobacco-leaves. These were now steeped in a calabash of water, which was then placed on the ground. The peaiman had provided himself with several bunches of green boughs cut from the bushes on the savannah. The entrance to the house having been closed, we were completely shut in—for the house, as usual among the savannah Indians, was walled and without windows or chimneys. The fires were put out, and all was dark. Besides the peaiman and myself, there were about thirty people in the house, most of them attracted by such a novel performance as the peai-ing of a white man. We all lay in our hammocks; and I was especially warned not to put foot to the ground, for the kenaimas would be on the floor, and would do dreadful things to me if they caught me.

All was now ready for the performance; but there was a pause. At last it appeared that the peaiman was shy of working in the presence of a white man. I did what I could to reassure him; and at last succeeded in this, by promising that I would not stir out of my hammock, that I would not look at anything—a promise which it would have been hard to break in that utter darkness—and that I would not attempt to lay hands on anything that might touch me. Then the ceremony began.

For a moment all was still, till suddenly the silence was broken by a burst of indescribable and really terrible yells and roars and shouts, which filled the house, shaking walls and roof, sometimes rising rhythmically to a roar, sometimes sinking to a low distant-sounding growl, which never ceased for six hours. Questions seemed to be thundered out and answers shouted back; words and sentences, questions and answers, following each other so closely that there was no pause in the sound. To me, knowing very little of the Macusi language, the meaning was unintelligible; but as long as I kept my senses a Macusi boy who spoke English, and who had slung his hammock close to mine, did his best to whisper into my ear some sort of a translation. It was the peaiman, he explained, roaring out his questions and commands to the kenaimas, and the kenaimas who were yelling and growling and shouting their answers.

Every now and then, through the mad din, there was a sound, at first low and indistinct, and then gathering in volume, as if some big winged thing came from far toward the house, passed through the roof, and then settled heavily on the floor; and again, after an interval, as if the same winged thing rose and passed away as it had come. As each of these mysterious beings came and went, the air, as if displaced by wings, was driven over my face. They were the kenaimas coming and going.

As each came, his yells were first indistinctly heard from far off, but grew louder and louder until, as he alighted on the floor of the house, they reached their height. The first thing each did was to lap up some of the tobacco-water, with an ostentatious noise, from the calabash on the floor. But while he lapped, the peaiman kept up the shouts, until the kenaima was ready to answer. When each kenaima had given an account of itself, and had promised not to trouble me, it flew rustling away. They came in the form of tigers, deer, monkeys, birds, turtles, snakes, and of Ackawoi and Arecuna Indians. Their voices were slightly different in tone, and they all shouted in voices which were supposed to be appropriate to their forms—but oddly enough, all hoarsely.

It was a clever piece of ventriloquism and acting. The whole long terrific noise came from the throat of the peaiman; or perhaps a little of it from that of his wife. The only marvel was that the man could sustain so tremendous a strain upon his voice and throat for six long hours. The rustling of the wings of the kenaimas, and the thud which was heard as each alighted on the floor, were imitated, as I afterwards found, by skilfully shaking the leafy boughs and then dashing them suddenly against the ground. The boughs, swept through the air close by my face, also produced the breezes which I had felt. Once, probably by accident, the boughs touched my face; and it was then that I discovered what they were, by seizing and holding some of the leaves with my teeth. Once, too, toward the end of the performance, and when I had lost nearly all consciousness, a hand was, I thought, laid upon my face. That, as will presently appear, was the crisis of my illness.

The effect of all this upon me was very strange. Before long I ceased to hear the explanations of the boy by my side, and passed into a sort of fitful sleep or stupor, probably akin to mesmeric trance. Incapable of voluntary motion, I seemed to be suspended somewhere in a ceaselessly surging din; and my only thoughts were a hardly-felt wonder as to the cause of the noise, and a gentle, fruitless effort to remember if there had once been a time before noise was. Now and then, when the noise all but died away for a few moments, during the intervals in which the peaiman was supposed to have passed out through the roof and to be heard from a great distance, I woke to half-consciousness. But always as he came back, and the noise grew again, I once more gradually fell into a state of stupor.

At last, when, toward morning, the noise had finally ended, I awoke thoroughly. The bars being taken away from the entrance of the house, I rushed out on the open savannah. It was a wild and pitch-dark night; rain fell heavily; thunder pealed incessantly; and every now and then lightning, flashing behind the far-off Pacaraima range, for a moment vividly showed the rugged edge of the dark mountains against the sky. Bare-headed, bare-footed, and coatless, I spent the short time before dawn out in the storm; and the savannah, the night, and the storm seemed strangely fresh and pleasant after the dark, close, noise-filled house.

It is perhaps needless to add that my head was anything but cured of its ache. But the peaiman, insisting that I must be cured, asked for payment. He even produced the kenaima, a caterpillar, which, he said, had caused the pain, and which he had extracted from my body at the moment when his hand had touched my face. I gave him a looking-glass which had cost fourpence; and he was satisfied.

# 12

# The *Angakoq* Uses a Peculiar Language and Defines Taboos

(1887)

*German-born American anthropologist Franz Boas played an impor-*
*tant role in moving anthropology away from ethnocentric views. He*
*wrote many articles contradicting racism and eugenics. He also taught*
*a generation of young anthropologists that cultures were to be appreci-*
*ated in their own terms. In the early 1880's, he spent a year living among*
*the Inuit ("Eskimo") of Baffin Island. Boas provided several pertinent*
*observations regarding their medicine-men or* angakoq.

[In Eskimo mythology] a great number of minor spirits are known. They are called Tornait, and appear in the shape of men, bears, or stones. By their help a man may become what is called angakoq, a kind of priest or wizard. The spirits help him to discover the causes of sickness and death, and therefore he is the medicine-man. In their incantations they use a peculiar language, which consists to a great extent of archaic roots, and it is remarkable that some of these words which I collected on the coast of Baffin Bay are found in the language of Alaskan tribes. This shows that a close connection existed in olden times between the Eskimo of North-eastern America and the inhabitants of Alaska. The angakoq, or the priest, exercises a great power over the minds of the Eskimo. His commands are strictly obeyed, and his prescriptions regarding the abstaining of certain kinds of work or food are rigidly observed. It is strange that the Eskimo, who have a very limited supply of food animals, should restrict themselves in regard to food. Still their regulations on this subject are numerous. For instance, it is absolutely impossible to induce them to eat walrus meat during the deer-hunting season, or *vice versa*. Seal and deer meat must not be brought into contact, and, although they are not at all cleanly, they wash themselves every time before changing from one food to the other. It is generally believed that the Eskimo are extremely filthy, but I can assure you that this is not so everywhere. . . .

After all the many little adventures, and after a long and intimate intercourse with the Eskimo, it was with feelings of sorrow and regret that I parted from my Arctic friends. I had seen that they enjoyed life, and a hard life, as we do; that nature is also beautiful to them; that feelings of friendship also root in the Eskimo heart; that, although the character of their life is so rude as compared to civilized life, the Eskimo is a man as we are; that his feelings, his virtues, and his shortcomings are based in human nature, like ours.

# 13

# The-Man-Who-Fell-from-Heaven
# Shamanizes Despite Persecution

## WENCESLAS SIEROSHEVSKI

### (1896)

*Wenceslas Sieroshevski, a Pole, was sent as a political exile to the land
of the Yakut people in Siberia for twelve years. On returning from exile,
he wrote a book about the Yakuts in Russian, which the Imperial Russian Geographical Society published in 1896. Sieroshevski noticed that
some shamans had more talent than others, and that their eyes changed
when they practiced their craft.*

A *shaman* whose name meant "The-man-who-fell-from-heaven," told
the author about his career as a *shaman*. He was sixty years old, of
middle stature, a dried up, muscular old man, although it was evident
that he had once been vigorous and active. Even when seen, he could
still perform shamanistic rites, jump and dance the whole night
through without becoming weary. He had travelled from the northern
to the southern extremities of the Yakut territory. His countenance
was dark and full of active expression. His features resembled the
Tungus type. The pupil of his eye was surrounded by a double ring of
a dull green colour. When he was practising his magic, his eyes took
on a peculiar, unpleasant dull glare, and an expression of idiocy, and
their persistent stare, as the author observed, excited and disturbed
those upon whom he fixed it. Another shaman who was observed had

the same peculiarities of the eyes. In general, there is in the appearance of a *shaman* something peculiar, which enabled the author, after some practice, to distinguish them with great certainty in the midst of a number of persons who were present. They are distinguished by a certain energy and mobility of the muscles of the face, which generally amongst the Yakuts are immobile. There is also in their movements a noticeable spryness. Besides this, in the north, they all without exception wear their hair long enough to fall on their shoulders. Generally they braid it behind the head into a queue, or tie it into a tuft. In the south, near the city of Yakutsk, where the clergy and government persecute them, and where they are compelled to hide, long hair is rare. "The-man-who-fell-from-heaven" declared that he did not like long hair because the little lice frisk about in it and torment him. He could not get rid of them without cutting it off. Some shamans are as passionately devoted to their calling as drunkards to drink. This man had several times been condemned to punishment; his professional dress and drum had been burned; his hair had been cut off, and he had been compelled to make a number of obeisances and to fast. He told the author, "We do not carry on this calling without paying for it. Our masters (the spirits) keep a zealous watch over us, and woe betide us afterwards if we do not satisfy them! But we cannot quit it; we cannot cease to practice shaman rites. Yet we do no evil." . . .

Observation justifies the division of *shamans* into great, middling and petty. Some of them dispose of light and darkness in such a masterly manner, also of silence and incantation; the modulation of the voice is so flexible; the gestures so peculiar and expressive; the blows of the drum and the tone of them correspond so well to the moment: and all is intertwined with such an original series of unexpected words, witty observations, artistic and often elegant metaphors, that involutarily you give yourself up to the charm of watching this wild and free evocation and a wild and free spirit.

# 14

# *Sh*amanism Is a Dangerously Vague Word

ARNOLD VAN GENNEP

(1903)

*French anthropological theorist Arnold Van Gennep coined the term* rite
of passage, *which has proved useful for the study of human societies.
One could say that becoming a shaman is a major rite of passage, but
Van Gennep did not approve of the word* shamanism.

We have inherited a certain number of very vague terms, which can be
applied to anything, or even to nothing; some were created by travelers and then thoughtlessly adopted by the dilettantes of ethnopsychology, and used any which way. The most dangerous of these vague
words is *shamanism*.

One finds it used, even in specialized journals, to signify a "reli-
gious form" of a certain kind. Thus one speaks of the shamanism of
Siberian populations, African Negroes, North, Central, and South
American Amerindians. . . .

But this is a strange abuse of language. There can be no shamanic
beliefs or cults, and therefore no shamanic religion, for the simple reason that the word does not designate a set of beliefs that manifest
themselves through a set of customs. It merely affirms the existence of
a certain kind of person who plays a religious and social role. Would
one speak of a sorcery-religion in medieval France or of a witch-

religion in Germany? By using the noun *shamanism* and the adjective *shamanic*, one has accepted the terms invented by eighteenth- and nineteenth-century explorers in Siberia. These explorers, who knew almost nothing about ethnography and general ethnopsychology, thought they had found a special, characteristic form of religious belief and practice. Then the word gained favor among the ignorant, general public and among amateurs of exotic euphonism. . . .

But as soon as one has some knowledge of the beliefs and customs not only of Siberians but of the semicivilized the world over, one realizes that they are more or less the same, that the Siberians are no exception and that it is pointless to borrow one of their words, to divert it from its etymological meaning and to apply it elsewhere, when other terms, which are more precise, comprehensive, and logical, exist.

"Shamanism" comes from *shaman (saman)*, a word used only by the Tungus, Buryats, and Yakuts. . . .

The shaman is a sorcerer who is essentially no different from the medicine men of the Amerindians, Negroes, Malaysians, etc. What, then, does the derived word *shamanism* mean? That one adores sorcerers and worships them? That is impossible, because the sorcerer is neither a spirit nor a god. Perhaps one believes in sorcerers and considers them to have special, magical, and supernatural powers? But that would not suffice to constitute a *religion;* Siberians are not the only ones to have individuals who serve as intermediaries between the divinities and ordinary humans; one does not refer to catholicism as *priestism*, to protestantism as *ministerism,* or to buddhism as *bonzism.* . . .

The word *sorcerer* is too evocative of modern or medieval Europe; for the semicivilized, it is better to use the word *shaman*. But when it comes to the word *shamanism,* which does not apply to anything definite, one would do better, it seems to me, to leave it out.

# 15

# "Doomed to Inspiration"

WALDEMAR BOGORAS

(1904)

*In the late nineteenth century, Waldemar Bogoras was exiled to north-eastern Siberia for his revolutionary activities. He decided to study the area's indigenous inhabitants. In 1900, the American Museum of Natural History mounted an expedition to the North Pacific and hired him to study the Chukchee people. In 1901, Bogoras fled Russia and settled in New York City, where he wrote* The Chukchee. *This book has since become an ethnographic classic because it is clear and detailed. Here Bogoras discusses the difficulties of becoming a Chukchee shaman.*

The shamanic call manifests itself in various ways. Sometimes it is an inner voice, which bids the person enter into intercourse with the "spirits." If the person is dilatory in obeying, the calling "spirit" soon appears in some outward, visible shape, and communicates the call in a more explicit way. . . .

Young people, as a rule, are exceedingly reluctant to obey the call, especially if it involves the adoption of some characteristic device in clothing or in the mode of life. They refuse to take the drum and to call the "spirits," leave the amulets in the field, from very fear, etc.

The parents of young persons "doomed to inspiration" act differently, according to temperament and family conditions. Sometimes they protest against the call coming to their child, and try to induce it to reject the "spirits" and to keep to the ordinary life. This happens mostly in the case of only children, because of the danger pertaining to the shamanistic call, especially in the beginning. The protest of the parents is, however, of no avail, because the rejection of the "spirits" is much more dangerous even than the acceptance of their call. A young man thwarted in his call to inspiration will either sicken and shortly die, or else the "spirits" will induce him to renounce his home and go far away, where he may follow his vocation without hindrance.

On the other hand, it is entirely permissible to abandon shamanistic performances at a more mature age, after several years of practice; and the anger of the "spirits" is not incurred by it. I met several persons who asserted that formerly they had been great shamans, but that now they had given up most of their exercises. As reason for this, they gave illness, age or simply a decrease of their shamanistic power, which in the course of time manifested itself. One said that because of illness he felt as if his arms and legs were frozen, and that thereafter they did not thaw, so that he was unable to "shake himself" well upon the drum. Another said that he and his "spirits" became tired of each other. Most of the cases, probably, were simply the result of recovery from the nervous condition which had made the persons in question fit subjects for the inspiration. While the shaman is in possession of the inspiration, he must practise, and cannot hide his power. Otherwise it will manifest itself in the form of bloody sweat or in a fit of violent madness similar to epilepsy.

There are parents who wish their child to answer the call. This happens especially in families rich in children, with large herds, and with several tents of their own. Such a family is not inclined to feel anxious about a possible loss of one of its members. On the contrary, they are desirous of having a shaman of their own—made to order, so to speak—a special solicitor before the "spirits," and a caretaker in all extraordinary casualties of life.

A shaman by the name of Tei'ñet, in the country near the Wolverene River, told me that, when the call came to him and he did not want to obey, his father gave him the drum and induced him to begin the exercise. After that he continued to feel "bashful" for several years.

On days of ceremonials he even fled from the camp and hid himself, lest his relatives should find him out and bring him back to camp, to show to the assembled people his newly acquired and growing skill.

For men, the preparatory stage of shamanistic inspiration is in most cases very painful, and extends over a long time. The call comes in an abrupt and obscure manner, leaving the young novice in much uncertainty regarding it. He feels "bashful" and frightened; he doubts his own disposition and strength, as has been the case with all seers, from Moses down. Half unconsciously and half against his own will, his whole soul undergoes a strange and painful transformation. This period may last months, and sometimes even years. The young novice, the "newly inspired," loses all interest in the ordinary affairs of life. He ceases to work, eats but little and without relishing the food, ceases to talk to people, and does not even answer their questions. The greater part of his time he spends in sleep.

Some keep to the inner room and go out but rarely. Others wander about in the wilderness, under the pretext of hunting or of keeping watch over the herd, but often without taking along any arms of the lasso or the herdsman. A wanderer like this, however, must be closely watched, otherwise he might lie down on the open tundra and sleep for three or four days, incurring the danger, in winter, of being buried in drifting snow. . . .

The preparatory period is compared by the Chukchee to a long, severe illness; and the acquirement of inspiration, to a recovery. There are cases of young persons who, having suffered for years from lingering illness (usually of a nervous character), at last feel a call to take to shamanistic practice, and by this means overcome the disease. Of course it is difficult to draw the line of demarcation, and all these cases finally come under one and the same class. The preparatory period of inspiration is designated by the Chukchee by a special term, meaning "he gathers shamanistic power." With weaker shamans and with women, the preparatory period is less painful, and the call to inspiration comes mainly in dreams.

To people of more mature age the shamanistic call may come during some great misfortune, dangerous and protracted illness, sudden loss of family or property, etc. Then the person, having no other resource, turns to the "spirits," and claims their assistance. It is generally considered that in such cases a favorable issue is possible only with the aid of the "spirits:" therefore a man who has withstood some extraordinary trial of his life is considered as having within himself the possibilities of a shaman, and he often feels bound to enter into closer relations with the "spirits," lest he incur their displeasure at his negligence and lack of gratitude. . . .

The single means used by the Chukchee shamans, novice or experienced, for communication with "spirits," is the beating of the drum and singing. . . .

The beating of the drum, notwithstanding its seeming simplicity, requires some skill, and the novice must spend considerable time before he can acquire the desired degree of perfection. This has reference especially to the power of endurance of the performer. The same may be said of the singing. The manifestations continue for several hours, during all which time the shaman exercises the most violent activity without scarcely a pause. After the performance he must not show any signs of fatigue, because he is supposed to be sustained by the "spirits;" and, moreover, the greater part of the exercise is asserted to be the work of the "spirits" themselves, either while entering his body, or while outside his body. The degree of endurance required for all this, and the ability to pass quickly from the highest excitement to a state of normal quietude, can, of course, be acquired only by long practice. Indeed, all the shamans I conversed with said that they had to spend a year, or even two years, before sufficient strength of hand, and freedom of voice, were given to them by the "spirits." Some asserted that during all this preparatory time they kept closely to the inner room, taking up the drum several times a day, and beating it as long as their strength would allow.

The only other means of training for inspiration, of which I am aware, is abstention from all fat and rich foods, as well as great moderation in eating. The same strictness is observed ever afterwards in the preparation for each individual performance, in which the shaman tries to abstain wholly from food.

Various tricks performed by the Chukchee shamans, including ventriloquism, have to be learned in the preparatory stage. However, I could obtain no detailed information on this point, since the shamans, of course, asserted that the tricks were done by "spirits," and denied having any hand whatever in proceedings of such a character. . . .

Most of the shamans I knew claimed to have had no teachers, but to have acquired their art by their own individual efforts. I am not aware of a single instance of the transfer of shamanistic power in the whole domain of Chukchee folklore.

# 16.

# Ventriloquist and Trickster Performances for Healing and Divination

VLADIMIR ILICH JOCHELSON

(1908)

*In the late nineteenth century, Russian ethnographer and linguist Vladimir Ilich Jochelson was exiled to eastern Siberia because of his revolutionary activities. He used the opportunity to study the area's indigenous inhabitants. In 1900 he participated in the Jesup North Pacific Expedition organized by the American Museum of Natural History, for which he produced a study called* The Koryak. *Jochelson differs from eighteenth-century observers: He explains the shaman's trick but does not debunk him. Jochelson also notices that shamans use fly-agaric mushrooms.*

During the entire period of my sojourn among the Koryak I had opportunity to see only two shamans. Both were young men, and neither enjoyed special respect on the part of his relatives. Both were poor men who worked as laborers for the rich members of their tribe. One of them was a Maritime Koryak from Alutor. He used to come to the village of Kamenskoye in company with a Koryak trader. He was a bashful youth. His features, though somewhat wild, were flexible and pleasant, and his eyes were bright. I asked him to show me proof of his shamanistic art. Unlike other shamans, he consented without waiting to be coaxed. The people put out the oil-lamps in the underground house in which he stopped with his master. Only a few coals were glowing on the hearth, and it was almost dark in the house. On the large platform which is put up in the front part of the house as the seat and sleeping-place for visitors, and not far from where my wife and I were sitting, we could just discern the shaman in an ordinary shaggy shirt of reindeer-skin, squatting on the reindeer-skins that covered the platform. His face was covered with a large oval drum.

Suddenly he commenced to beat the drum softly and to sing in a plaintive voice: then the beating of the drum grew stronger and stronger; and his song—in which could be heard sounds imitating the howling of the wolf, the groaning of the cargoose, and the voices of other animals, his guardian spirits—appeared to come sometimes from the corner nearest to my seat, then from the opposite end, then again from the middle of the house, and then it seemed to proceed from the ceiling. He was a ventriloquist. Shamans versed in this art are believed to possess particular power. His drum also seemed to sound, now over my head, now at my feet, now behind, now in front of me. I could see nothing; but it seemed to me that the shaman was moving around us, noiselessly stepping upon the platform with his fur shoes, then retiring to some distance, then coming nearer, lightly jumping, and then squatting down on his heels.

All of a sudden the sound of the drum and the singing ceased. When the women had relighted their lamps, he was lying, completely exhausted, on a white reindeer-skin on which he had been sitting before the shamanistic performance. The concluding words of the shaman, which he pronounced in a recitative, were uttered as though spoken by the spirit whom he had summoned up, and who declared that the "disease" had left the village, and would not return.

The shaman's prediction suited me admirably, for one of the old Koryak had forbidden his children to go into the house where I stopped to take measurements, saying that they would die if they allowed themselves to be measured. He also tried to stir up the other Koryak against me, pointing out to them that an epidemic of measles had broken out after the departure of Dr. Slunin's expedition, and that the same thing might take place after I left.

I made an appointment with the shaman's master to have him call on me, together with the shaman, on the following day. I wished to take a record in writing of the text of the incantations which I had heard; but when I woke up in the morning, I was informed that the shaman had left at daybreak.

I saw another shaman among the Reindeer Koryak of the Taigonos Peninsula. He had been called from a distant camp to treat a syphilitic patient who had large ulcers in his throat that made him unable to swallow. I was not present at the treatment of the patient, since the latter lived in another camp, at a distance of several miles from us, and I learned of the performance of the rite only after it was over. The Koryak asserted that the patient was relieved immediately after the shamanistic exercises, and that he drank two cups of tea without any difficulty. Among other things, the shaman ordered the isolation to the patient from his relatives, lest the spirits that had caused the disease might pass to others. A separate tent was pitched next to the main tent for the patient and his wife, who was taking care of him. I lived in the house of the patient's brother, the official chief of the Taigonos Koryak. At my request he sent reindeer to bring the shaman. The shaman arrived. His appearance did not inspire much confidence.

In order to obtain a large remuneration, he refused at first, under various pretexts, to perform his art. I asked him to "look at my road;" that is, to divine whether I should reach the end of my journey safely. The official chief said that this performance must take place in my own tent, and not in that of some one else; but the shaman declared that his spirits would not enter a Russian lodging, and that he would be in deadly peril if he should call up spirits for a foreigner. Finally it was decided that the peril for the shaman would be eliminated by making his remuneration large enough to completely satisfy the spirits. I promised to give the shaman, not only a red flannel shirt, which he liked very much, but also a big Belgian knife. I had offered him first the choice of one of the two articles; but he declared that his spirits liked one as well as the other.

Another difficulty arose over the drum. The chief himself found a way out of it by means of casuistry. He gave his own drum, saying that a family drum must not be taken into another Koryak's house, but that it was permissible to take it into mine. The drum was brought into my tent by one of the three wives of the chief. It was in its case, because the drum must not be taken out of the house without its cover. A violation of this taboo may result in bringing on a blizzard.

During the shamanistic exercises there were present, besides my wife and myself, the chief, his wife who had brought the drum, my cossack, and the interpreter. The shaman had a position on the floor in a corner of the tent, not far from the entrance. He was sitting with his legs crossed, and from time to time he would rise to his knees. He beat the drum violently, and sang in a loud voice, summoning the spirits. As he explained to me after the ceremony, his main guardian spirits were One-who-walks-around-the-Earth, Broad-soled-One (one of the mythical names of the wolf), and the raven. The appearance of the spirits of these animals was accompanied by imitations of sounds characteristic of their voices. Through their mediation he appealed to The-One-on-High with the following song; which was accompanied by the beating of the drum:

(It is) good that (he) should arrive.
Also I should well myself also reach home.

That is, "Let him reach home safely, and let me also reach home safely." Suddenly, in the midst of the wildest singing and beating of the drum, he stopped, and said to me, "The spirits say that I should cut myself with a knife. You will not be afraid?" "You may cut yourself, I am not afraid," I replied. "Give me your knife, then. I am performing my incantations for you, so I have to cut myself with your knife," said he. To tell the truth, I commenced to feel somewhat uneasy; while my wife, who was sitting on the floor by my side, and who was completely overwhelmed by the wild shrieks and the sound of the drum, entreated me not to give him the knife. . . .

I took from its sheath my sharp "Finnish" travelling-knife, that looked like a dagger, and gave it to him. The light in the tent was put out; but the dim light of the arctic spring night (it was in April), which penetrated the canvas of the tent, was sufficient to allow me to follow the movements of the shaman. He took the knife, beat the drum, and sang, telling the spirits that he was ready to carry out their wishes. After a little while he put away the drum, and, emitting a rattling sound from his throat, he thrust the knife into his breast up to the hilt. I noticed, however, that after having cut his jacket, he turned the knife downward. He drew out the knife with the same rattling in his throat, and resumed beating the drum. Then he turned to me, and said that the spirits had secured for me a safe journey over the Koryak land, and predicted that the Sun-Chief—i.e., the Czar—would reward me for my labors.

Contrary to my expectations, he returned the knife to me (I thought he would say that the knife with which he had cut himself must be left with him), and through the hole in his jacket he showed spots of blood on his body. Of course, these spots had been made before. However, this cannot be looked upon as mere deception. Things visible and imaginary are confounded to such an extent in primitive consciousness, that the shaman himself may have thought that there was, invisible to others, a real gash in his body, as had been demanded by the spirits. The common Koryak, however, are sure that the shaman actually cuts himself, and that the wound heals up immediately. . . .

Many shamans, previous to their seances, eat fly-agaric [mushroom] in order to get into ecstatic states. Once I asked a Reindeer Koryak, who was reputed to be an excellent singer, to sing into the phonograph. Several times he attempted, but without success. He evidently grew timid before the invisible recorder; but after eating two fungi, he began to sing in a loud voice, gesticulating with his hands. I had to support him, lest he fall on the machine; and when the cylinder came to an end, I had to tear him away from the horn, where he remained bending over it for a long time, keeping up his songs.

# 17.

# "A Motley Class of Persons"

ROLAND B. DIXON

(1908)

*American anthropologist Roland B. Dixon wrote a useful survey called "Some Aspects of the American Shaman." It shows that a good deal of information was already available on the subject at the beginning of the twentieth century. Dixon made a start at classifying what makes a shaman, and how a shaman is made.*

In any study of the religious beliefs and ceremonials of savage or semi-civilized peoples, either special or comparative, the shaman stands easily as one of the foremost figures. On almost every side of their religious life his influence makes itself felt, and his importance reaches out beyond the limits of religion into the domain of social life and organization and governmental control. By some the term shaman is confined, and perhaps rightly, within somewhat narrow limits; if I may be pardoned the liberty, I shall here extend rather than restrict the meaning of the term, and shall use it as applying to that motley class of persons, found in every savage community, who are supposed to have closer relations with the supernatural than other men, and who, according as they use the advantages of their position in one way or another, are the progenitors alike of the physician and the sorcerer, the prophet, the teacher, and the priest.

Although fundamentally the shaman is everywhere much alike, yet there are not inconsiderable differences apparent, both in his character and position. . . .

One of the broadest distinctions which may be made, in connection with the making of shamans, is that of sex—whether the practice of shamanism is open freely to both sexes, or is more or less restricted to one or the other. In this particular, America is at one with most of the rest of the world in that, predominantly, shamans are male. It by no means follows, however, that women are entirely excluded, for indeed there are few cases known where men exclusively perform this important function. Among various tribes, in both North and South America, the number of women as compared to men in the profession is small, and in some instances no mention is made of women shamans at all. Yet in these cases there are often indications from other sources that they really did exist. We ought to expect, also, that in those tribes where the shaman was already well advanced on the way to becoming a priest, that the proportion of women would in most cases be very small. Opposed to this prevalence of men as shamans, we find in several sections women shamans equalling or even exceeding the men in importance, as in northern California, or among some of the Carib tribes. The element of sex appears again in another way, as among the tribes of Patagonia, where there was a curious custom which prescribed the wearing of female clothing by male shamans. This assumption of the apparel of the opposite sex seems rare in America, but somewhat analogous conditions exist among various tribes of northeastern Asia. In general, then, it appears that in America women are widely permitted to become shamans, male shamans even in some cases having to assume women's dress, and that the tendency toward the exclusion of women is not as strong as, for example, in much of Polynesia or in Australia.

Next to questions of sex, one of the most important distinctions lies in heredity. In numerous instances the position of shaman descends by inheritance, in either the male or female line, according to the prevailing system of tribal descent. In most such cases the assumption of shamanhood is not merely permissive, but mandatory, and refusal by the heir to accept the responsibilities was punished by the spirits with sickness or death.

Contrasted with this hereditary principle, we find many tribes where it plays at best but a small part. That the position is anywhere regarded as exclusively to be attained by inheritance seems not to be the case. More commonly the hereditary element is only moderately developed, and the position of shaman may equally well be obtained as a result of individual initiative, the man or woman seeking to acquire the gift, the position being regarded as open to all. This conscious seeking is further not ruled out by inheritance; for while by inheritance the individual may secure one or two guardian spirits, for example, he often exerts himself to acquire others in addition.

Contrasted both with the idea of inheritance and of conscious seeking, there is not infrequently something like a supposed selection of the individual by the supernatural beings who force him to enter the ranks of the shamans, and who punish refusal with death. More rarely, perhaps, the selection is human, not divine; for the older shamans select those youths whom they regard as most likely to make good successors to themselves, and teach them the art, or train them to be their assistants. In such cases often the selection is made because of certain psychic qualities which the youth is thought to possess, such as a tendency to epileptic attacks.

Where the future shaman is designated, either by heredity or by the spirits, indications are usually early apparent. These signs are in part purely subjective and personal, taking the form of dreams, visions, or extraordinary experiences; and partly patent to the world at large, in a growing abstraction of manner, a tendency toward solitude, or in some cases more or less frequent cataleptic seizures. To those who inherit their position, or have it thrust upon them by higher power, these things come naturally, whereas the seekers after shamanhood must induce them artificially and consciously. To refuse to heed the call of heredity or the mandates of the gods is to bring down on the individual's head the wrath of the beings by whose aid the shaman accomplishes his results, and such bold persons are punished by disease, loss of reason, or death. In the case of the individual seeker after shamanhood, the attitude is not, after all, very different from that of the ordinary seeker for a personal guardian or manitou. Both are consciously asking aid of the divine beings, and both employ as a whole similar methods, but the powers so gained are employed by one professionally, whereas the other looks at them in quite a different light.

Whatever the sex, and in whatever manner the novice comes to be a member of the craft, the sources of his power, and the means by which he accomplishes his purposes are mainly four: He may derive his aid and secure his guardian from among the host of animal spirits; or from local spirits of various sorts and those of natural phenomena; or from the ghosts of the dead; or, lastly, from the greater deities themselves. Of these, the first seems to be by far the most common in America as a whole; and where, in some cases, the guardian spirits are not themselves animal, it sometimes occurs that the shaman's powers are secured, at least in some degree, through their aid. Various local or disembodied spirits, or those of natural phenomena, seem perhaps the next most common source of power, and these are often conceived of as human or semi-human in form. A ghostly origin for the shaman's power is, on the whole, rather rare; but we may see one form of the idea in the Tlingit method, adopted as a last resort by those seeking to acquire shamanistic strength, of sleeping on a grave, or biting off the finger of a corpse. That the power of the shaman comes directly or indirectly from one of the higher deities seems, also, a comparatively restricted belief in America. Such instances, however, as that of the Mohave are striking, for here not only is the shaman supposed to secure his strength from the greater deities, but to have so secured it before birth, in the mythic age. . . .

It goes without saying almost, that the most widespread method is that of fasting and solitude. The weakening of the body and the stimulation of the imagination through these means is almost universally regarded as one of the most efficient ways of getting into communication with the unseen world, and is employed alike by the shaman novice and by the seeker for spiritual aid of all sorts. Very frequently there is added to this requirement of fasting and solitude that of bodily cleanliness. This may be attained by frequent bathing in remote lakes or streams, by the use of the sudatory, or by either of these means, with the added requirement of rubbing the body or scenting it with fragrant herbs and roots. Not infrequently, also, this exterior cleanliness must be accompanied by an inner cleansing as well, and we have then the use of various sorts of purgatives and emetics, as among the Muskogi, the Caribs, and other tribes. The underlying principle in this is, in many instances, clearly that the supernatural beings are displeased by bodily uncleanliness, and attracted by its opposite, and will therefore refuse to come to an applicant who does not present himself clean and sweet-smelling, or at least without the smell of mankind.

These means alone are, however, often thought to be inadequate unless supplemented by some sort of offering or sacrifice. Such sacrifices are as a rule not great, and consist of a few beads, a little tobacco, or in some cases the offering of a few drops of the applicant's blood. Such gifts are accompanied by a brief prayer to the spirit for aid. Animal sacrifice, under such conditions, seems almost if not quite unknown in America.

The use of drugs to induce a stupor, in which the shaman novice is visited by the spirits, is in the northern continent rather rare, but appears much more frequently in South America, where the use of drugs is reported, or may be inferred, over large areas. That dreams are also a most important element in the initiation of the shaman's association with the supernatural beings is well known, and these are as a rule made more vivid by the fasting and solitude which, as already stated, almost invariably form part of the preliminary training.

# 18

# Seeking Contact with Spirits Is Not Necessarily Shamanism

FRANZ BOAS

(1910)

*Franz Boas did fieldwork among native North Americans over decades, from Baffin Island to New Mexico. This gave him a vantage point from which to generalize with a clear eye. People often confuse vision quests with shamanism. Here Boas discusses how the two differ, but he also notes that they can lead to each other.*

Perhaps the most characteristic of North American Indian methods of gaining control over supernatural powers is that of the acquisition of one of them as a personal protector. Generally this process is called the acquiring of a manito; and the most common method of acquiring it is for the young man during the period of adolescence to purify himself by fasting, bathing, and vomiting, until his body is perfectly clean and acceptable to the supernatural beings. At the same time the youth works himself by these means, by dancing, and sometimes also by means of drugs, into a trance, in which he has a vision of the guardian spirit which is to protect him throughout life. These means of establishing communication with the spirit world are in very general use, also at other periods of life. The magic power that man thus acquires may give him special abilities; it may make him a successful hunter, warrior, or shaman; or it may give him power to acquire wealth, success in gambling, or the love of women. . . .

Protection against disease is also sought by the help of superhuman powers. These practices have two distinct forms, according to the fundamental conception of disease. Disease is conceived of principally in two forms—either as due to the presence of a material object in the body of the patient, or as an effect of the absence of the soul from the body. The cure of disease is intrusted to the shamans or medicine-men, who obtain their powers generally by the assistance of guardian spirits, or who may personally be endowed with magic powers. It is their duty to discover the material disease which is located in the patient's body, and which they extract by sucking or pulling with the hands; or to go in pursuit of the absent soul, to recover it, and to restore it to the patient. Both of these forms of shamanism are found practically all over the continent but in some regions—for instance, in California—the idea of material bodies that cause sickness is particularly strongly developed; while in other regions the idea of the absence of the soul seems to be more marked. In treating the patient, the shamans almost everywhere use various means to work themselves into a state of excitement, which is produced by singing, by the use of the drum and rattle, and by dancing. The belief also widely prevails that unpropitious conditions may counteract the work of the shaman, and that for this reason particular care must be taken to remove all disturbing and impure elements from the place where the shamanistic performance is held. When the shaman has to have intercourse with the spirits, whom he visits in their own domain, or when he has to pursue the soul of the patient, we find frequently sleight-of-hand employed, such as the tying of the hands of the shaman, who, when his soul leaves the body, is believed to free himself with the help of the spirits.

The belief that certain individuals can acquire control over the powers has also led to the opinion that they may be used to harm enemies. The possession of such control is not always beneficial, but may be used also for purposes of witchcraft. Hostile shamans may throw disease into the bodies of their enemies or they may abduct their souls. They may do harm by sympathetic means, and control the will-power of others by the help of the supernatural means at their disposal. Witchcraft is everywhere considered as a crime, and is so punished.

# 19.

# "The Shaman Practices on the Verge of Insanity"

## MARIE ANTOINETTE CZAPLICKA
## (1914)

*Polish-born anthropologist Marie Antoinette Czaplicka wrote a thesis at Oxford University in which she used the literature on Siberian shamans and summarized the medicalized view that shamans are mentally unstable.*

Although hysteria (called by some writers "Arctic hysteria") lies at the bottom of the shaman's vocation, yet at the same time the shaman differs from an ordinary patient suffering from this illness in possessing an extremely great power of mastering himself in the periods between the actual fits, which occur during the ceremonies. [As Sieroshevski wrote:] "A good shaman ought to possess many unusual qualities, but the chief is the power, acquired by tact and knowledge, to influence the people round him." His reserved attitude has undoubtedly a great influence on the people among whom he lives. He must know how and when to have his fit of inspiration, which sometimes rises to frenzy, and also how to preserve his high "tabooed" attitude in his daily life....

Whether his calling be hereditary or not, a shaman must be a capable—nay, an inspired person. Of course, this is practically the same thing as saying that he is nervous and excitable, often to the verge of insanity. So long as he practices his vocation, however, the shaman never passes this verge. It often happens that before entering the calling persons have had serious nervous affections. Thus a Chukchee female shaman, Telpina, according to her own statement, had been violently insane for three years, during which time her household had taken precautions that she should do no harm to the people or to herself.

[As Jochelson wrote:] "I was told that people about to become shamans have fits of wild paroxysms alternating with a condition of complete exhaustion. They will lie motionless for two or three days without partaking of food or drink. Finally they retire to the wilderness, where they spend their time enduring hunger and cold in order to prepare themselves for their calling."

To be called to become a shaman is generally equivalent to being afflicted with hysteria; then the accepting of the call means recovery. [Bogoraz wrote:] "There are cases of young persons who, having suffered for years from lingering illness (usually of a nervous character), at last feel a call to take up shamanistic practice and by this means overcome the disease."

# PART FOUR

# The Understanding
# Deepens

In the first half of the twentieth century, anthropologists began listening closely to shamans and recording what they said about themselves. This is when their understanding deepened.

Throughout this period, anthropologists and ethnopsychiatrists debated whether shamans were mentally deranged. Claude Lévi-Strauss appeared to settle the issue by twisting it around and saying that shamans were more like psychoanalysts than psychotics. But the debate raged on.

Mircea Eliade had another ax to grind in his grand synthesis *Shamanism: Archaic Techniques of Ecstasy*. He wanted the shaman to go to heaven. Eliade defined *shamanism* as "techniques of ecstasy" or soul-flight (in Greek, the word *ekstasis* means "standing outside oneself"). Eliade emphasized "celestial" flights over "infernal" ones.

"Descents to the underworld, the struggle against evil spirits, but also the increasingly familiar relations with 'spirits' that result from their 'embodiment' or in the shaman's being 'possessed' by 'spirits,' are innovations, most of them recent," Eliade wrote. "The specific element of shamanism is not the incorporation of spirits by the shaman, but the ecstasy provoked by the ascension to the sky or by the descent to Hell: the incorporation of spirits and possession by them are universally distributed phenomena, but they do not belong necessarily to shamanism in the strict sense."

But Eliade's distinctions ultimately appear to have more to do with his own religious beliefs than with the facts. When one goes back to the primary accounts of Arctic shamanism that Eliade used to fashion his soaring overview, one finds that shamanism and spirit possession regularly occur together.

It turns out that acting as a medium for spirits, spirit possession, and shamanism occur on a continuum. They all involve trance states and contact with spirits, but each one has its specific character. Mediums rarely operate with music, while shamans and possession cults almost always do. Similarly, while acting as a medium for spirits does not necessarily involve the conception of a cosmos, shamanism and possession cults usually do. Finally, a shamanic session differs from a possession cult, such as the vodoun ceremony in Haiti, in that the shaman's audience usually remains passive; participants may go into trance, but it is the shaman, rather than the audience, who performs in the ceremony.

These distinctions explain why there are surprisingly few accounts of shamanism in Africa, which is thought to be the cradle of humanity. Most cases of trance states and spirit communication in Africa involve possession rather than shamanism. But some cases defy easy classification. Lorna Marshall, for example, describes medicine men among the !Kung Bushmen of South-West Africa who seem to operate as shamans: They go into trance while singing and treat the sick by drawing out illness and casting it back to the spirits. But contrary to the "classical" shamans of Asia and the Americas, who tend to operate alone, half of all male Bushmen are medicine men; shamanism among them is more a collective affair than an individual one. And the !Kung women, who are not shamans, sing and clap ardently while the medicine men go into deep trance; they play an active role, which is uncharacteristic of most shamanic audiences.

Further illustrating the confusion about shamanism in Africa, Marshall did not call the !Kung medicine men "shamans" when they appear to do the work of shamans. Anthropologist Siegfried Nadel, on the other hand, described "shamans" among the Nyima of Sudan who seemed in fact to be mediums. They went into trances in seances to contact spirits for clients without performing music of any kind. Although Nadel stated that the activities he observed among these people corresponded "in all the essentials to the classical shamanism of Central Asia and North West America," he seemed to be describing mediums rather than shamans. So while Marshall's report is included here, Nadel's is not.

Even though African people appear to enter into contact with spirits by being possessed by them, rather than by calling them and controlling them, as in shamanism, it is possible that shamanic practices may be more widespread in Africa than is generally acknowledged. Furthermore, finding clear-cut limits between mediums, possession cults, and shamanism is ultimately somewhat arbitrary. In Haitian vodoun, for example, those who participate in *loa* ceremonies, and whom the spirits possess, often do not remember what happened to them during the possession; if they do, it it is generally considered that they have not gone into deep enough trances. But the *loa* priest or priestess eventually learns to see in trance, a process called *la prise des yeux*. This enables them essentially to become shamans in that they can control their own trances. As Gilbert Rouget points out in his book *Music and Trance: A Theory of the Relations between Music and Possession:* "Shamanic trance and possession trance . . . can thus alternate in one and the same person. Or, if one prefers, one and the same person can undergo in succession these two forms of trance. It seems that no one can experience them simultaneously."

There are clear shamanic elements in Haitian vodoun, such as commerce with spirits through trance states involving music, and healing conducted by the vodoun priest or priestess. Yet, vodoun has been considered by most authorities as separate from shamanism and is classified under "possession." We have hewed to this classical classification and have not included reports on vodoun or other possession cults in this volume.

In 1944, Alfred Métraux defined the shaman as "any individual who maintains by profession and in the interest of the community an intermittent commerce with spirits, or who is possessed by them." While Métraux's definition is appealing in its simplicity and evenhandedness, it is perhaps ultimately too broad, as it also fits African and Haitian possession cults. So we would add to Métraux's definition: Shamanism involves a kind of theater in which the shaman performs and the audience remains an audience.

In possession cults, such as vodoun, the audience is encouraged to become actively engaged in the drama of spirit possession. In shamanism it is the shaman who is on stage and is the dramatic actor.

# 20

# Near-Death Experience

## IVALO AND KNUD RASMUSSEN

### (1929)

*Danish anthropologist Knud Rasmussen was born in Greenland in 1879. He grew up in contact with the Inuit ("Eskimo"), whose language he learned. He studied in Denmark but conducted most of his work independently of institutions. From 1921 to 1924 he led the Danish expedition to Arctic North America, during which he interviewed several shamans (known locally as* angakut). *Rasmussen took pains to write down people's stories word for word. His texts on shamanism have been widely quoted because of their quality. Rasmussen is a shining light of ethnographic understanding. Here he quotes a man called Ivalo, who tells how his relative Niviatsian became a shaman.*

Niviatsian, Aua's cousin, was out hunting walrus with a number of other men near Iglulik; some were in front of him and others behind. Suddenly a great walrus came up through the ice close beside him, grasped him with his huge fore-flippers, just as a mother picks up her little child, and carried him off with it down into the deep. The other men ran up, and looking down through the hole in the ice where the walrus had disappeared, they could see it still holding him fast and trying to pierce him with its tusks. After a little while it let him go, and rose to the surface, a great distance off, to breathe. But Niviatsian, who had been dragged away from the hole through which he had first been pulled down, struggled with arms and legs to come up again. The men could follow his movements, and cut a hole about where they expected him to come up, and here my father actually did manage to pull him up. There was a gaping wound over his collarbone, and he was breathing through it; the gash had penetrated to the lung. Some of his ribs were broken, and the broken ends had caught in one of his lungs, so that he could not stand upright.

Niviatsian lay for a long time unconscious. When he came to himself, however, he was able to get on his feet without help. The wound over the collarbone was the only serious one; there were traces of the walrus's tusks both on his head and in different parts of his body, but it seemed as if the animal had been unable to wound him there. Old folk said that this walrus had been sent by the Mother of the Sea Beasts, who was angry because Niviatsian's wife had had a miscarriage and concealed the fact in order to avoid the taboo.

Niviatsian then went with his companions in towards land, but he had to walk a little way apart from them, on ice free from footmarks. Close to land, a small snow hut was built, and he was shut in there, laid down on a sealskin with all his wet clothes on. There he remained for three days and three nights without food or drink, this he was obliged to do in order to be allowed to live, for if he had gone up at once to the unclean dwellings of men after the ill-treatment he had received, he would have died.

All the time Niviatsian was in the little snow hut, the shaman up at the village was occupied incessantly in purifying his wife and his old mother, who were obliged to confess in the presence of others all their breaches of taboo, in order to appease the powers that ruled over life and death. And after three days, Niviatsian recovered, and had now become a great shaman. The walrus, which had failed to kill him, became his first helping spirit. That was the beginning.

# 21

# Seeking Knowledge in the Solitude of Nature

## IGJUGÂRJUK AND KNUD RASMUSSEN

### (1930)

*Knud Rasmussen quotes Inuit shaman Igjugârjuk on how he became a shaman. Igjugârjuk's words have the ring of truth.*

"When I was to be a shaman, I chose suffering through the two things that are most dangerous to us humans, suffering through hunger and suffering through cold. First I hungered five days and was then allowed to drink a mouthful of warm water; the old ones say that only if the water is warm will Pinga and Hila notice the novice and help him. Thereafter I went hungry another fifteen days, and again was given a mouthful of warm water. After that I hungered for ten days, and then could begin to eat. . . .

"These days of 'seeking for knowledge' are very tiring, for one must walk all the time, no matter what the weather is like and only rest in short snatches. I am usually quite done up, tired, not only in body but also in head, when I have found what I sought.

"We shamans in the interior have no special spirit language, and believe that the real angatkut do not need it. On my travels I have sometimes been present at a seance among the saltwater-dwellers, for instance among the coast people at Utkuhigjalik. These angatkut never seemed trustworthy to me. It always appeared to me that these

salt-water angatkut attached more weight to tricks that would aston-
ish the audience, when they jumped about the floor and lisped all sorts
of absurdities and lies in their so-called spirit language; to me all this
seemed only amusing and as something that would impress the ignorant. A real shaman does not jump about the floor and do tricks, nor
does he seek by the aid of darkness, by putting out the lamps, to make
the minds of his neighbours uneasy. For myself, I do not think I know
much, but I do not think that wisdom or knowledge about things that
are hidden can be sought in that manner. True wisdom is only to be
found far away from people, out in the great solitude, and it is not
found in play but only through suffering. Solitude and suffering open
the human mind, and therefore a shaman must seek his wisdom there.

"But during my visits to the salt-water shamans . . . I have never
openly expressed my contempt for their manner of summoning their
helping spirits. A stranger ought always to be cautious, for—one may
never know—they may of course be skilful in magic and, like our
shamans, be able to kill through words and thoughts. This that I am
telling you now, I dare confide to you, because you are a stranger from
a far away country, but I would never speak about it to my own kins-
men, except those whom I should teach to become shamans. While I
was at Utkuhigjalik, people there had heard from my wife that I was a
shaman, and therefore they once asked me to cure a sick man, a man
who was so wasted that he could no longer swallow food. I summoned
all the people of the village together and asked them to hold a song-
feast, as is our custom, because we believe that all evil will shun a
place where people are happy. And when the song-feast began, I went
out alone into the night. They laughed at me, and my wife was later on
able to tell me how they mocked me, because I would not do tricks to
entertain everybody. But I kept away in lonely places, far from the village, for five days, thinking uninterruptedly of the sick man and wish-
ing him health. He got better, and since then nobody at that village has
mocked me."

.   .   .

*Rasmussen goes on to note:*

Thus did Igjugârjuk speak about himself and his special powers, and the whole of the characteristic I have given him elsewhere will, I hope, make it obvious that he himself believed everything he told me. Nor had he in fact any reason for lying or exaggerating. I never attempted to contradict him, even if some of his accounts seemed quite improbable to me. For instance, I could not understand that a man could survive thirty to fifty degrees of cold, sitting in a tiny snow hut without taking any nourishment, simply a little tepid water twice during the whole period. I was afraid of making him cautious by doubting or asking him questions, and after all what I wanted to get to know, here as elsewhere, was these people's own beliefs. And there is not the slightest doubt that they themselves believed that the holy art itself, which consisted in being able to see into the riddles of life, imparted to novices and practitioners some special power that enabled them to go through what ordinary mortals would not be able to survive.

The religious ideas of the Caribou Eskimos, and especially those of the Pâdlermiut, are among the most primitive I have found among all the Eskimos I visited throughout the whole expedition. The mistress of the animals of the hunt, Pinga, lives somewhere up in the air or in the sky, and is often named quite indiscriminately with Hila; she is the guardian of all life, both man and animal, but she does not offer man eternal hunting grounds like the godhead of the coast dwellers; she collects all life on the land itself, and makes it eternal solely in this manner, that everything living appears there.

When an animal or a person dies, the soul leaves the body and flies to Pinga who then lets the life or the soul rise again in another being, either man or animal. As a rule there is no fear of death, and I remember that Igjugârjuk would sometimes say half jokingly, that he had undoubtedly been so imperfect as a human being that his soul, when it went to Pinga after his death, would only be allowed to rise again as a little, burrowing lemming.

## 22.

# Summoning the Spirits
# for the First Time

BLACK ELK AND JOHN G. NEIHARDT

(1932)

*In 1931, poet John G. Neihardt recorded the life story of Black Elk, an old Oglala Sioux. Black Elk had lived in the days when the Sioux controlled their territory and hunted bison. As a young man he fought in the battle of the Little Big Horn. In the following passage Black Elk summons the spirits for his first cure.*

One day in the Moon of Fatness (June), when everything was blooming, I invited One Side to come over and eat with me. I had been thinking about the four-rayed herb that I had now seen twice—the first time in the great vision when I was nine years old, and the second time when I was lamenting on the hill. I knew that I must have this herb for curing, and I thought I could recognize the place where I had seen it growing that night when I lamented.

After One Side and I had eaten, I told him there was a herb I must find, and I wanted him to help me hunt for it. Of course I did not tell him I had seen it in a vision. He was willing to help, so we got on our horses and rode over to Grass Creek. Nobody was living over there. We came to the top of a high hill above the creek, and there we got off our horses and sat down, for I felt that we were close to where I saw the herb growing in my vision of the dog.

We sat there awhile singing together some heyoka songs. Then I began to sing alone a song I had heard in my first great vision:

"In a sacred manner they are sending voices."

After I had sung this song, I looked down towards the west, and yonder at a certain spot beside the creek were crows and magpies, chicken hawks and spotted eagles circling around and around.

Then I knew, and I said to One Side: "Friend, right there is where the herb is growing." He said: "We will go forth and see." So we got on our horses and rode down Grass Creek until we came to a dry gulch, and this we followed up. As we neared the spot the birds all flew away, and it was a place where four or five dry gulches came together. There right on the side of the bank the herb was growing, and I knew it, although I had never seen one like it before, except in my vision.

It had a root about as long as to my elbow, and this was a little thicker than my thumb. It was flowering in four colors, blue, white, red, and yellow.

We got off our horses, and after I had offered red willow bark to the Six Powers, I made a prayer to the herb, and said to it: "Now we shall go forth to the two-leggeds, but only to the weakest ones, and there shall be happy days among the weak."

It was easy to dig the herb, because it was growing in the edge of the clay gulch. Then we started back with it. When we came to Grass Creek again, we wrapped it in some good sage that was growing there.

Something must have told me to find the herb just then, for the next evening I needed it and could have done nothing without it.

I was eating supper when a man by the name of Cuts-to-Pieces came in, and he was saying: "Hey, hey, hey!" for he was in trouble. I asked him what was the matter, and he said: "I have a boy of mine, and he is very sick and I am afraid he will die soon. He has been sick a long time. They say you have great power from the horse dance and the heyoka ceremony, so maybe you can save him for me. I think so much of him."

I told Cuts-to-Pieces that if he really wanted help, he should go home and bring me back a pipe with an eagle feather on it. While he was gone, I thought about what I had to do; and I was afraid, because I had never cured anybody yet with my power, and I was very sorry for Cuts-to-Pieces. I prayed hard for help. When Cuts-to-Pieces came back with the pipe, I told him to take it around to the left of me, leave it there, and pass out again to the right of me. When he had done this, I sent for One Side to come and help me. Then I took the pipe and went to where the sick little boy was. My father and my mother went with us, and my friend, Standing Bear, was already there.

I first offered the pipe to the Six Powers, then I passed it, and we all smoked. After that I began making a rumbling thunder sound on the drum. You know, when the power of the west comes to the two-leggeds, it comes with rumbling, and when it has passed, everything lifts up its head and is glad and there is greenness. So I made this rumbling sound. Also, the voice of the drum is an offering to the Spirit of the World. Its sound arouses the mind and makes men feel the mystery and power of things.

The sick little boy was on the northeast side of the tepee, and when we entered at the south, we went around from left to right, stopping on the west side when we had made the circle.

You want to know why we always go from left to right like that. I can tell you something of the reason, but not all. Think of this: Is not the south the source of life, and does not the flowering stick truly come from there? And does not man advance from there toward the setting sun of his life? Then does he not approach the colder north where the white hairs are? And does he not then arrive, if he lives, at the source of light and understanding, which is the east? Then does he not return to where he began, to his second childhood, there to give back his life to all life, and his flesh to the earth whence it came? The more you think about this, the more meaning you will see in it.

As I said, we went into the tepee from left to right, and sat ourselves down on the west side. The sick little boy was on the northeast side, and he looked as though he were only skin and bones. I had the pipe, the drum and the four-rayed herb already, so I asked for a wooden cup, full of water, and an eagle bone whistle, which was for the spotted eagle of my great vision. They placed the cup of water in front of me; and then I had to think awhile, because I had never done this before and I was in doubt.

I understood a little more now, so I gave the eagle-bone whistle to One Side and told him how to use it in helping me. Then I filled the pipe with red willow bark, and gave it to the pretty young daughter of Cuts-to-Pieces, telling her to hold it, just as I had seen the virgin of the east holding it in my great vision.

Everything was ready now, so I made low thunder on the drum, keeping time as I sent forth a voice. Four times I cried "Hey-a-a-hey," drumming as I cried to the Spirit of the World, and while I was doing this I could feel the power coming through me from my feet up, and I knew that I could help the sick little boy.

I kept on sending a voice, while I made low thunder on the drum, saying: "My Grandfather, Great Spirit, you are the only one and to no other can any one send voices. You have made everything, they say, and you have made it good and beautiful. The four quarters and the two roads crossing each other, you have made. Also you have set a power where the sun goes down. The two-leggeds on earth are in despair. For them, my Grandfather, I send a voice to you. You have said this to me: The weak shall walk. In vision you have taken me to the center of the world and there you have shown me the power to make over. The water in the cup that you have given me, by its power shall the dying live. The herb that you have shown me, through its power shall the feeble walk upright. From where we are always facing (the south), behold, a virgin shall appear, walking the good red road, offering the pipe as she walks, and hers also is the power of the flowering tree. From where the Giant lives (the north), you have given me a sacred, cleansing wind, and where this wind passes the weak shall have strength. You have said this to me. To you and to all your powers and to Mother Earth I send a voice for help."

You see, I had never done this before, and I know now that only one power would have been enough. But I was so eager to help the sick little boy that I called on every power there is.

I had been facing the west, of course, while sending a voice. Now I walked to the north and to the east and to the south, stopping there where the source of all life is and where the good red road begins. Standing there I sang thus:

"In a sacred manner I have made them walk.
A sacred nation lies low.
In a sacred manner I have made them walk.
A sacred two-legged, he lies low.
In a sacred manner, he shall walk."

While I was singing this I could feel something queer all through my body, something that made me want to cry for all unhappy things, and there were tears on my face.

Now I walked to the quarter of the west, where I lit the pipe, offered it to the powers, and, after I had taken a whiff of smoke, I passed it around.

When I looked at the sick little boy again, he smiled at me, and I could feel that the power was getting stronger.

I next took the cup of water, drank a little of it, and went around to where the sick little boy was. Standing before him, I stamped the earth four times. Then, putting my mouth to the pit of his stomach, I drew through him the cleansing wind of the north. I next chewed some of the herb and put it in the water, afterward blowing some of it on the boy and to the four quarters. The cup with the rest of the water I gave to the virgin, who gave it to the sick little boy to drink. Then I told the virgin to help the boy stand up and to walk around the circle with him, beginning at the south, the source of life. He was very poor and weak, but with the virgin's help he did this.

Then I went away.

Next day Cuts-to-Pieces came and told me that his little boy was feeling better and was sitting up and could eat something again. In four days he could walk around. He got well and lived to be thirty years old.

Cuts-to-Pieces gave me a good horse for doing this; but of course I would have done it for nothing.

When the people heard about how the little boy was cured, many came to me for help, and I was busy most of the time.

This was in the summer of my nineteenth year (1882), in the Moon of Making Fat.

# 23.

# The Shaman's Assistant

SERGEI M. SHIROKOGOROFF

(1935)

*Russian ethnographer Sergei M. Shirokogoroff is the first academic ob-
server we know who realized the importance of the shaman's assistant.
He also stated in a footnote that he participated in several shamanic sessions, acting as the shaman's assistant. This showed that he had gained
a deeper understanding of shamanism by participating in it. Shirokogoroff was several decades ahead of his colleagues on this count.*

In the matter of technique, a great part of the success of a performance
depends upon the assistant. From a description of the assistant's functions the actual role of the assistant will be clear. As far as I know,
there are two terms for the "assistant", namely, *erów* and *jăr'i.* . . .

The assistance of *erów* or *jăr'i* consists in helping the shaman to
maintain his *ecstasy* and to find out what the spirit says and wants,
when it is introduced into the shaman. Thus, the assistant, at the beginning of the performance, prepares the drum and helps the shaman
to dress himself. During the performance he changes and dries the
drum, if necessary, but this may be done by any one of the audience.
When the shaman sings, the assistant must "help" him with the repetition of the refrains, and usually other people follow the assistant.
When the shaman can no longer do himself the drumming, the assistant carries on the drumming and in this way "helps" the shaman to
maintain his ecstasy. The assistant may also maintain and enforce

the state of ecstasy by rhythmically screaming and by exciting the shaman. When the spirit enters the shaman, the assistant asks various questions and even bargains and quarrels with the spirit, if necessary. When the shaman falls down unconscious, the assistant watches him to know the moment when the shaman must be brought back to consciousness. When the shaman is in a state of ecstasy, the assistant takes the drum and continues the drumming, both for maintaining the shaman's state of ecstasy and for controlling the behaviour of the audience. These functions are very important for a successful carrying out of the whole performance as regards the result, the assurance of the smoothness of the performance and the shaman's personal safety. A good assistant, who is familiar with the shaman's character, his way of performing, his language and complex of spirits etc., may make the performance easy and smooth, and would get out of it a much greater result, than an assistant who lacks the qualities and fitness. An assistant, who is not experienced in general and who does not know the shaman whom he is assisting, may turn the performance into a torture for the shaman and will lessen the results of the shamanizing. Thus there are good and bad assistants, and good assistants are rare. The quality of an assistant depends upon his familiarity with the shamanizing, his acquaintance with the shaman, and his general intelligence. No assistants are met with among some Tungus groups that have been investigated. For instance, among the Reindeer Tungus of Transbaikalia I have not heard of assistants, although there were some persons who usually helped the shamans by keeping time, singing refrains, etc. The Tungus of Manchuria told me that the institution of *erów (jãr'i)* is a recent one, and that originally there were no assistants. I admit that this statement is correct. . . .

During the performance of the annual sacrifice, when the spirits come one after another into the shaman, the latter asks the question: *takam'i takaraku?* — "do you recognize?" — which greatly abbreviates the performance if the assistant can guess at once. When the assistant cannot guess, the shaman gives a hint by naming the row *(faiðan)*, and the assistant usually enumerates, one after another, the spirits, until he

91

reaches the introduced spirit. Therefore, the shamans like to have assistants experienced in the work. Usually *ta jăr'i* knows by heart all the ritualistic recitals of spirits and the whole ritual. Some forms of shamanizing, as will be shown, may require several assistants, so that "leading assistants" are differentiated from ordinary ones.

Anyone may become an assistant to a shaman: a man, a woman, a young or elderly person. However, among the Manchus, a woman does not perform the functions of an assistant. The shaman may have one and the same assistant, or he may have several assistants, or no assistant at all. The function of the assistant may as well be carried out by persons incidentally present.* Generally speaking assistants are not persons of fixed and definite social standing, but at the same time if there are several assistants, one of them may be preferred by the shaman. Such an assistant may thus assume a special social function, whence a special social position will distinguish him, or her. As a special characteristic of the assistants it should be noted that, almost as a rule, they are not inclined to become themselves shamans. One of the reasons is perhaps that the assistant must not allow himself to be overcome by ecstasy, but must carefully follow the shaman, to observe and, when needed, to come to his assistance. There is a special selection of persons who are not susceptible to ecstasy, but who understand the essentials of the performance. If besides the performing shaman, there were another shaman, the latter might perform the duties of an assistant. As will be shown, the old shaman who is "teaching" a young one, may perform the duties of assistant too. As a matter of fact, in his

---

*During my work among the Tungus and Manchus, when I was acquainted with the technique of shamanizing and especially the language, I sometimes performed the duties of an assistant. The first time when I ventured to do it was an exceptional case among the Birareen. The shaman had no assistant and was in a rather difficult position, the reason being that some Chinese were present who were very hostile to the shaman, so that the usual assistants did not do their duty, under the pressure of "public opinion." Since the case seemed to me exceptional, I began assisting, and as I did not disturb the shaman in shamanizing, it was very encouraging for me and opened new possibilities for my investigations, and especially for the penetration into the psychology of the shamans and into the techniques of the performance.

first performances the new shaman is usually assisted by experienced shamans.

When a shaman is performing, helping is not confined to his assistant alone. When a shamanizing is difficult, the people present at the performance may assist the shaman, as well. Besides drying the drum, and especially in forming a sympathetic audience, help is, first of all, lent by the singing of refrains. In observing shamanizing, I have found out that the functions of assistants are usually performed by men, while a great number of females make up the chorus. Among the Manchus the females are less active than males, and in some performances of clan shamanizing they are even not present.

# 24.

# Shamans Charm Game

WILLARD Z. PARK

(1938)

*American anthropologist Willard Z. Park lived with the Paviotso (or Northern Paiute) people of western Nevada in the early 1930's and studied their shamanism. Then he wrote a book called* Shamanism in Western North America. *Here Park describes how "antelope shamans" charm game. Park got his information from old people who had memories of conversations with antelope shamans from the previous generation. Park arrived one generation too late to learn the fine detail of the shaman's role in hunting. By the beginning of the twentieth century, the Paviotso were no longer hunting antelope, because their lands had all been taken up by white ranchers.*

The antelope-drive is called by a shaman who has the antelope spirit as power. He first sends out scouts to find a herd of antelope, but if anyone sees a herd he may go to an antelope shaman and tell him where the animals are. Some shamans are said to find the antelope herds simply by dreaming. In the spring, when food supplies are exhausted, there is often a strong public demand for the antelope shaman to exercise his power.

When the herd of antelope has been found, the procedure is first to build a corral of sagebrush-bark rope under the direction of the antelope shaman at a place which he has previously selected. . . . When the rope has been prepared beforehand, the corral can be finished in a day. That night a dance is held either at the camp established near by or within the corral. Apparently there is not a fixed rule for the length of the dance: several said that it lasts only a few hours, others that it is not over until morning. In the latter event, the dancers go out at daylight to drive in the antelope. During the dance the shaman sings his antelope-songs, goes into a trance, or otherwise performs in order to charm the antelope and make them docile when they are driven into the corral.

Music for the singing and dancing in the charming rite is frequently provided by rubbing a rasp made by wrapping a bow-string around a piece of horn. The notched-stick rasp was reported by two informants. Several others told of rubbing an arrow across a taut bow-string to provide musical accompaniment for the singing and dancing. The rattles customarily employed in the curing ceremony seem never to be used in charming antelope. . . .

Men, women, and children participate in the antelope-drive. Only women who are pregnant or menstruating are excluded. It is believed that the presence of a woman in either of these conditions causes the antelope to break through the corral fence and escape. Several informants said that the husbands of menstruating and pregnant women were also prohibited from taking part in the drive.

When the antelope shaman calls people together for a drive, he warns them about their behavior. Sexual intercourse among the married is forbidden during the several days required to build the corral. The tabu on sexual relations lasts until the antelope have been slaughtered. It is also forbidden for young people to flirt. People participating in the drive are not supposed to relieve themselves anywhere near the fence of the corral. The loss of any personal property within the corral is believed to weaken the fence; consequently everyone is warned to watch personal possessions carefully. These rules and prohibitions are not in force during the communal hunts held for other game. . . .

It is clear that the antelope shaman's performance has an important place in the shamanistic complex of the Paviotso. But as has been pointed out, the charming of game through the exercise of the shaman's power is confined entirely to the antelope-drive. The plan of procedure is highly variable, but the basic belief in the control of the antelope by supernatural power is clear. Antelope-charming, then, is the one well-recognized function of the shaman which is not a part of the all-pervading belief in curing. In fact, it is the only important shamanistic performance of the Paviotso that is not heavily charged with beliefs about the cause and control of disease.

# 25

# Climbing the Twisted Ladder to Initiation

ALFRED MÉTRAUX

(1944)

*Swiss anthropologist Alfred Métraux wrote a fine survey of South American shamanism called* The Shaman in the Indigenous Civilizations of the Guyanas and the Amazon. *Métraux was known for his extensive and precise research. Here he provides a broad definition of the shaman: "a person who maintains by profession and in the interest of the community an intermittent commerce with spirits, or who is possessed by them." And he lists several key elements of South American shamanism: use of tobacco or bark teas to contact spirits, initiation through fasting, dancing, singing, sexual abstinence, and out-of-body experiences involving ladders. Métraux also points out the shaman's fundamental ambivalence: To help people, shamans must be able to harm them.*

The magician's functions, techniques, and attributes present a remarkable uniformity across the forest tribes of the Guyanas and the Amazon Basin. These fundamental similarities justify a global treatment despite the linguistic and cultural differences between tribes dispersed across this immense area. Except for the Apinayé, the Gé groups from the Brazilian plateau have been omitted from this description, because shamanism is hardly developed among them, and is even absent sometimes.

The magico-religious practices of the Indians of the tropical rain forest include a spectacular element that has long drawn the attention of travellers. They make up an aspect of the indigenous cultures that are well known, at least in their exterior manifestations. The magician's character has particularly excited the curiosity and the verve of French missionaries and travellers who described the habits and customs of the Tupinamba in Brazil and of the Caribs of Guyana and the West Indies. Following their example, we will call the agent of the supernatural in the indigenous societies of tropical South America *piai:* This word, of Tupi and Carib origin, belongs to the vocabulary of the different languages spoken from the Guyanas to Paraguay. It is synonymous with the Siberian term *shaman,* which designates any individual who maintains by profession and in the interest of the community an intermittent commerce with spirits or who is possessed by them.

Shamanism is a profession that is almost essentially masculine; it is not closed to women, but the latter only play an important role in a very small number of tribes. In the medical domain, which is the shaman's par excellence, women only practice easy cures that require the administration of simple medicines and the recitation of charms. They do not perform in the dramatic sessions during which the spirits are evoked.

The intensity of religious experiences, which is the very condition for shamanic practices, gives the *piai* a position that is both privileged and marginal within their group. There is no doubt that this "vocation" attracts a certain elite of intelligence and character. Is the Amazonian shaman a neurotic? In the current state of our knowledge, it is impossible to answer this question. One will nonetheless note that shamans are recruited among those people who are predisposed to mysticism or who are unstable. Trance opens the doors for them to the supernatural and brings them ecstasies and states of crisis in which their temperament delights. Let us not forget that shamanism, even if it is practiced by neurotics, is in no way a pathological manifestation. It is a technique of communication with the world of spirits that is in no way abnormal in the eyes of the group. The shaman's function is to heal the sick, and those who make a profession of it are obviously the first to benefit from the calming effects of the trance and from communication with supernatural beings.

Ancient and contemporary travellers took pleasure in denouncing *piai* as impostors who exploit the naïveté of their companions. This remains the point of view of many unenlightened missionaries. However, there is no lack of examples to prove their good faith and honesty. If they themselves fall ill, do they not call upon one of their colleagues? A great number of shamans show themselves to be scrupulous in the exercise of their art. They rarely refuse to assume the often dangerous responsibility of a medical treatment, and during the cure they often demonstrate zeal and energy. The trances are sometimes hard and tiresome. Many shamans would no doubt refrain from provoking them if they did not believe in their efficacy. . . .

The apprentice shaman must pass through a period of retreat during which he observes continence and different food taboos. He must notably abstain from eating meat. . . .

During the retreat periods, the future shaman must drink bark teas and vomit them in order to enter into contact with the spirits. It is particularly important that he enters into a relationship through these teas with the "spirits of the ladder or the rungs," which will help his soul leave his body and fly, or which will allow the spirits of the forest to descend into his body and occupy it. The Akawaio say that by absorbing and vomiting these bark teas "the spirit of the bark or other spirits can install themselves inside the body." Indeed, "vomited tree bark becomes Imawali. Imawali is a forest spirit and trees possess this spirit."

The novice must also accustom himself to drinking tobacco juice and to vomiting it occasionally. Tobacco attracts the spirits during the sessions and helps the shaman's spirit fly away. The spirit of tobacco is closely associated to the spirit of the *kumalak* bird, which is a kind of kite. This bird is the main auxiliary of the magician, who borrows its wings. The shaman, drunk on tobacco juice, rises above the mountains followed by the *kumalak* bird. Both wander in this way, "seeing all and discovering all." Other birds, especially those that live in the mountain where the spirits dance, teach the shaman and lend him their wings so that he can come and dance with them. A long rustling sound indicates that the shaman's spirit has flown back, and a thud on the ground proves he has landed. Upon return from his aerial excursions, the shaman gives the borrowed wings back to his auxiliary. The novice must therefore try to establish contact with the *kumalak* spirit when he drinks tobacco juice and when he sings. By imposing food restrictions on himself and by vomiting, the shaman, who has become thin, turns into a prop for the wings, which will take him to the spirits' world. The songs that play such an important role in the exercise of the profession are called *malik,* after the name of the ornaments that symbolize the *kumalak* bird's wings. They describe the flight of the shaman's soul and his adventures in the regions of the spirits. These are "wing songs" or "flight songs." Under the master's directions, the novice learns the techniques of the profession: drinking tobacco juice, singing the spirits' songs, and shaking the packet of leaves, the rustling of which creates the illusion of the approach or departure of a spirit. These lessons can occur in the shaman's hut or in the forest. Sometimes they are given by the spirit of a dead shaman. During the public session that will consecrate him as a shaman, the novice, who has drunk vast quantities of tobacco juice, "dies," that is to say, his soul deserts his body. His master helps him search for his soul and bring it back to earth. From that moment on the postulant can "shamanize" on his own. . . .

In the tribe of the Caribs of Barama, the master takes charge of a small group of students whom he gathers together in a specially constructed hut. He starts by showing them how to make a rattle. He then gives them strong tobacco tea, which plunges them into a trance state during which they visit the land of "water spirits," which they will learn to invoke through magical songs.

Later, after executing frenetic dances under the joint influence of tobacco smoke and juice, the novices enter into a relationship with spirit jaguars. They feel themselves turn into jaguars, walk on all fours, and roar. They must then cross a great fire, which bars the path to the river, while continuing to imitate the jaguar. They run down to the river, scorched and drunk on tobacco juice, to catch fish and worms, so as to ensure the cooperation of aquatic spirits.

Three months of fasting and continence follow these ordeals. The novices observe various taboos, including that of fire and vapor. They avoid these so as not to frighten the spirits that they are seeking to frequent. In order to acquire the dexterity needed to shoot their magical arrows with precision, they practice archery on a cotton ball suspended by a thread. . . .

The initiation's object is to lead the novice's soul to the beyond, where he will meet not only his familiar spirits but also his future supernatural opponents. The means deployed to obtain these visions, despite the complexity of their details, are rather simple. They consist above all of ferocious fasts, frenetic dances, and massive absorption of tobacco smoke and juice.

In between dances, the novices sit on a caiman-shaped bench. They are completely blinded by the hot pepper that has been rubbed into their eyes, and they listen to their master tell them about the supernatural beings and their attributes. The visions provoked by the intoxication of tobacco juice are naturally very influenced by the mythical tales told by the initiator. Invariably, the candidate believes himself to be transported to the land of spirits. Like Dante, he is met at the threshold of the beyond by a protector spirit who becomes his mentor. The latter says: "Come, novice. You will climb to heaven on the ladder of Grandfather vulture. It is not far." He climbs a kind of twisting ladder and reaches the first level of heaven, where he crosses Indian villages and towns inhabited by whites. Then the novice meets a very beautiful woman. This is the spirit of water who gets him to dive into the river. There she teaches him charms and magical formulas. The novice and his guide reach the other bank and go to the intersection of Life and Death. The future shaman can then freely go to the

"Land Without Evening" or the "Land Without Dawn." His mysterious companion then reveals to him the fate of souls after death. Suddenly the candidate is brought back to earth by a strong feeling of pain. The master has just applied a torture instrument to his skin called *maraké,* which consists of a plait that contains large poisonous ants in its interstices. . . .

The main function of the shaman is to cure illnesses. He carries out this task by convoking, in spectacular sessions, the spirits responsible for the ill or, on the contrary, those he expects can help. These dramatic cures invariably end with massages, fumigations, and suckings practiced on the patients to extract the "ill" from their body in the form of different pathological objects.

His other attributes are multiple: to predict the future, interpret signs or omens, stop the natural elements from harming humans, charm game, distribute magical strength to those who need it, and organize and preside over religious ceremonies and dances.

All medicine men are also sorcerers who can kill at a distance. To help people, shamans must be able to harm them; this ambivalence in their personality is one of the most striking characteristics of South American shamanism.

Everywhere shamans enjoy a prestige and an authority that are often considerable, but it is only among the Guarani and in several other tribes that they officially accumulate political and mystical power.

Shamanism dominates the religious life of the Indians of the Guyanas and of the Amazon. Except for certain half-religious, half-profane ceremonies, shamanic sessions are the simplest means for them to enter into contact with the supernatural. The Indian's attitude toward the spirits contains fear and a certain familiarity. The shaman is above all the individual who uses, for the benefit of all, the superior power of the spirits and who thwarts their evils if necessary. Where the influence of the Andean civilizations has not made itself felt, the Indians live in a universe peopled by spirits, of which the shaman is the only master.

# 26

# Aboriginal Doctors Are Outstanding People

ADOLPHUS PETER ELKIN

(1945)

*In 1945, Australian anthropologist Adolphus Peter Elkin published a book called* Aboriginal Men of High Degree. *Elkin cast a favorable light on indigenous society in a time where such open-mindedness was unusual, and he directly challenged the idea that shamans were mentally ill.*

A number of writers refer to the native doctor as an "impostor," "the greatest scamp of the tribe," or "as a rule the most cunning man in the tribe and a great humbug." These opinions, however, are based on superficial observation. When a native doctor sucks a magical bone out of a sick person's abdomen and shows it to those around and to the patient, he is not a mere charlatan, bluffing his fellows because he introduced and produced the bone at the psychological moment by sleight of hand. Nor is he just play-acting for effect when, having rubbed the affected part of his patient in the "correct" manner, he gathers an invisible something in his hands and, solemnly walking a few steps away, casts "it" into the air with a very decided jerk of the arms and opening of the hands. These are two of a number of traditional methods that he has learned, and in which he and all believe—methods for extracting the ill from the patient and so giving the latter assurance (often visible) of his cure. The cause has been removed.

We should remember that if a medicine man himself becomes ill, he calls in a fellow practitioner to treat him in one of the accepted ways, although he knows all the professional methods (which we might call tricks). He also desires earnestly, like all other sick people, assurance that the cause of his pain or illness has been extracted and cast away, or that his wandering soul (if that be the diagnosis) has been caught and restored. The actions and chantings and production of "bones" and "stones" are but the outward expression and means of the doctor's personal victory over one or both of two factors: first, the malevolent activities of some person practicing sorcery on the sick man or woman; and second, the patient's willingness to remain ill or even to die. This latter must be counteracted and the will to be healthy and to live be restored. . . .

To sum up: Medicine men are not impostors. They practice their profession in the way that they and their fellow tribesfolk have inherited, and that they believe, and have found, to be effective. If a doctor's efforts fail, it means that he was summoned too late, or that the power of the distant sorcerer was too great, or that the patient had broken a very important taboo, or that the spirits of the "dead" would not be deprived of the company of the sick person's spirit; all of which finds an echo in our own experiences and attitudes.

It is reported, however, that an impostor may occasionally appear (like our charlatan) who claims to possess power and knowledge, hoping thereby to gain prestige of goods. But the shallowness of his claims is eventually seen through. In any case, a medicine man must be able to maintain his prestige and "doctor personality" by success in his specialization or by convincing his tribesmen that his explanations of failures are satisfactory. Otherwise, faith in him will wane, and he will realize that he has lost his powers. He will recall that he has broken one or more of the taboos, on the observance of which the maintenance of his power depends. For example, a doctor must not drink hot water, must not be bitten by certain ants; must not be immersed in salt water, and must not eat certain foods. As the infringement of some of these may be accidental, the discredited practitioner has an honorable way out. In other cases, he can no longer practice because he has ceased to dream of the spirits of the dead. In some tribes, at least, a doctor who breaks the food taboos associated with his profession is discredited; indeed, it is only one with a very powerful personality who would dare risk his reputation and practice in this way.

To practice a profession so "hedged about" with forms of "ritual" behavior that can be observed by all is at least some guarantee that the person concerned is genuine. Impostors are unlikely to appear except in a condition of tribal and cultural disintegration, when cunning persons might think there is an opportunity to gain some position of privilege. Moreover, unthinking and credulous white men sometimes encourage the medicine man to play on their desire for mystery. He recognizes what the white man hopes to hear, and desires to pay for, and lowering his voice to tones of secrecy, he relates satisfying tales of magic and mystery. But look at the glint of merriment in the old doctor's eyes, as he thinks to himself, "White man 'nother kind; white man fool."

If the superficial observation of medicine men as scoundrels and impostors is not true, is it possible that it arises from the fact that these men are really clever, endowed with knowledge above the average and marked by strong personalities? Beneath the unkempt hair, above a naked body or one clothed in the white man's cast-offs, and in an immobile face shine shrewd, penetrating eyes—eyes that look you all the way through—the lenses of a mind that is photographing your very character and intentions. I have seen those eyes and felt that mind at work when I have sought knowledge that only the man of high degree could impart. I have known white people who almost feared the eyes of a *karadji,* so all-seeing, deep, and quiet did they seem. This clever man was definitely an outstanding person, a clear thinker, a man of decision, one who believed, and acted on the belief, that he possessed psychic power, the power to will others to have faith in themselves.

As a result of my own experience and of a close examination of reports on the subject, I am satisfied that medicine men are, generally speaking, persons of special knowledge, self-assurance, and initiative, and that association with them quickly reveals this fact. . . .

It is obvious that a medicine man, at least one who has not lost his *mana*, his power and prestige, must stand out in his community. He is superior in knowledge, in experience, and in psychic power, and this must be reflected in his attitude and general bearing, especially when he is confronted with the abnormal or unexpected. It is for this reason that he seems to be somewhat reserved except toward his fellow doctors, even though he is usually well liked.

Moreover, the medicine man's personality is not an individual phenomenon. Because of his "making" and training and deeds, a special social personality is ascribed to him by his fellows: He is essential to their social well-being and to the maintenance of satisfactory relations with the unseen—with the spirits of the dead and of the bush, with the rainbow serpent and the sky-being, and with sorcerers in strange places.

For all these reasons, we can say that the medicine man is a man of special, and often outstanding, personality.

It has been maintained that medicine men are abnormal and neurotic. At first sight, there might seem to be some justification for holding that there is something strange or queer about men who claim to have had their "insides" exchanged for spirit-insides, to carry quartz stones, bones, and spirit-snakes in their bodies—who claim to be able to converse with the dead, to travel invisibly through space, to visit the sky land, and so on. But no observer records that Aboriginal medicine men, or sorcerers, are, apart from their occult powers and intellectual attainments, other than normal Aboriginal personalities. They live the ordinary family and social life and take part in the regular ritual and ceremonial life of their tribe like any other initiated men. . . .

Aboriginal culture does not put any premium on the epileptic or abnormal of any sort. It is rather an expression of a world of order and normality, deriving from the long-past dreamtime of the culture-heroes, through the present, to the future.

Finally, emphasis should be placed on the fact that a medicine man's life is one of self-discipline, preceded by training, of social responsibility, and of contact with powerful forces or spiritual beings. He must work coolly and deliberately when his services are required, and not as some mental disturbance dictates or disposes. He does not seek the necessary knowledge or power through drug or violent dance but rather through quietness and receptivity, meditation and recollection, observation and inference, concentration and decision. His is a profession for which he has been duly prepared and trained. It is not a kink, though it is possible that sometimes a man may be misled into believing that he "was made" in some dream experience, but that alone will not accredit him. In the same way, we must distinguish among ourselves the well-trained and accredited psychotherapist and analyst from the amateur with a psychoanalytical or similar kink. It is the latter who is usually somewhat abnormal, and who seems unable to see through himself, or to realize that he should do so.

In other words, the real medicine man is a professional individual of special training whose personality, from the point of view of the community, reaches a high degree of normality.

# 27.

# Shamans as Psychoanalysts

## CLAUDE LÉVI-STRAUSS
## (1949)

*French anthropologist Claude Lévi-Strauss pointed out the common ground between shamanism and psychoanalysis in an essay called "The Effectiveness of Symbols." His analysis refers to the transcript of a shamanic curing session among the Cuna Indians of Panama. Lévi-Strauss crystallized the difference between the practical symbolist and the psychoanalyst, and got it really clear: The shaman speaks, whereas the psychoanalyst listens.*

The cure would consist, therefore, in making explicit a situation originally existing on the emotional level and in rendering acceptable to the mind pains which the body refuses to tolerate. That the mythology of the shaman does not correspond to an objective reality does not matter. The sick woman believes in the myth and belongs to a society which believes in it. The tutelary spirits and malevolent spirits, the supernatural monsters and magical animals, are all part of a coherent system on which the native conception of the universe is founded. The sick woman accepts these mythical beings or, more accurately, she has never questioned their existence. What she does not accept are the incoherent and arbitrary pains, which are an alien element in her system but which the shaman, calling upon the myth, will re-integrate within a whole where everything is meaningful.

Once the sick woman understands, however, she does more than resign herself; she gets well. But no such thing happens to our sick when the causes of their diseases have been explained to them in terms of secretions, germs, or viruses. We shall perhaps be accused of paradox if we answer that the reason lies in the fact that microbes exist and monsters do not. And yet, the relationship between germ and disease is external to the mind of the patient, for it is a cause-and-effect relationship; whereas the relationship between monster and disease is internal to his mind, whether conscious or unconscious: It is a relationship between symbol and thing symbolized, or, to use the terminology of linguists, between sign and meaning. The shaman provides the sick woman with a language, by means of which unexpressed, and otherwise inexpressible, psychic states can be immediately expressed. And it is the transition to this verbal expression—at the same time making it possible to undergo in an ordered and intelligible form a real experience that would otherwise be chaotic and inexpressible—which induces the release of the physiological process, that is, the reorganization, in a favorable direction, of the process to which the sick woman is subjected.

In this respect, the shamanic cure lies on the borderline between our contemporary physical medicine and such psychological therapies as psychoanalysis. Its originality stems from the application to an organic condition of a method related to psychotherapy. How is this possible? A closer comparison between shamanism and psychoanalysis—which in our view implies no slight to psychoanalysis—will enable us to clarify this point.

In both cases the purpose is to bring to a conscious level conflicts and resistances which have remained unconscious, owing either to their repression by other psychological forces or—in the case of childbirth—to their own specific nature, which is not psychic but organic or even simply mechanical. In both cases also, the conflicts and resistances are resolved, not because of the knowledge, real or alleged, which the sick woman progressively acquires of them, but because this knowledge makes possible a specific experience, in the course of which conflicts materialize in an order and on a level permitting their free development and leading to their resolution. This vital experience is called *abreaction* in psychoanalysis. We know that its precondition is the unprovoked intervention of the analyst, who appears in the conflicts of the patient through a double transference mechanism, as flesh-and-blood protagonist and in relation to whom the patient can restore and clarify an initial situation which has remained unexpressed or unformulated.

All these characteristics can be found in the shamanic cure. Here, too, it is a matter of provoking an experience; as this experience becomes structured, regulatory mechanisms beyond the subject's control are spontaneously set in motion and lead to an orderly functioning. The shaman plays the same dual role as the psychoanalyst. A prerequisite role—that of listener for the psychoanalyst and of orator for the shaman—establishes a direct relationship with the patient's conscious and an indirect relationship with his unconscious. This is the function of the incantation proper. But the shaman does more than utter the incantation; he is its hero, for it is he who, at the head of a supernatural battalion of spirits, penetrates the endangered organs and frees the captive soul. In this way he, like the psychoanalyst, becomes the object of transference and, through the representations induced in the patient's mind, the real protagonist of the conflict which the latter experiences on the border between the physical world and the psychic world. The patient suffering from neurosis eliminates an individual myth by facing a "real" psychoanalyst; the native woman in childbed overcomes a true organic disorder by identifying with a "mythically transmuted" shaman.

This parallelism does not exclude certain differences, which are not surprising if we note the character—psychological in the one case and organic in the other—of the ailment to be cured. Actually the shamanic cure seems to be the exact counterpart to the psychoanalytic cure, but with an inversion of all the elements. Both cures aim at inducing an experience, and both succeed by recreating a myth which the patient has to live or relive. But in one case, the patient constructs an individual myth with elements drawn from his past; in the other case, the patient receives from the outside a social myth which does not correspond to a former personal state. To prepare for the abreaction, which then becomes an "adreaction," the psychoanalyst listens, whereas the shaman speaks.

# 28.

# Using Invisible Substances
# for Good and Evil

ALFRED MÉTRAUX

(1949)

> *The theme of magic darts and invisible substances appears several times in this anthology. It is a recurrent theme among shamans, in particular in South America. Swiss anthropologist Alfred Métraux provided one of the first detailed examinations of the subject in the* Handbook of South American Indians *(published by the United States government).*

The shaman's power often was identified with his breath or with tobacco smoke, which materialized his breath and added to it the efficacy of tobacco. The purifying and strengthening power of breath and tobacco smoke played an important part in magic treatments and other magic rites.

The shaman's power also has been described by some authorities as a mysterious substance which the magician carried in his body. The gestures of shamans during their magic operations suggested that they were handling some invisible stuff which they removed from the patient's body or transmitted to persons or even things to enhance their excellence. The *Apapocuva-Guaraní* shamans, for instance, were given a substance by the spirits which, in turn, they could communicate to other people to increase their vitality. . . .

There is no basic difference between the magic substance—an invisible but tangible stuff—and the arrows, crystals, and thorns that sometimes lodge in the shaman's body. These objects really are materializations of the shaman's power that is sometimes conceived of in the more abstract and vague form of "magic substance." The guardian spirit or familiar of the shaman likewise is a personification of the same power rather than a different entity coexisting with the notion of invisible substance. Magic substance, pathogenic objects, and guardian spirits are three different aspects of the same fundamental but vaguely conceived notion of magic power.

Some concrete examples may illustrate the point. Among several tribes of the upper Amazon the magic substance is closely connected with invisible thorns and darts which are soaked in it.

There is also association between crystals and magic force among the *Cubeo*, where the shaman put into the head of the novice small pieces of crystal that ate up his brains and eyes, replacing these organs and becoming his "power."

The rock crystals also are spirits. According to the Barama *Carib*, each category of spirits was represented by a different kind of stone, the possession of which ensured to the shaman power over the class of spirits identified with the stones. Toward the end of the initiation, stones were passed from the novice's mouth through his arms to open a passage for a magic missile. The crystals and spirits are identical. The magic weapons are endowed with life, for after performing the task assigned to them, they return to the shaman's body.

When a *Yaguá* shaman died, the darts in his body went into the person of a disciple. If a shaman had no heir, the darts flew in the air until they found a shaman into whose body they could enter. . . .

Since shamans were by definition "carriers of invisible arrows or magic substances" they were provided with powerful weapons that could be used as well for good and evil. Without his negative power, the shaman could not be a doctor. A shaman who used his weapons only to attack enemies outside the community would have a good reputation and would be regarded as the best servant of the group. It was only when he turned against members of his own group that he provoked hatred, distrust, and, in the end, sometimes revenge.

The magic substance which was the shaman's strength and which he used to heal and strengthen his clients, became a mortal weapon when it was turned against an enemy. "The power of the shaman is identical with the poison" that kills. The *Guaraní* shaman struck at his foes by casting into them the magic substance recovered from the body of his patients. The *Chiquito* shaman carried in his stomach a blackish substance which was fatal to those in whom it was injected with criminal intent. . . .

The punishment which the Indians meted out to witches was proportionate to the fear with which they regarded them. The most cruel acts committed by Indians were always those against shamans who had forfeited their trust. The *Campa* not only slaughtered the guilty shaman, but also his family, and destroyed his goods.

# 29

# The Shamanin Performs a Public Service with Grace and Energy

VERRIER ELWIN

(1955)

*British anthropologist Verrier Elwin lived among the Saora people of India. He described the prominent role of their female shamans, whom he called "shamanin," in particular in treating the sick.*

Every shamanin is called to her sacred duties at about the time of puberty as a result of a remarkable dream-experience (which is paralleled in the experience of the shamans) which results in her "marriage" to a tutelary from the Under World. This spiritual marriage is not generally a bar to marriage on earth . . . for the Saoras have no special belief in the magical efficacy of chastity, and the girl usually marries a human husband after a few years. But her dream-lord seems to be equally real to her; to hear a shamanin talking, it is not always easy to say which of her two husbands means more to her.

This experience may follow or precede some formal training in divination. Sometimes a girl whose family has had no previous association may be called to it in a dream and the dream-husband himself may teach her the art. More commonly a girl belongs to a family where the shamanin tradition already exists; the mother or, as so often, the father's sister is a shamanin and begins to prepare the little girl from an early age for her future life. The dream-experiences, therefore, are not unexpected (though the convention is to regard them as a great surprise) and this is why they follow a regular pattern, conditioned by the mythology and the social tradition.

The dream which forces a girl into her profession and seals it with supernatural approval takes the form of visits of a suitor from the Under World who proposes marriage with all its ecstatic and numinous consequences. This "husband" is a Hindu, well-dressed and handsome, wealthy, and observant of many customs to which the Saoras are strangers. He comes, according to tradition, in the depth of night; when he enters the room the whole household is laid under a spell and sleeps like the dead.

In nearly every case, the girl at first refuses, for the profession of shamanin is both arduous and beset with dangers. The result is that she begins to be plagued with nightmares: her divine lover carries her to the Under World or threatens her with a fall from a great height. She generally falls ill; she may even be out of her wits for a time, and wanders pathetically dishevelled in the fields and woods. The family then takes a hand. Since in most cases the girl has been having training for some time, everyone knows what she is in for, and even if she herself does not tell her parents what is happening they usually have a shrewd idea. But the proper thing is for the girl herself to confess to her parents that she has been "called," that she has refused, and that she is now in danger. This immediately relieves her own mind of its burden of guilt and sets the parents free to act. They at once arrange the girl's marriage with her tutelary. . . .

After the marriage, the shamanin's spirit-husband visits her regularly and lies with her till dawn. He may even take her away into the jungle for days at a time, feeding her there on palm wine. In due course a child is born and the ghostly father brings it every night to be nursed by the girl. But the relationship is not primarily a sexual one; the important thing is that the tutelary husband should inspire and instruct his young wife in her dreams, and when she goes to perform her sacred duties he sits by her and tells her what to do.

At first a girl sits with other shamanins until she is thoroughly adept and experienced, for this is a profession where mistakes may lead to tragic consequences. When she is completely ready the young shamanin starts her own practice and she will soon be in as great a demand as any of the others. . . .

It is in the treatment of the sick that a shamanin finds her greatest scope and fulfillment. Her methods of diagnosis and cure are varied and ingenious; she uses the fan and the lamp, the bow and the sword, handfuls of rice and pots of wine. Now she dances in ecstasy, now lies lost to the world in trance. When she has found the cause of disease or tragedy, she is at infinite pains to heal the wounds; she sucks infection from her patient's body, burns it with flashes of gunpowder, bites and kisses it, massages it to expel the evil, orders the sacrifice of goat or buffalo, directs the village artist in the composition of sacred pictures flattering to the spirits, dedicates pots, speaks healing and consoling words. She works ceaselessly, for she is inspired not only by pride in her profession, but also by her love for the tribal community she serves. . . .

Women have a high and honoured place in Saora society. Protected by their innocence and their fidelity, they move freely about their lovely hills; gay and happy, their laughter and their singing echoes at all hours among the palms. They have an important role alike in festivity and funeral; their voice is not unheard in tribal and village affairs; they can more than hold their own with their men. It would be hard to find women more industrious; they toil laboriously in terraced field and remote swidden, and when they return home the work of the spinning-wheel or the kitchen fills what might well be hours of leisure. But this is not mere drudgery; because they are free and self-reliant, respected and loved by their menfolk, adored by their children, their life is full, interesting and satisfying.

To this happy state of affairs the institution of the shamanin has made its contribution. For here is a body of women dedicated to the public service and fulfilling that dedication with grace and energy. Here are women, believed to be vitally in touch with supernatural affairs, on whom one can rely, women who respond to the needs of the sick and anxious with professional thoroughness and affectionate concern. For the shamanin really cares about her patients.

The shamanin is indeed an impressive and honorable figure. She lives a dedicated life on the boundary between this life and the next. A young girl like Sondan of Bungding had the absorbed look of the idealist and dreamer; she knew herself to be someone apart; she must not enter too much into the ordinary business of life or be stained by vulgar contacts; quiet, dignified, efficient, she made one think of a world of values foreign to this. The mysterious other-world "below" was already more real to her almost maiden imagination than the coarse realities of earth. And even bustling business-like efficient little Amiya, who was a thoroughly "this-world" type, did by her obstinate and lifelong refusal to seek carnal pleasure in the world of temptation that enveloped her, establish the priority of spiritual things. The dedication, the sacrifice, the tutelary came first.

To the sick and lonely, the shamanin is the nurse and friend, the guide, the analyst. To the stranger's eye, she may be just one more dirty old village woman; but to the Saora whose life is broken by tragedy, she may well be an angel of strength and consolation.

# 30

# "The Shaman Is Mentally Deranged"

## GEORGE DEVEREUX

### (1956)

*French anthropologist and star ethnopsychiatrist George Devereux took a Freudian stance that may seem extreme, but which contains elements of truth. Retrospectively it seems clear that some shamans are somewhat deranged some of the time, to put it mildly.*

Many tribes stress the painfulness of the budding shaman's psychic experiences. In some instances individuals who receive such supernatural "calls" flatly refuse to comply with them—exactly the way the Plains Indian refused to obey the vision which instructed him to become a transvestite, and killed himself instead. Among the Sedang Moi, a person who receives the "call" may even drink his own urine, in the hope that this act will so depreciate him in the sight of his divine sponsors that they will take back the power they had given him. The Mohave believe that a potential shaman who refuses to accept the call becomes insane. The writer personally interviewed such a man who had spent some time in a state hospital with the—to our mind questionable—diagnosis of manic depressive psychosis. Both he and his tribe felt that his psychotic episode was due to his refusal to become a practicing shaman.

There is also evidence that even those who do accept the "call" feel that their mode of life is ego dystonic, and therefore commit vicarious suicide. Thus, we are inclined to suspect that older healing shamans among the Mohave turn into witches precisely because witches are killed. In fact, Mohave society actually expects witches to incite others to kill them. There is no real psychological difference between this type of vicarious suicide and the suicide of the Plains Indian who refused to become a berdache.

In brief, there is no reason and no excuse for not considering the shaman as a severe neurotic and even as a psychotic.

In addition, shamanism is often also culture dystonic. This is a point which is amply documented but often systematically overlooked. Thus, the shaman is quite often what we called elsewhere a "trouble unit" in society. The Mohave say that shamans are both crazy and cowardly. The Siberian shaman is usually wretchedly poor and is not highly regarded. The Sedang bitterly resent their shamans, particularly because of their rapaciousness. In fact, this very human resentment — reflecting insight into the fact that the shaman is culturally dystonic — even contaminates the attitudes of members of higher religions toward their truly saintly members. The saint is a troublemaker from the viewpoint of workaday life. Even so gentle a man as St. Francis of Assisi did not have an easy time of it, and the savior of France, St. Joan of Arc, was burned at the stake as a heretic before being canonized. The opposition of primitive priesthood to shamans is, moreover, conspicuous and chronic.

Briefly stated, we hold that the shaman is mentally deranged. This is also the opinion of Kroeber and Linton [both fellow anthropologists].

# 31

# Clever Cords and Clever Men

RONALD ROSE

(1957)

*Australian writer Ronald Rose starts by describing the initiation of a young "clever man," as Australian Aborigines call shamans. Then he investigates by questionnaire a mysterious component of Aborigine shamanship. Known as "clever cords," they bear close similarities to the invisible substances and magic darts described by Amazonian shamans. Rose leaves the mystery intact.*

For as many moons as their hands had fingers the two of them had been preparing for this supreme moment. For the first few months older relatives, specially appointed, had been instructing them in tribal lore and ritual, in the meaning of manhood, on their responsibilities and their rights as men. They had been shown some of the sacred tribal churinga. Then some of the doctors had taught them about themselves, shown them how injuries can be borne without pain, taught them something of the control of fear—but they were afraid now. The doctors had introduced them to an inner life of contemplation that, to the aborigines, is a mark of manhood.

There followed for them a long period of isolation from the tribe with but short intervals of contact with a few men of the totem when cicatrices had been cut and weals burned on their chest, back, and arms. They had lived amidst comparative plenty in the bush but were allowed to hunt and eat only a few of the animals about them, and subsist on a restricted variety of roots and berries. Despite hunger they dared not violate the taboos for they knew that this privation was necessary to become a man. And they knew, too, that back in the main camp the doctors knew what they were doing, could see them with their clever-eyes, or were perhaps floating unseen above them on their magic watching them, always watching them.

They were being watched now.

Suddenly, from behind them, out of the silence, came the booming "oowah, oowah" of a bull-roarer and, as if in answer, "oowahwah" from another directly ahead. Then, all round them, booming, filling their ears with vibrating, restless tempo, came the roar. And into the pale light stepped a man, his body covered with clay and ochre, feathers and blood, whirling a sacred bull-roarer on its cord of human hair, dancing slowly, deliberately, toward them. His body quivered and the white cockatoo down seemed like a restless cloud clinging to him.

Other men came from the shadows, all painted, some twirling roarers, some with spears. There were dancers, too, their bodies gleaming yellow as the dawn light warmed.

Abruptly the noise ceased and before them, as if coming from nowhere, stood a huge man at whom all the other men looked with awe. Or was it a man? Was it Baieme come from the Eternal Dream Time?

He looked closely at them and they could see fires burning in his eyes. "Watch me," he said. He laid on his back. His body gave a shiver and his mouth opened. Some of the men gasped almost inaudibly. From his mouth the boys saw a thing come forth, a live thing that was not a snake, nor was it a cord. But it looked like a cord and moved like a snake. Slowly it issued from the gaping, quivering jaws, the length of a man's finger but not so thick. It moved about on the man's face and became longer, almost as long as a man's arm. It left his mouth and crawled in the grass. Then it returned to the man's body.

After a time the big man left and there was another man before them, an old man whose gums were toothless and whose beard was very white, like the cockatoo down. This man was telling them to look at him, showing them a large, bright crystal that stole the light from the dawn and dazzled their eyes. The old man was speaking to them, but the words were only sounds whose meaning was lost in the warmth of the sun he held in his hand. Soon the boys felt something moving on their bodies, things that felt like snakes and spiders. One of the boys breathed deeply and relaxed, sinking into a state of repose that was almost sleep. He felt these things, but he was not afraid.

The other lad had begun to tremble. Perspiration broke out on his cold skin and he became tense. There seemed to be a multitude of reptiles about him, sliding over his body. He thought he felt the sharp stab of fangs in his leg and it went numb. For a moment a cry choked itself in his throat; then he jumped to his feet and screamed, shivered, and screamed again. Some men grasped him and led him sobbing away. He had failed. He would not be "made." Death must now follow his disgrace. Grim-faced men returned silently to the clearing and the drama went on.

The remaining lad then witnessed a series of displays. Clever-men appeared to lie on their backs and clever-ropes exuded from their mouths, their navels. The cords seemed to rise into the air, and the old fellows climbed hand over hand up them to treetop height. Then some of them moved from the top of one tree to the top of another by means of the cords, which swayed out into space. The boy had been told that clever-men could travel vast distances in no time with the aid of such cords: now he was seeing for himself some of these marvelous things.

Some of the doctors walked straight to the trunks of big eucalyptus-trees and appeared to melt into them, reappearing a moment later on the other side.

The boy saw the doctors produce from within themselves great numbers of gleaming quartz crystals, grinning as the wet crystals that seemed to come from within them were taken from between pituri-stained teeth. Each old doctor formed a small pile of crystals beside him. These, too, were part of his power, symbols of the sacred water that each had acquired during his making as a clever-man. With these the doctor could perform many miracles: the crystals warned him of the approach of enemies, he was assisted by them in making his cures, he could project one or more into an enemy and thus kill him. There seemed to be a friendly competition between the old doctors to see who could produce the greatest number of crystals.

The boy was conscious that old scars on his back and chest were being opened and fresh cicatrices were being cut. The oldest of the doctors, those who had the greatest number of crystals, those who had climbed the trees with their cords, or passed through them, clustered about him and his "making" was completed. . . .

This is how initiation ceremonies were described for me by Tjalka-lieri and other natives. Naturally the pattern differed from area to area and from tribe to tribe, but basically it was the same. A native who has been "through the ring" (initiation ceremonies on the coast occur at circular borah grounds) or "given the rule" is highly thought of in detribalized groups of aborigines now. There were many interesting features about these descriptions, and one that certainly required investigation was that of the magic cord.

Such magic cords or magic ropes figure prominently in aboriginal mythology and are related to the mythological snakes, especially the rainbow snake, that occur in the vast explanatory legends of aboriginal lore. . . .

We vigorously pursued an investigation of the magic cord among these people. Most of the information came through a comprehensive questionnaire by which the natives were asked about a wide variety of magical experiences and beliefs.

Half the natives interviewed had actually seen a magic cord, they claimed. . . .

Owen, a well-educated native, had seen Eric Walker produce a magic cord only a few years previously.

"We were walking along in the bush—three or four of us—talking about the old-time powers of the doctors. Eric Walker said to us, 'I got a clever-rope. I'll show it to you.' He lay down on the ground and his face was all twisted up and he breathed heavy. We all watched him and I was pretty frightened.

"Soon we saw something coming out of Eric's mouth. It was alive and moving about."

"How thick was it?"

"It was no thicker than your little finger and sandy in colour. It had a sort of blunt head. It moved about like a snake. We were all awful frightened; then it went back and Eric woke up again."

"How long was it?"

"We only saw about six inches that time, but a couple of days later, when we were all together again, Eric said, 'You fellows ought to see all that clever-rope of mine' and he lay down again. Well, the whole rope came out this time. It was as long as your arm and it crawled about in the grass like it was alive. Then it went back into his body."

"You're sure it wasn't a snake—you'd recognize a snake?"

"Oh, nothing like a snake, no."

"Or an earthworm?"

Owen laughed aloud. "If you had seen it, you would know it wasn't a worm. It wasn't the colour of a worm."

"You know what we mean by hypnotism, Owen? You've told me that you've seen white men at theaters making others go to sleep and seem to see things that are not there. Would Eric Walker have done this, do you think?"

"Oh, no." Owen laughed again. "No, not that. This was real clever stuff."

"I see. Did Eric tell you beforehand what you were going to see, and then you saw it?"

"Yes."

Here was a suggestion of hypnotism at work. . . .

One afternoon we were conducting some of our tests on a cottage veranda and paused briefly from these to talk about the cord. There was quite a crowd on the veranda—Danny Sambo, a full-blood initiate of the Gidabul tribe, Bert Mercy, a Nogwadjil from the region of Coff's Harbour, Joe Culham, a seventy-one-year-old Mullunjarli native, and a number of young men, mostly of the Bundulung-speaking group.

125

Bert Mercy said he had often seen magic cords. Usually they were black, at other times sandy, and they were never thicker than a single strand of horsehair. . . .

"The doctors find their cords in creeks," he said. "I have seen them myself in clear waters. But you only find them when you're not looking for them. When the doctors find them, they tie a knot in them and take them into themselves. Then they get cleverer."

"How would that make them cleverer?"

"They can cure people who are sick, make storms, travel long ways in the skies . . ."

"And keep danger away," interrupted Joe Culham.

"And catch people," said Tom Kenny.

All eyes turned toward him. "Yes. I seen people caught with a cord. My grandfather had a cord. It was about four feet long, and he told me he used it to catch people, and when he did this they died."

"Did you ever see the cord, Tom?"

"Yes, lots of time. I seen my grandfather break up a storm with that same cord. He took it out and whirled it round his head."

"Did it seem to be alive?"

"Yes. And it had a flat head like some of those snakes."

So the accounts were recorded. And from these eye-witness accounts we built up a picture of the cord that differed somewhat from the second-hand or mythologically embellished accounts.

Mostly the cord was inches long rather than feet, and a couple of feet at most, sandy to black in colour, very thin rather than thick, and seemed to be alive. Usually it came from the doctor's mouth, and sometimes he pulled it from his mouth and sucked it back again later.

Further enlightening information came from Willie Mackenzie, a Yinliburra native, who said he had seen a clever-man take a thin cord, about nine inches long, from his mouth. It was like a fine thread. He held it over the glowing coals of a fire, and it crawled up into his hand. Then he returned it to his mouth. The cord seemed to tie itself into knots, he said.

With basic data like this we were left with a number of things to explain. For example, could all or part of the reports be explained by hypnotism? Did the informants really see something? If they did, could the ordinary sleight-of-hand tricks of doctors explain what they saw?

Could the cords be, for example, sinews of animals, or perhaps living creatures?. . .

But the existing evidence was complicated in a rather strange way. The phenomenon of the magic cord as recounted by aborigines closely resembled the phenomenon of ectoplasm reported by spiritualists and others and the stories throughout mythology (to which the *Gordius* worm, which is found in other parts of the world, has no doubt made its contribution), so that the mundane explanation advanced might not be the complete one.

In the case of the aborigines it appeared not to be "all done with mirrors." But was it all done with hypnotism? Or was there yet another possible answer?. . .

The question of the magic cord is not yet fully resolved. I am thoroughly convinced that hypnotism plays a major part and is probably associated with the *Gordius* worm, or animal sinews, or spittle manipulation, or some other such form of deception.

# 32.

# Singing Multifaceted Songs

VILMOS DIÓSZEGI

(1958)

> *Hungarian anthropologist Vilmos Diószegi conducted a year-long study of Siberian shamans. One day he persuaded a shaman called Kizlasov to make a recording of his songs. To do this, they left the shaman's isolated log cabin and traveled to a sawmill equipped with an electric generator, to power the anthropologist's tape recorder. (Battery-powered tape recorders did not come into their own until the 1960's.)*

The machine is already humming, the old man raises his voice. Like the murmur of a faraway waterfall, the monotonous noise of the generator pervades the room. It blends with the song of the shaman, until the forceful intensity of the song does not overpower the sound of the machine.

It is true that I am hearing a shaman's song recited *viva voce* for the first time in my life, I witness this performance for the first time, I have never before seen how they conjure up the spirits, but I have to confess, rather embarrassedly, I was immensely impressed by it.

And this is just a simple demonstration.

There is no devout congregation watching the shaman and truly fearing the invoked spirits. The playful reflections of the fire are missing, there is no flaming or glowing fire here, casting strange shadows upon the walls of the yurt, suggesting the presence of the assembling spirits. Nobody throws twigs or branches and weeds into the fire, so that their overpowering smoke might let the clouded eyes see all that the shaman is singing about. Kizlasov has no drum, suggesting with its faster or slower, stronger or weaker beats, whether the mounted shaman gallops or ambles only, whether he is coming or going, further and further away. The ceremonial garb is lacking too, with its innumerable metal bells, straining the nerves with their tinkling, jingling sound and whose several hundreds of coloured ribbons make the human likeness of the whirling shaman improbable with their fluttering. There is no dance, the movements of which help to represent and explain all the shaman wants to indicate and depict. And, last but not least, I have absolutely no faith in the supernatural power of the shaman and no faith in his spirits, which have been instilled in every Sagay from the cradle on. And still . . .

It was an unforgettable experience.

Hardly had the old man begun his song than he was entirely immersed in it. There was no drum in his hands but with his right hand he kept beating out the rhythm as if he were holding a drumstick, slowly first, then faster, then in syncopated time. The voice filled the empty room, it echoed from the bare walls and it poured forth incessantly from the shaman's mouth, first slowly, then it became sputtering, then it was conversational, then it grew into a song again, then it was a monologue, after that it formed questions and answers, now it was soft, and after that resounding, it was high-pitched and then a deep bass, once it was only like a soft whistle, another time it was like the neighing of a horse.

I realized it now: no pencil, no tape recorder can ever capture this. This should be exempted from oblivion by a sound-film. However, it could never be the same without the original environment and that does not exist any more.

Very probably, the shaman could not remain indifferent any more than an actor could if he performed to an enthusiastic audience and not to an empty room. What an enthralling force shamanizing might have been about fifty or a hundred years ago . . . we can only imagine.

But the text, the heretofore entirely unknown Sagay shaman-song had at least been recorded. Science will, no doubt, be able to make use of it. The only question is, shall we ever be able to interpret it correctly? The rhythm of the text, the melody and the meaning of the separate words may be captured, but would we ever grasp what is behind them? The inner tension, the secret meaning of the different melodious motives and the innermost, hidden significance of certain expressions might remain an eternal mystery.

# 33

# !Kung Medicine Dance

LORNA MARSHALL

(1962)

*American anthropologist Lorna Marshall carried out fieldwork among the !Kung Bushmen in South-West Africa. (The exclamation mark indicates that the k is sounded as a throaty click.) She described the activities of medicine men, who cure people by going into trance while singing, drawing out sickness and casting it back to the spirits. Marshall did not refer to these men as shamans, but she describes a rare instance of shamanism in Africa.*

The ceremonial curing dance is the one religious act which has form and in which the people are united. The purpose of the dance is to cure sickness and to drive away evil. If there is actual sickness among the people or if real misfortune has come upon them, the dance will be held especially to cure these ills. But the people dance often when no one is actually known to be sick, and when no particular misfortune has come, to drive away evil which might be there but which one cannot see, and to feel protected by goodness. . . .

After several dances have been danced the medicine men begin to cure. The !Kung do not have sorcerers, witches, or witch doctors, and do not believe that the divine beings enter into the medicine men or speak through them. Almost all the !Kung men are medicine men. They do not all choose to practice, for one reason or another, but there are always several in a band who are active. Medicine men receive no rewards other than their inner satisfactions and emotional release. I know that some of them feel a deep responsibility for the welfare of their people and great anxiety and concern if their curing fails, and a corresponding satisfaction if it prevails. Others of them appear to be less concerned about the people whom they try to cure and more inwardly turned.

When the medicine men are curing, all of them experience varying degrees of self-induced trance, which includes a period of frenzy and a period of semi-consciousness or deep unconsciousness. They may become stiff or froth at the mouth or lie still as if in coma. Some of them habitually remain in trance only a short time, others for hours. One man used to remain in a semi-trance for most of the day following a dance.

A Bushman curing cannot be fully described in words; it must be heard and I give only an outline here. The medicine man begins by dancing and singing with the others whatever medicine song is being sung. He then leaves the line of dancing men and leans, still singing, over the person he is going to cure. He places one hand on the person's chest, one on his or her back, and flutters his hands. The !Kung believe that in this way he draws the sickness, real or potential, out of the person through his own arms into himself. He grunts with shuddering, gurgling, gasping grunts which intensify in tempo and pitch into shrieks and reach a high, piercing, quavering yell. Finally the medicine men throws up his arms to cast the sickness out, hurling it into the darkness back to *Gauwa* [an evil spirit] or the *gauwasi* [spirits in general], with a sharp yelping cry or *"Kai Kai Kai."* This shows that it is heavy work to draw the sickness out. The effect of the sound on one observer, myself, was striking—gooseflesh and a stopping of the breath which made it seem as though the heart stood still an instant. A medicine man goes to every person present, leaning over each to cure, even the babies, who, amazingly, seldom cry, though he gurgles and gasps right into their ears. If someone is actually sick, he returns to him again and again through the night.

After the curing has been going on for some time, medicine men begin to reach their state of frenzy. They no longer go around to the people, their spasms of grunting and shrieking become more frequent and violent, their stomachs heave, they stagger and sway. They rush to the fire, trample it, pick up the coals, set fire to their hair. Fire activates the medicine in them. People hold them to keep them from falling and beat out the flames. They rush out into the darkness, where *Gauwa* and the *gauwasi* are lurking. They hurl burning sticks and swear at them. "Filthy face! Take away the sickness you have brought." "Uncovered penis! You are bad. You want to kill us. Go away." "*Hishe*, you are a liar. This man will not die." At this point they may fall into deep unconsciousness or sink down semi-conscious, eyes closed, unable to walk.

The medicine men who have not reached their full frenzy or who have passed through it attend those who are in it. The !Kung believe that at such a time the medicine man's spirit leaves his body and goes out to meet *Gauwa* and the *gauwasi*. They call this "half death." It is a dangerous time and the man's body must be watched over and kept warm. The medicine men lean over the one who is in trance. They blow in his ears to open them. They take sweat from their armpits and rub him. Some fall over on to him in trance themselves and are in turn rubbed and cared for by the others. The women must sing and clap ardently while a man is in deep trance. He needs the good medicine of the music to protect him.

The curing dance draws people of a Bushman band together into concerted action as nothing else does. They stamp and clap and sing with such precision that they become like an organic being. In this close configuration—together—they face the gods. They do not plead, as they do in their individual supplications, for the favour of the divine, all-powerful beings, and do not praise them for goodness. Instead, the medicine men, on behalf of the people, releasing themselves from ordinary behaviour by trance and overcoming fear and inaction, throw themselves into combat with the gods and try to force them with hurled sticks and hurled words to take away the evils they might be bringing.

The violence and excitement of the ceremony have the effect, as in a drama, I believe, of releasing the emotions of the people and purging them, in Aristotle's sense. Fear and hostility find outlet and the people have acted together to protect themselves. In this there is solace and hope.

# PART FIVE

# The Observers
# Take Part

Historian of religions Mircea Eliade declared in his classic work on shamanism: "Narcotics are only a vulgar substitute for 'pure' trance. . . . [T]he use of intoxicants (alcohol, tobacco, etc.) is a recent innovation and points to a decadence in shamanic technique. Narcotic intoxication is called on to provide an *imitation* of a state that the shaman is no longer capable of attaining otherwise." Scholars debated this point for decades. Many saw a personal bias in Eliade's use of the term *decadence.* They also criticized him for lumping all inebriants under the term *narcotics* and for failing to recognize the central role of hallucinogens in many forms of shamanism. Anthropologist Peter Furst said that Eliade told him in the last years of his life that he had "discarded his view of the use of hallucinogenic plants as 'degeneration' of the shamanic techniques of ecstasy."

Anthropologist Bronislaw Malinowski developed the method of "participant observation" in the 1910's, but it was not until decades later that anthropologists and ethnographers began using this method to study shamans by actively participating in their sessions.

However, academic observers did not hurry to participate in shamanic ordeals such as extended fasts in nature. It seems they preferred to try the more direct route of the hallucinogenic plants used by certain shamans, particularly in Central and South America. Eating acrid mushrooms or drinking a bitter brew did not require too much self-sacrifice. But the reports they wrote deal mostly with observing oneself among shamans, rather than observing shamans. It does not suffice to take plant hallucinogens to understand shamans.

Nevertheless, western observers who participated in shamanic sessions involving hallucinogenic plants found that they could have experiences similar to those described by shamans. Gordon Wasson experienced flying out of his body. Barbara Myerhoff saw the *axis mundi*. Michael Harner felt he was dying and learned about life from giant reptilian creatures.

This led observers to take shamans more seriously.

# 34

# Smoking Huge Cigars

FRANCIS HUXLEY

(1956)

*British anthropologist Francis Huxley lived with the Urubú and the*
*Tembé people in the Brazilian Amazon in the 1950's. Having lost their*
*shamans, the Urubú applied to the Tembé for instruction in that field.*
*Tembé shamans consume enormous quantities of strong tobacco, which*
*takes strong practice. Try as he might, Huxley would cough after only a*
*few such "cruel lungfuls."*

By the evening, everyone in the village had come crowding into our
hut with their hammocks, which they slung here and there between the
house-posts. . . . There was a small pile of tawari cigars on the table,
which I'd provided from my tobacco; made from hard tobacco sliced
fine and rubbed between the hands, put into a thin sheet of tawari
bark which is then rolled up tight and tied with narrow strips of itself.
One such tawari, a foot long and half an inch thick, was lit and given
to Chico, who started humming to warm himself up; then he turned
and said to me, "I'll sing six or seven songs for them all." He sat in
Pari's hammock, with Pari at his side, the rest of us, men, women and
children, each with a tawari, sitting or standing where we could.

After humming the tune to himself a few times—all Tembé tunes
were pleasing and elegant, some sounding remarkably like Gregorian
chants, in contrast to the whooping or groaning songs of the Urubus—
and beating time with the maraca Toi had lent him, Chico started

singing properly, and soon was on his feet, singing his loudest. The others, not knowing the words, all hoo'd and hay'd as best they could, supporting the tune while Chico started on his cigar. He played with it at first, crumpling the end slightly between his fingers and blowing, so that a stream of sparks went up into the roof; Toi at once followed suit, with Tero playing the fool with his cigar, using it like a hose. Then Chico started to inhale—no dainty puffs, but taking the smoke with great sucking gasps right into his lungs, working his shoulders like bellows to get as much smoke in as possible in the quickest time, and then out again, suck blow, suck blow, till I was sure he'd have to take a mouthful of pure air in order not to suffocate; on he went without even a cough. Admittedly, it's not all smoke that one breathes in: the mouth isn't clamped to the end of the cigar, but a small space left open which lets the air mix with the smoke, thus letting the lungs take in a great volume at great speed. But it must take a lot of practice: I cough after a couple of such cruel lungfuls. A good shaman, however, will smoke five or six tawaris eighteen inches long in one night, and while he'll do quite a bit of coughing he'll sing till dawn without losing his voice.

Chico sang quite well, for a young man: he didn't yet have the resonance his father had, which makes listening to Tembé songs a pleasure even when they go on all night. But the others were a bar behind him all the time, and when they couldn't find the tune they'd sing *hé hé* as a stopgap in a neutral tone of voice; while the women, like dreadful oboes played windily in their top reaches, sang—whatever the song and whatever the place in the song—a guttural yodel of four notes, always just out of key. Chico was soon drowned by all this noise, by the women's descant and the men's roaring whoops and *hé hé*'s.

After every other verse or so, Chico would sigh exhaustedly—ehh! ohhh!—and take another twenty lungfuls of tobacco smoke. Then—if he wasn't caught by a fit of coughing, which came on him later—he'd start immediately into the succeeding verses. Ehh! Ohhh! the other men around him sighed, just to be in things; filled their lungs with smoke, roared out of tune, and blew showers of sparks into the air. It was really a remarkable sight, since it was a very dark moonless night, and my paraffin lamp had been put out: all one could see was a large number of burning cigar ends, glowing and fading, sometimes emitting showers of sparks, and from time to time illuminating some dim, ruddy face anxiously sucking. The smoke filled the air, curling slowly out of the hut, and the noise was magnificent.

Chico, drunk with tobacco smoke and also, doubtless, with too much oxygen, started groaning deep in his chest till he left the ordinary songs that he'd been singing up till then, and started on a true shaman song, to summon Mikur the opossum from the jungle to aid him in the cure he was going to do. Soon he fell down on his back on to the ground, where he lay groaning miserably: the others all stopped singing, which they shouldn't have done, puffed idly at their cigars and chatted a bit; at length they started singing again, urged by the women. Four minutes later Chico was on his feet once more singing louder than ever, possessed by the opossum spirit. One of the children had a pain in her side, and while everyone continued singing, Chico palped the place, blew smoke over it directly from the end of his cigar, blew some more from his mouth. Then he sucked the place several times, after having filled his mouth with smoke, and vigorously blew into his closed fist, which he then flung away from himself, opening his fingers at the same time, to get rid of what he had sucked out. Finally he filled his mouth again with smoke, and blew it through his hand on to the place, and was finished. He showed what had been causing the trouble—a rather nasty little object, I think a piece of meat he'd kept in his mouth since supper. . . .

But there was one trick Chico could not manage, that of killing a man at a distance by magic. To do this, the shaman "softens" a specially made wooden caruwa and blows it, with a puff of spiritually charged breath, towards the man; no matter how far away he is, the caruwa will find the man, enter his body and kill him. Chico was unable to perform this sorcerer's trick because he had once touched a corpse, and that one corrupting contact had bled him of his power. This is one of the paradoxes that are so common among the Indians.

When a shaman, or a sorcerer, falls into a trance he is said to be "manon-manon," dead-dead, and only then is he able to converse with the spirits that come to inhabit him; and his ability to do this confers on him a kind of immortality, since after every such "death" he wakes up, or is "born" again. To confuse this spiritual death with a physical one, however, is fatal, and if he should touch a dead body his magic is short-circuited, leaving him empty of power.

In order to keep his power intact, the shaman has to lead a somewhat secluded life. He is greatly admired, for if the power to do things is a kind of commonplace magic, the power to make things do themselves is irresistible: Indians take great delight in a watch, or a magnet, or any more or less self-moving object. But the shaman's power, which he derives from a dangerous and laborious mastery of the spirits, must be used productively if he is not to turn into a sorcerer, and his power into black magic. A good shaman has tricks, but his reputation rests on the cures he effects: that is, he may not keep his power to himself. If he does, and uses it selfishly, he may be put to death: a fate which has overtaken several Tembé shamans in the past, and is in fact the occupational hazard of shamans throughout South America.

# 35

# "I Was a Disembodied Eye Poised in Space"

R. GORDON WASSON

(1957)

*American banker and mushroom enthusiast R. Gordon Wasson was the first person to describe eating hallucinogenic mushrooms with a Mexican shaman. Unlike many of the texts in this anthology, Wasson's account was read by hundreds of thousands of people in* Life *magazine. The Mazatec shaman's name was Maria Sabina, but Wasson called her "Eva Mendez," in a fruitless attempt to protect her privacy. This article inspired a surge of hippie tourism that weighed heavily on indigenous villages in southern Mexico for many years.*

On the night of June 29–30, 1955, in a Mexican Indian village so remote from the world that most of the people still speak no Spanish, my friend Allan Richardson and I shared with a family of Indian friends a celebration of "holy communion" where "divine" mushrooms were first adored and then consumed. The Indians mingled Christian and pre-Christian elements in their religious practices in a way disconcerting for Christians but natural for them. The rite was led by two women, mother and daughter, both of them *curanderas*, or shamans. The proceedings went on in the Mixeteco language. The mushrooms were of a species with hallucinogenic powers; that is, they cause the eater to see visions. We chewed and swallowed these acrid mushrooms, saw visions, and emerged from the experience awestruck. We had come from afar to attend a mushroom rite but had expected nothing so staggering as the virtuosity of the performing *curanderas* and the astonishing effects of the mushrooms. Richardson and I were the first white men in recorded history to eat the divine mushrooms, which for centuries have been a secret of certain Indian peoples living far from the great world in southern Mexico. No anthropologists had ever described the scene that we witnessed. . . .

We could stay only a week or so: we had no time to lose. I went to the *municipio* or town hall, and there I found the official in charge, the *síndico,* seated alone at his great table in an upper room. He was a young Indian, about 35 years old, and he spoke Spanish well. His name was Filemon. He had a friendly manner and I took a chance. Leaning over his table, I asked him earnestly and in a low voice if I could speak to him in confidence. Instantly curious, he encouraged me. "Will you," I went on, "help me learn the secrets of the divine mushroom?" and I used the Mixeteco name, *'nti sheeto,* correctly pronouncing it with glottal stop and tonal differentiation of the syllables. When Filemon recovered from his surprise he said warmly that nothing could be easier. He asked me to pass by his house, on the outskirts of town, at siesta time.

Allan and I arrived there at about 3 o'clock. Filemon's home is built on a mountainside, with a trail on one side at the level of the upper story and a deep ravine on the other. Filemon at once led us down the ravine to a spot where the divine mushrooms were growing in abundance. After photographing them we gathered them in a cardboard box and then labored back up the ravine in the heavy moist heart of that torrid afternoon. Not letting us rest Filemon sent us high up above his house to meet the *curandera,* the woman who would officiate at the mushroom rite. A connection of his, Eva Mendez by name, she was a *curandera de primera categoria,* of the highest quality, *una Señora sin mancha,* a woman without stain. We found her in the house of her daughter, who pursues the same vocation. Eva was resting on a mat on the floor from her previous night's performance. She was middle-aged, and short like all Mixetecos, with a spirituality in her expression that struck us at once. She had presence. We showed our mushrooms to the woman and her daughter. They cried out in rapture over the firmness, the fresh beauty and abundance of our young specimens. Through an interpreter we asked if they would serve us that night. They said yes.

About 20 of us gathered in the lower chamber of Filemon's house after 8 o'clock that evening. Allan and I were the only strangers, the only ones who spoke no Mixeteco. Only our hosts, Filemon and his wife, could talk to us in Spanish. The welcome accorded to us was of a kind that we had never experienced before in the Indian country. Everyone observed a friendly decorum. They did not treat us stiffly, as strange white men; we were of their number. The Indians were wearing their best clothes, the women dressed in their *huipiles* or native costumes, the men in clean white trousers tied around the waist with strings and their best serapes over their clean shirts. They gave us chocolate to drink, somewhat ceremonially, and suddenly I recalled the words of the early Spanish writer who had said that before the mushrooms were served, chocolate was drunk. I sensed what we were in for: at long last we were discovering that the ancient communion rite still survived and we were going to witness it. . . .

At about 10:30 o'clock Eva Mendez cleaned the mushrooms of their grosser dirt and then, with prayers, passed them through the smoke of resin incense burning on the floor. As she did this, she sat on a mat before a simple altar table adorned with Christian images, the Child Jesus and the Baptism in Jordan. Then she apportioned the mushrooms among the adults. She reserved 13 pair for herself and 13 pair for her daughter. (The mushrooms are always counted in pairs.) I was on tiptoe of expectancy: she turned and gave me six pair in a cup. I could not have been happier: this was the culmination of years of pursuit. She gave Allan six pair too. His emotions were mixed. His wife Mary had consented to his coming only after she had drawn from him a promise not to let those nasty toadstools cross his lips. Now he faced a behavior dilemma. He took the mushrooms, and I heard him

143

mutter in anguish, "My God, what will Mary say!" Then we ate our mushrooms, chewing them slowly, over the course of a half hour. They tasted bad—acrid with a rancid odor that repeated itself. Allan and I were determined to resist any effects they might have, to observe better the events of the night. But our resolve soon melted before the onslaught of the mushrooms.

Before midnight the Señora (as Eva Mendez is usually called) broke a flower from the bouquet on the altar and used it to snuff out the flame of the only candle that was still burning. We were left in darkness and in darkness we remained until dawn. For a half hour we waited in silence. Allan felt cold and wrapped himself in a blanket. A few minutes later he leaned over and whispered, "Gordon, I am seeing things!" I told him not to worry, I was too. The visions had started. They reached a plateau of intensity deep in the night, and they continued at that level until about 4 o'clock. We felt slightly unsteady on our feet and in the beginning were nauseated. We lay down on the mat that had been spread for us, but no one had any wish to sleep except the children, to whom mushrooms are not served. We were never more wide awake, and the visions came whether our eyes were opened or closed. They emerged from the center of the field of vision, opening up as they came, now rushing, now slowly, at the pace that our will chose. They were in vivid color, always harmonious. They began with art motifs, angular such as might decorate carpets or textiles or wallpaper or the drawing board of an architect. Then they evolved into palaces with courts, arcades, gardens—resplendent palaces all laid over with semiprecious stones. Then I saw a mythological beast drawing a regal chariot. Later it was as though the walls of our house had dissolved, and my spirit had flown forth, and I was suspended in midair viewing landscapes of mountains, with camel caravans advancing slowly across the slopes, the mountains rising tier above tier to the very heavens. Three days later, when I repeated the same experience in the same room with the same *curanderas*, instead of mountains I saw river estuaries, pellucid water flowing through an endless expanse of reeds down to a measureless sea, all by the pastel light of a horizontal

sun. This time a human figure appeared, a woman in primitive costume, standing and staring across the water, enigmatic, beautiful, like
a sculpture except that she breathed and was wearing woven colored
garments. It seemed as though I was viewing a world of which I was
not a part and with which I could not hope to establish contact. There
I was, poised in space, a disembodied eye, invisible, incorporeal, seeing but not seen.

The visions were not blurred or uncertain. They were sharply fo-
cused, the lines and colors being so sharp that they seemed more real
to me than anything I had ever seen with my own eyes. I felt that I was
now seeing plain, whereas ordinary vision gives us an imperfect view;
I was seeing the archetypes, the Platonic ideas, that underlie the imperfect images of everyday life. The thought crossed my mind: could
the divine mushrooms be the secret that lay behind the ancient Mysteries? Could the miraculous mobility that I was now enjoying be the
explanation for the flying witches that played so important a part in
the folklore and fairy tales of northern Europe? These reflections
passed through my mind at the very time that I was seeing the visions,
for the effect of the mushrooms is to bring about a fission of the spirit,
a split in the person, a kind of schizophrenia, with the rational side
continuing to reason and to observe the sensations that the other side
is enjoying. The mind is attached as by an elastic cord to the vagrant
senses.

Meanwhile the Señora and her daughter were not idle. When our
visions were still in the initial phases, we heard the Señora waving her
arms rhythmically. She began a low, disconnected humming. Soon the
phrases became articulate syllables, each disconnected syllable cutting
the darkness sharply. Then by stages the Señora came forth with a
full-bodied canticle, sung like very ancient music. It seemed to me at
the time like an introit to the Ancient of Days. As the night progressed
her daughter spelled her at singing. They sang well, never loud, with
authority. What they sang was indescribably tender and moving, fresh,
vibrant, rich. I had never realized how sensitive and poetic an instrument
the Mixeteco language could be. Perhaps the beauty of the Señora's

performance was partly an illusion induced by the mushrooms; if so, the hallucinations are aural as well as visual. Not being musicologists, we know not whether the chants were wholly European or partly indigenous in origin. From time to time the singing would rise to a climax and then suddenly stop, and then the Señora would fling forth spoken words, violent, hot crisp words that cut the darkness like a knife. This was the mushroom speaking through her, God's words, as the Indians believe, answering the problems that had been posed by the participants. This was the Oracle. At intervals, perhaps every half hour, there was a brief intermission, when the Señora would relax and some would light cigarets.

At one point, while the daughter sang, the Señora stood up in the darkness where there was an open space in our room and began a rhythmic dance with clapping or slapping. We do not know exactly how she accomplished her effect. The claps or slaps were always resonant and true. So far as we know, she used no device, only her hands against each other or possibly against different parts of her body. The claps and slaps had pitch, the rhythm at times was complex, and the speed and volume varied subtly. We think the Señora faced successively the four points of the compass, rotating clockwise, but are not sure. One thing is certain: this mysterious percussive utterance was ventriloquistic, each slap coming from an unpredictable direction and distance, now close to our ears, now distant, above, below, here and yonder, like Hamlet's ghost *hic et ubique*. We were amazed and spellbound, Allan and I.

There we lay on our mat, scribbling notes in the dark and exchanging whispered comments, our bodies inert and heavy as lead, while our senses were floating free in space, feeling the breezes of the outdoors, surveying vast landscapes or exploring the recesses of gardens of ineffable beauty. And all the while we were listening to the daughter's chanting and to the unearthly claps and whacks, delicately controlled, of the invisible creatures darting around us.

The Indians who had taken the mushrooms were playing a part in the vocal activity. In the moments of tension they would utter exclamations of wonder and adoration, not loud, responsive to the singers and harmonizing with them, spontaneously yet with art.

On that initial occasion we all fell asleep around 4 o'clock in the morning. Allan and I awoke at 6, rested and heads clear, but deeply shaken by the experience we had gone through. Our friendly hosts served us coffee and bread. We then took our leave and walked back to the Indian house where we were staying, a mile or so away.

# 36.

# Fear, Clarity, Knowledge, and Power

CARLOS CASTANEDA

(1968)

*Anthropologist Carlos Castaneda lived a life shrouded in mystery. Few photos of him were published. And although there is some evidence he was born in Peru, even his place of birth and original nationality have been questioned. Castaneda claimed to have apprenticed himself to a Yaqui sorcerer named "don Juan." And his work seems to have been based in part on some real research, at least in the beginning. But other anthropologists have cast serious doubts on the ethnographic integrity of his reports. The extent to which Castaneda made up his accounts is an open question, but he appears to have used literary devices to trick his readers into suspending their disbelief, even from the beginning. Castaneda did not call don Juan a shaman, but his books ignited an unprecedented interest in shamanism. And in this passage from his first book, Castaneda seems to have put his finger on the essence of the shaman's path. Don Juan's "enemies of a man of knowledge" echo numerous other accounts of the challenges of practicing shamanism.*

Saturday, April 8, 1962

In our conversations, don Juan consistently used or referred to the phrase "man of knowledge," but never explained what he meant by it. I asked him about it.

"A man of knowledge is one who has followed truthfully the hardships of learning," he said. "A man who has, without rushing or without faltering, gone as far as he can in unraveling the secrets of power and knowledge."

"Can anyone be a man of knowledge?"

"No, not anyone."

"Then what must a man do to become a man of knowledge?"

"He must challenge and defeat his four natural enemies."

"Will he be a man of knowledge after defeating these four enemies?"

"Yes. A man can call himself a man of knowledge only if he is capable of defeating all four of them."

"Then, can *anybody* who defeats these enemies be a man of knowledge?"

"Anybody who defeats them becomes a man of knowledge."

"But are there any special requirements a man must fulfill before fighting with these enemies?"

"No. Anyone can try to become a man of knowledge; very few men actually succeed, but that is only natural. The enemies a man encounters on the path of learning to become a man of knowledge are truly formidable; most men succumb to them."

"What kind of enemies are they, don Juan?"

He refused to talk about the enemies. He said it would be a long time before the subject would make any sense to me. . . .

"To be a man of knowledge has no permanence. One is never a man of knowledge, not really. Rather, one becomes a man of knowledge for a very brief instant, after defeating the four natural enemies."

"You must tell me, don Juan, what kind of enemies they are."

He did not answer. I insisted again, but he dropped the subject and started to talk about something else.

Sunday, April 15, 1962

As I was getting ready to leave, I decided to ask him once more about the enemies of a man of knowledge. I argued that I could not return for some time, and it would be a good idea to write down what he had to say and then think about it while I was away.

He hesitated for a while, but then began to talk.

"When a man starts to learn, he is never clear about his objectives. His purpose is faulty; his intent is vague. He hopes for rewards that will never materialize for he knows nothing of the hardships of learning.

"He slowly begins to learn—bit by bit at first, then in big chunks. And his thoughts soon clash. What he learns is never what he pictured, or imagined, and so he begins to be afraid. Learning is never what one expects. Every step of learning is a new task, and the fear the man is experiencing begins to mount mercilessly, unyieldingly. His purpose becomes a battlefield.

"And thus he has stumbled upon the first of his natural enemies: Fear! A terrible enemy—treacherous, and difficult to overcome. It remains concealed at every turn of the way, prowling, waiting. And if the man, terrified in its presence, runs away, his enemy will have put an end to his quest."

"What will happen to the man if he runs away in fear?"

"Nothing happens to him except that he will never learn. He will never become a man of knowledge. He will perhaps be a bully, or a harmless, scared man; at any rate, he will be a defeated man. His first enemy will have put an end to his cravings."

"And what can he do to overcome fear?"

"The answer is very simple. He must not run away. He must defy his fear, and in spite of it he must take the next step in learning, and the next, and the next. He must be fully afraid, and yet he must not stop. That is the rule! And a moment will come when his first enemy retreats. The man begins to feel sure of himself. His intent becomes stronger. Learning is no longer a terrifying task.

"When this joyful moment comes, the man can say without hesitation that he has defeated his first natural enemy."

"Does it happen at once, don Juan, or little by little?"

"It happens little by little, and yet the fear is vanquished suddenly and fast."

"But won't the man be afraid again if something new happens to him?"

"No. Once a man has vanquished fear, he is free from it for the rest of his life because, instead of fear, he has acquired clarity—a clarity of mind which erases fear. By then a man knows his desires; he knows how to satisfy those desires. He can anticipate the new steps of learning, and a sharp clarity surrounds everything. The man feels that nothing is concealed.

"And thus he has encountered his second enemy: Clarity! That clarity of mind, which is so hard to obtain, dispels fear, but also blinds.

"It forces the man never to doubt himself. It gives him the assurance he can do anything he pleases, for he sees clearly into everything. And he is courageous because he is clear, and he stops at nothing because he is clear. But all that is a mistake; it is like something incomplete. If the man yields to this make-believe power, he has succumbed to his second enemy and will be patient when he should rush. And he will fumble with learning until he winds up incapable of learning anything more."

"What becomes of a man who is defeated in that way, don Juan? Does he die as a result?"

"No, he doesn't die. His second enemy has just stopped him cold from trying to become a man of knowledge; instead, the man may turn into a buoyant warrior, or a clown. Yet the clarity for which he has paid so dearly will never change to darkness and fear again. He will be clear as long as he lives, but he will no longer learn, or yearn for, anything."

"But what does he have to do to avoid being defeated?"

"He must do what he did with fear: he must defy his clarity and use it only to see, and wait patiently and measure carefully before taking new steps; he must think, above all, that his clarity is almost a mistake. And a moment will come when he will understand that his clarity was only a point before his eyes. And thus he will have overcome his second enemy, and will arrive at a position where nothing can harm him anymore. This will not be a mistake. It will not be only a point before his eyes. It will be true power.

"He will know at this point that the power he has been pursuing for so long is finally his. He can do with it whatever he pleases. His ally is at his command. His wish is the rule. He sees all that is around him. But he has also come across his third enemy: Power!

"Power is the strongest of all enemies. And naturally the easiest thing to do is to give in; after all, the man is truly invincible. He commands; he begins by taking calculated risks, and ends in making rules, because he is a master.

"A man at this stage hardly notices his third enemy closing in on him. And suddenly, without knowing, he will certainly have lost the battle. His enemy will have turned him into a cruel, capricious man."

"Will he lose his power?"

"No, he will never lose his clarity or his power."

"What then will distinguish him from a man of knowledge?"

"A man who is defeated by power dies without really knowing how to handle it. Power is only a burden upon his fate. Such a man has no command over himself, and cannot tell when or how to use his power."

"Is the defeat by any of these enemies a final defeat?"

"Of course it is final. Once one of these enemies overpowers a man there is nothing he can do."

"Is it possible, for instance, that the man who is defeated by power may see his error and mend his ways?"

"No. Once a man gives in he is through."

"But what if he is temporarily blinded by power, and then refuses it?"

"That means his battle is still on. That means he is still trying to become a man of knowledge. A man is defeated only when he no longer tries, and abandons himself."

"But then, don Juan, it is possible that a man may abandon himself to fear for years, but finally conquer it."

"No, that is not true. If he gives in to fear he will never conquer it, because he will shy away from learning and never try again. But if he tries to learn for years in the midst of his fear, he will eventually conquer it because he will never have really abandoned himself to it."

"How can he defeat his third enemy, don Juan?"

"He has to defy it, deliberately. He has to come to realize the power he has seemingly conquered is in reality never his. He must keep himself in line at all times, handling carefully and faithfully all that he has learned. If he can see that clarity and power, without his control over himself, are worse than mistakes, he will reach a point where everything is held in check. He will know then when and how to use his power. And thus he will have defeated his third enemy.

"The man will be, by then, at the end of his journey of learning. And almost without warning he will come upon the last of his enemies: Old age! This enemy is the cruelest of all, the one he won't be able to defeat completely, but only fight away.

"This is the time when a man has no more fears, no more impatient clarity of mind—a time when all his power is in check, but also the time when he has an unyielding desire to rest. If he gives in totally to his desire to lie down and forget, if he soothes himself in tiredness, he will have lost his last round, and his enemy will cut him down into a feeble old creature. His desire to retreat will overrule all his clarity, his power, and his knowledge.

"But if the man sloughs off his tiredness, and lives his fate through, he can then be called a man of knowledge, if only for the brief moment when he succeeds in fighting off his last, invincible enemy. That moment of clarity, power, and knowledge is enough."

# 37.

# "I Found Myself Impaled
# on the Axis Mundi"

BARBARA MYERHOFF

(1974)

> *Barbara Myerhoff studied anthropology at the University of California*
> *Los Angeles at the same time as Carlos Castaneda. She went on to be-*
> *come the first anthropologist, with Peter Furst, to accompany the Hui-*
> *chol Indians of Mexico on their pilgrimage across the desert during*
> *which they hunt for the hallucinogenic peyote cactus. To prepare for this,*
> *Myerhoff ate peyote under the supervision of Huichol shaman Ramón*
> *Medina Silva. The following is an account of her experience.*

"Ramón," I asked, "What would I see if I were to eat peyote?" "Do
you want to?" he replied unexpectedly. "Yes, very much." "Then come
tomorrow, very early and eat nothing tonight or tomorrow. Only drink
a little warm water when you get up in the morning." The Huichols,
unlike the neighboring Cora and Tarahumara Indians, have no fear of
peyote. Ordinary men, women, and children take it frequently with no
sickness or frightening visions, as long as the peyote they use has been
gathered properly during an authentic peyote hunt. Ramón assured
me that the experience in store for me would be beautiful and important and I trusted him and his knowledge completely by this time.

   The next morning he led me into the little hut and began feeding
me the small green "buttons" or segments, one after another, perhaps

a dozen or more in all. He cut each segment away from the large piece he held and prepared it in no way that I could see, for the small pieces I was given retained all their skin, dirt, and root. The tiny fuzzy white-gray hairs that top each segment were intact and only the small button-most portion of the root had been pared off. The buttons were very chewy and tough, and unspeakably bitter-sour. My mouth flooded with saliva and shriveled from the revolting flavor, but no nausea came. "Chew well," Ramón urged me. "It is good, like a tortilla, isn't it?" But I was no longer able to answer.

After giving me what he felt was the proper dosage, Ramón indicated that he was going to wait outside and directed me to lie down quietly and close my eyes. For a long time I heard him singing and playing his little violin and then there were new sounds of comings and goings and soft laughter. "They've all come to stare at me and laugh," I thought. "Come on," I imagined them saying to each other. "Peek inside, we've got a *gringa* in there and we've given her a weed. You can get those anthropologists to eat anything if you tell them it's sacred. She thinks she's going to have a vision!"

But these thoughts were more amusing than ominous, for I really did not believe that Ramón would deceive me. After an inestimable period of time I began to be aware of a growing euphoria; I was flooded with feelings of goodwill. With great delight I began to notice sounds, especially the noises of the trucks passing on the highway outside. Although I discovered that I couldn't move, I was able to remain calm when it occurred to me that this was of no consequence because there was no other place that I wanted to be. My body assumed the rhythm of the passing trucks, gently wafting up and down like a scarf in a breeze. Time and space evaporated as I floated about in the darkness and vague images began to develop. I realized that I could keep track of what was happening to me and remember it if I thought of it not as a movielike flow of time but as a discrete series of events like beads on a string. I could go from one to the next and though the first was perhaps out of sight, it had not disappeared as do events in ordinary chronology. It was like a carnival with booths spread about to which I could always return to regain an experience, a Steppenwolf-like magical theater. The problem of retaining my experience was thus solved. There remained only the hazard of getting lost. But Ramón had prepared me for this; though he was outside the hut, I felt that as my guide and craftsman, he had left me a thread by means of which I could trace and retrace my peregrinations through the labyrinth and thus return safely from any far-flung destination. Assured by this notion, I started out.

The first "booth" found me impaled on an enormous tree with its roots buried far below the earth and its branches rising beyond sight, toward the sky. This was the Tree of Life, the *axis mundi* or world pole which penetrates the layers of the cosmos, connecting earth with underworld and heaven, on which shamans ascend in their magical flights. The image was exactly the same as a Mayan glyph which I was to come across for the first time several years after this vision occurred.

In the next sequence, I beheld a tiny speck of brilliant red flitting about a forest darkness. The speck grew as it neared. It was a vibrant bird who, with an insouciant flicker, landed on a rock. It was Ramón as psychopomp, as Papageno—half-man, magic bird, bubbling with excitement. He led me to the next episode which presented an oracular, gnomelike creature of macabre viscosity. I asked *the question,* the one that had not been out of my mind for months, "What do myths *mean?*" He offered his reply in mucid tones, melting with a deadly portentousness that mocked my seriousness. "The myths signify—nothing. They mean *themselves.*" Of course! They *were* themselves, nothing equivalent, nothing translated, nothing taken from another more familiar place to distort them. They had to be accepted in their own terms. I was embarrassed that as an aspirant anthropologist I had to be told this basic axiom of the discipline, but I was amused and relieved for in a vague way I had known it all along.

My journey ended many booths later, as I sat concentrating on a mythical little animal, aware that the entire experience was drawing to a close. The little fellow and I had entered a yarn painting and he sat precisely in the middle of the composition. I watched him fade and finally disappear into a hole and I made an extra effort to concentrate on him, convinced that a final lesson — a grand conclusion — was about to occur. Just as he vanished, an image flicked into the corner of my vision. In the upper righthand quadrant of the painting, another being had just jumped out of sight. I had missed him and *he* was the message. There it was! I had lost my lesson by looking for it too directly, with dead-center tight focus, with will and impatience. It was a practice which I knew fatal to understanding anything truly unique. It was my Western rationality, honed by formal study, eager to simplify, clarify, dissect, define, categorize, and analyze. These techniques, exercised prematurely, are antithetical to good ethnographic work and this I was to learn and learn and forget and relearn. The message could emerge anywhere on the canvas; one had to be alert, patient, receptive to whatever might occur, at any moment, in whatever ambiguous, unpredictable form it assumed, reserving interpretation for a later time. In the years to come, the vision was to serve as a mnemonic for this principle and help me keep it in the foreground of my consciousness for all that was ahead.

*War-ne-la, a Female Kwakiutl Shaman of the Koskimo, British Columbia, 1914.*

*Tlingit Shaman, Juneau, Alaska,* © *1900.*

*Tlingit Shaman from Taku.*

*Tlingit Shaman.*

*Female Nootka Shaman from Clayoquot Sound, Vancouver Island.*

PHOTGRAPH BY EDWARD S. CURTIS, © 1914. ROYAL BRITISH COLUMBIA
MUSEUM, VICTORIA, PN 5410. REPRODUCED BY PERMISSION.

*Hupa Female Shaman, California, 1923.*
PHOTOGRAPH BY EDWARD S. CURTIS.

*The Eskimo Shaman Najagneq from the island of Nunivak.*
PHOTOGRAPH TAKEN IN 1924 DURING THE FIFTH DANISH EXPEDITION
TO THULE UNDER THE LEADERSHIP OF KNUD RASMUSSEN.
REPRODUCED BY PERMISSION OF THE HEIRS OF KNUD RASMUSSEN.

*The 104-year-old Lacandon Shaman Chan K'in Viejo, Guatemala, 1991.*

PHOTOGRAPH BY CINDY KARP. REPRODUCED BY
PERMISSION OF BLACK STAR, NY.

# 38.

# A Shaman Loses Her Elevation
# by Interacting with Observers

MARIA SABINA AND ALVARO ESTRADA

(1977)

*Mazatec shaman Maria Sabina became famous after Gordon Wasson published an article about her in* Life *magazine. But Sabina discovered that outside attention had drawbacks. It caused mushroom-seeking foreigners to invade her village, and it diminished the feeling of elevation the mushrooms gave her. Alvaro Estrada, a Mazatec journalist, interviewed her twenty years after Wasson's initial visit. He translated her words into Spanish and published them as an "oral autobiography." Their book is a beautiful pearl.*

The next day, somebody brought three fair-haired men over to my house. One of them was Mr. Wasson. Someone had told the foreigners that I was ill, but without telling them that a drunk had wounded me with pistol shots. One of the guests listened to my chest. He put his head on my chest to listen to my heartbeat, he took my temples in his hands, and he also put his head on my back. The man was making signs of intelligence as he touched me. Finally he said words that I did not understand; he was speaking a language that was not Spanish. I do not even understand Spanish.

One night soon after, the foreigners attended one of my evening ceremonies. Later I found out that Wasson had been filled with wonder; and that he even said that another person in Huautla, who claimed to be a Wise one *(sabio)*, was just a liar; that he knew nothing. In fact, it was the sorcerer Venegas . . .

When the foreigners took the *sacred children* [mushrooms] with me, I did not feel anything bad. The ceremony was a good one. I had different visions. I managed to *see* places I had never been able to imagine. I went to the places where the foreigners came from. I saw cities. Big cities. Many houses, big houses.

Wasson came back several times. He brought his wife and his daughter. Different people also came with him. . . .

Wasson, his family, and his friends left and did not come back. It has been years since I saw them, but I know his wife is dead. Wasson came back one time all by himself, two or three years ago. The last time I saw him, he told me: "Maria Sabina, you and I will live for long years."

After Wasson's first visits, many foreigners came to ask me to do evening ceremonies for them. I asked them if they were ill, but they said they were not, that they only came "to know God." These people had many objects with which they took what they called photographs; they also took my voice. Later, they brought me papers in which one could see me. I keep several papers in which I appear. I keep them, though I do not know what they say about me.

It is true that Wasson and his friends were the first foreigners who came to our village in search of the *sacred children*, and who did not take them to heal from an illness. Their reason was that they wanted to find God.

Before Wasson, nobody took the mushrooms simply to find God. One had always taken them to heal the sick. . . .

The first time I did an evening ceremony in front of foreigners, I did not think anything bad could come of it. The order to put myself at their disposal came straight from the municipal authority, with the recommendation of the mayor, Cayetano Garcia, who is a friend of mine. But what happened? Well, many people came to *find God*, people of all colors and all ages. The young ones were the least respectful, you know; they take the *children* any time and any place. They do not do it

167

at night and they do not follow the indications of those who know, nor do they do it because they are ill, to heal themselves.

But from the moment the foreigners came to find God, the *sacred children* lost their purity. They lost their force, one has spoiled them. From now on, they will no longer have an effect. There is nothing one can do about it.

Before Wasson, I felt that the *sacred children* elevated me. I no longer have that feeling. The force has diminished. If Cayetano had not brought the foreigners . . . the *sacred children* would still have their power.

# 39

# "I Felt Like Socrates
# Accepting the Hemlock"

MICHAEL HARNER

(1980)

*American anthropologist Michael Harner lived several years among the Jívaro and Conibo people in the Western Amazon. Here he describes his first experience with the hallucinogenic brew* ayahuasca. *He found to his amazement that the extraordinary creatures he saw in his visions were quite familiar to his indigenous informants. This excerpt comes from a book called* The Way of the Shaman, *which describes shamanic techniques that anybody can practice.*

My first prolonged fieldwork as an anthropologist took place more than two decades ago on the forested eastern slopes of the Ecuadorian Andes among the Jívaro [HEE-varo] Indians, or *Untsuri Shuar*. The Jívaro were famous at that time for their now essentially vanished practice of "head-shrinking," and for their intensive practice of shamanism, which still continues. I successfully collected a great deal of information on their culture during 1956 and 1957, but remained an outside observer of the world of the shaman.

A couple of years later, the American Museum of Natural History invited me to make a year-long expedition to the Peruvian Amazon to study the culture of the Conibo Indians of the Ucayali River region. I accepted, delighted to have an opportunity to do more research on the fascinating Upper Amazon forest cultures. That fieldwork took place in 1960 and 1961.

Two particular experiences I had among the Conibo and the Jívaro were basic to my discovering the way of the shaman in both those cultures. . . .

I had been living for the better part of a year in a Conibo Indian village beside a remote lake off a tributary of the Río Ucayali. My anthropological research on the culture of the Conibo had been going well, but my attempts to elicit information on their religion met with little success. The people were friendly, but reluctant to talk about the supernatural. Finally they told me that if I really wished to learn, I must take the shamans' sacred drink made from *ayahuasca,* the "soul vine." I agreed, with both curiosity and trepidation, for they warned me that the experience would be very frightening.

The next morning my friend Tomás, the kind elder of the village, went into the forest to cut the vines. Before leaving, he told me to fast: a light breakfast and no lunch. He returned midday with enough *ayahuasca* vines and leaves of the *cawa* plant to fill a fifteen gallon pot. He boiled them all afternoon, until only about a quart of dark liquid remained. This he poured into an old bottle and left it to cool until sunset, when he said we would drink it.

The Indians muzzled the dogs in the village so that they could not bark. The noise of barking dogs could drive a man who had taken *ayahuasca* mad, I was told. The children were cautioned to be quiet, and silence came over the small community with the setting of the sun.

As the brief equatorial twilight was replaced by darkness, Tomás poured about a third of the bottle into a gourd bowl and gave it to me. All the Indians were watching. I felt like Socrates amidst his Athenian compatriots, accepting the hemlock—it occurred to me that one of the alternate names people in the Peruvian Amazon gave *ayahuasca* was "the little death." I drank the potion quickly. It had a strange, slightly bitter taste. I then waited for Tomás to take his turn, but he said that he had decided not to participate after all.

They had me lie down on the bamboo platform under the great

thatched roof of the communal house. The village was silent, except for the chirping of crickets and the distant calls of a howler monkey deep in the jungle.

As I stared upward into the darkness, faint lines of light appeared. They grew sharper, more intricate, and burst into brilliant colours. Sound came from far away, a sound like a waterfall, which grew stronger and stronger until it filled my ears.

Just a few minutes earlier I had been disappointed, sure that the *ayahuasca* was not going to have any effect on me. Now the sound of rushing water flooded my brain. My jaw began to feel numb, and the numbness was moving up to my temples.

Overhead the faint lines became brighter, and gradually interlaced to form a canopy resembling a geometric mosaic of stained glass. The bright violet hues formed an ever-expanding roof above me. Within this celestial cavern, I heard the sound of water grow louder and I could see dim figures engaged in shadowy movements. As my eyes seemed to adjust to the gloom, the moving scene resolved itself into something resembling a huge fun house, a supernatural carnival of demons. In the center, presiding over the activities, and looking directly at me, was a gigantic, grinning crocodilian head, from whose cavernous jaws gushed a torrential flood of water. Slowly the waters rose, and so did the canopy above them, until the scene metamorphosed into a simple duality of blue sky above and sea below. All creatures had vanished.

Then, from my position near the surface of the water, I began to see two strange boats wafting back and forth, floating through the air towards me, coming closer and closer. They slowly combined to form a single vessel with a huge dragon-headed prow, not unlike that of a Viking ship. Set amidships was a square sail. Gradually, as the boat gently floated back and forth above me, I heard a rhythmic swishing sound and saw that it was a giant galley with several hundred oars moving back and forth in cadence with the sound.

I became conscious, too, of the most beautiful singing I have ever heard in my life, high-pitched and ethereal, emanating from myriad voices on board the galley. As I looked more closely at the deck, I could make out large numbers of people with the heads of blue jays and the bodies of humans, not unlike the bird-headed gods of ancient Egyptian tomb paintings. At the same time, some energy-essence began to float from my chest up into the boat. Although I believed myself to be an atheist, I was completely certain that I was dying and that the bird-headed people had come to take my soul away on the boat. While the soul-flow continued from my chest, I was aware that the extremities of my body were growing numb.

Starting with my arms and legs, my body slowly began to feel like it was turning to solid concrete. I could not move or speak. Gradually, as the numbness closed in on my chest, toward my heart, I tried to get my mouth to ask for help, to ask the Indians for an antidote. Try as I might, however, I could not marshal my abilities sufficiently to make a word. Simultaneously, my abdomen seemed to be turning to stone, and I had to make a tremendous effort to keep my heart beating. I began to call my heart my friend, my dearest friend of all, to talk to it, to encourage it to beat with all the power remaining at my command.

I became aware of my brain. I felt—physically—that it had become compartmentalized into four separate and distinct levels. At the uppermost surface was the observer and commander, which was conscious of the condition of my body, and was responsible for the attempt to keep my heart going. It perceived, but purely as a spectator, the visions emanating from what seemed to be the nether portions of my brain. Immediately below the topmost level I felt a numbed layer. Which seemed to have been put out of commission by the drug—it just wasn't there. The next level down was the source of my visions, including the soul boat.

Now I was virtually certain I was about to die. As I tried to accept my fate, an even lower portion of my brain began to transmit more visions and information. I was "told" that this new material was being presented to me because I was dying and therefore "safe" to receive these revelations. These were the secrets reserved for the dying and the dead, I was informed. I could only very dimly perceive the givers of these thoughts: giant reptilian creatures reposing sluggishly at the lowermost depths of the back of my brain, where it met the top of the spinal column. I could only vaguely see them in what seemed to be gloomy, dark depths.

Then they projected a visual scene in front of me. First they showed me the planet Earth as it was eons ago, before there was any life on it. I saw an ocean, barren land, and a bright blue sky. Then black specks dropped from the sky by the hundreds and landed in front of me on the barren landscape. I could see that the "specks" were actually large, shiny, black creatures with stubby pterodactyl-like wings and huge whale-like bodies. Their heads were not visible to me. They flopped down, utterly exhausted from their trip, resting for eons. They explained to me in a kind of thought language that they were fleeing from something out in space. They had come to the planet Earth to escape their enemy.

The creatures then showed me how they had created life on the planet in order to hide within the multitudinous forms and thus disguise their presence. Before me, the magnificence of plant and animal creation and speciation—hundreds of millions of years of activity— took place on a scale and with a vividness impossible to describe. I learned that the dragon-like creatures were thus inside of all forms of life, including man.* They were the true masters of humanity and the entire planet, they told me. We humans were but the receptacles and servants of these creatures. For this reason they could speak to me from within myself.

These revelations, welling up from the depths of my mind, alternated with visions of the floating galley, which had almost finished taking my soul on board. The boat with its blue-jay headed deck crew was gradually drawing away, pulling my life force along as it headed towards a large fjord flanked by barren, worn hills. I knew I had only

---

*In retrospect one could say they were almost like DNA, although at that time, 1961, I knew nothing of DNA.

a moment more to live. Strangely, I had no fear of the bird-headed people; they were welcome to have my soul if they could keep it. But I was afraid that somehow my soul might not remain on the horizontal plane of the fjord but might, through processes unknown but felt and dreaded, be acquired or re-acquired by the dragon-like denizens of the depths.

I suddenly felt my distinctive humanness, the contrast between my species and the ancient reptilian ancestors. I began to struggle against returning to the ancient ones, who were beginning to feel increasingly alien and possibly evil. Each heart beat was a major undertaking. I turned to human help.

With an unimaginable last effort, I barely managed to utter one word to the Indians: "Medicine!" I saw them rushing around to make an antidote, and I knew they could not prepare it in time. I needed a guardian who could defeat dragons, and I frantically tried to conjure up a powerful being to protect me against the alien reptilian creatures. One appeared before me; and at that moment the Indians forced my mouth open and poured the antidote into me. Gradually, the dragons disappeared back into the lower depths; the soul boat and the fjord were no more. I relaxed with relief.

The antidote radically eased my condition, but it did not prevent me from having many additional visions of a more superficial nature. These were manageable and enjoyable. I made fabulous journeys at will through distant regions, even out into the Galaxy; created incredible architecture; and employed sardonically grinning demons to realize my fantasies. Often I found myself laughing aloud at the incongruities of my adventures.

Finally, I slept.

Rays of sunlight were piercing the holes in the palm-thatched roof when I awoke. I was still lying on the bamboo platform, and I heard the normal, morning sounds all around me: the Indians conversing, babies crying, and a rooster crowing. I was surprised to discover that I felt refreshed and peaceful. As I lay there looking up at the beautiful woven pattern of the roof, the memories of the previous night drifted across my mind. I momentarily stopped myself from remembering more in order to get my tape recorder from a duffel bag. As I dug into the bag, several of the Indians greeted me, smiling. An old woman, Tomás' wife, gave me a bowl of fish and plantain soup for breakfast. It tasted extraordinarily good. Then I went back to the platform, eager to put my night's experiences on tape before I forgot anything.

The work of recall went easily except for one portion of the trance that I could not remember. It remained blank, as though a tape had been erased. I struggled for hours to remember what had happened in that part of the experience, and I virtually wrestled it back into my consciousness. The recalcitrant material turned out to be the communication from the dragon-like creatures, including the revelation of their role in the evolution of life on this planet and their innate domination of living matter, including man. I was highly excited at rediscovering this material, and could not help but feel that I was not supposed to be able to bring it back from the nether regions of the mind.

I even had a peculiar sense of fear for my safety, because I now possessed a secret that the creatures had indicated was only intended for the dying. I immediately decided to share this knowledge with others so that the "secret" would not reside in me alone, and my life would not be in jeopardy. I put my outboard motor on a dugout canoe and left for an American evangelist mission station nearby. I arrived about noon.

The couple at the mission, Bob and Millie, were a cut above the average evangelists sent from the United States: hospitable, humorous, and compassionate. I told them my story. When I described the reptile with water gushing out of his mouth, they exchanged glances, reached for their Bible, and read to me the following line from Chapter 12 in the Book of Revelation:

And the serpent cast out of his mouth water as a flood . . .

They explained to me that the word "serpent" was synonymous in the Bible with the words "dragon" and "Satan." I went on with my narrative. When I came to the part about the dragon-like creatures fleeing an enemy somewhere beyond the Earth and landing here to hide from their pursuers, Bob and Millie became excited and again read me more from the same passage in the Book of Revelation:

> And there was a war in heaven: Michael and his angels fought against the dragon; and the dragon fought and his angels, and prevailed not; neither was their place found any more in heaven. And the great dragon was cast out, that old serpent, called the Devil, and Satan, which deceiveth the whole world: he was cast out into the earth, and his angels with him.

I listened with surprise and wonder. The missionaries, in turn, seemed to be awed by the fact that an atheistic anthropologist, by taking the drink of the "witch doctors," could apparently have revealed to him some of the same holy material in the Book of Revelation. When I had finished my account, I was relieved to have shared my new knowledge, but I was also exhausted. I fell asleep on the missionaries' bed, leaving them to continue their discussion of the experience.

That evening, as I returned to the village in my canoe, my head began to throb in rhythm with the noise of the outboard motor; I thought I was going mad; I had to stick my fingers in my ears to avoid the sensation. I slept well, but the next day I noticed a numbness or pressure in my head.

I was now eager to solicit a professional opinion from the most supernaturally knowledgeable of the Indians, a blind shaman who had made many excursions into the spirit world with the aid of the *ayahuasca* drink. It seemed only proper that a blind man might be able to be my guide to the world of darkness.

I went to his hut, taking my notebook with me, and described my visions to him segment by segment. At first I told him only the highlights; thus, when I came to the dragon-like creatures, I skipped their arrival from space and only said, "There were these giant black animals, something like great bats, longer than the length of this house, who said that they were the true masters of the world." There is no word for dragon in Conibo, so "giant bat" was the closest I could come to describe what I had seen.

He stared up toward me with his sightless eyes, and said with a grin, "Oh, they're always saying that. But they are only the Masters of Outer Darkness."

He waved his hand casually toward the sky. I felt a chill along the lower part of my spine, for I had not yet told him that I had seen them, in my trance, coming from outer space.

I was stunned. What I had experienced was already familiar to this barefoot, blind shaman. Known to him from his own explorations of the same hidden world into which I had ventured. From that moment on I decided to learn everything I could about shamanism.

# 40.

# Experiencing the Shaman's
# Symphony to Understand It

HOLGER KALWEIT

(1987)

*German ethnologist Holger Kalweit visited a shaman in a Tibetan
refugee camp in India, and realized the importance of the observer's inner participation. Ceasing to observe allowed Kalweit to understand
what the shaman was doing. Others think that one of the points of in-
dulging in shamanically-induced trance states is to observe them.*

Six of us take our places in this tiny shelter built by the Indian government for refugees. A window with broken panes provides only a
minimum of light, but an additional beam of light from the open smoke
hole falls on the floor, which is of beaten earth. Tin boxes piled one
on top of another, as with so many oracles, constitutes the altar. On a
broken-down bed in the corner, an infant lies under a tent of fly
screening. As for the rest, nothing but the once-white walls. A few pictures of bodhisattvas and saints over the would-be altar make up the
house shrine. The *lhapa*, the god-man, takes his shaman's pouch from
the wall, and we hand him some incense sticks, half of which are lit at
once. . . .

We now learn that, in addition to healing, he can allow us only
three questions in a session. Now he begins to sing softly. Presently he
adds drum and bell as accompaniment and looks into his copper mir-

ror. Gradually, he gets into the swing of it. The drum turns faster, the chant becomes more penetrating, the bell strikes harder and harder. Only when he is sufficiently into the trance—or, as the Tibetans say, when the god is completely ready to enter into him—does he put on his apron, drop the lotus-shaped shoulder drape over his head, tie a red cloth around his forehead. Then, finally, he puts the crown of painted cardboard on over that.

Now the trance deepens. A soft, almost melodic whistling is heard. The old man, who is now possessed, trembles slightly. He kneels, still facing the altar, and sings indefatigably as he sprinkles water from the little bowls with a spoon and then tosses rice over us and into the air as a blessing. It takes a good while for the trance to become firmly established. From time to time the chanting swells. The god-man, who not long earlier was joking with me and mischievously suggesting that I have my ailments treated by a doctor, has now completely gone beyond. The drumbeats come ever faster, and the muttered chanting becomes more articulate. His body sways to and fro, back and forth, and wild glances from the corners of his eyes fall upon us. We are told that with these looks he sees the gods and spirits approaching.

While this is going on, his daughter continually works to keep him free of the tangle of *khataks* [ceremonial scarves]. And as the drumming and ringing mount to a deafening crescendo, the god—for it is he who now governs the body of the *lhapa*—jumps to his feet. The trembling of the body has now subsided. The *lhapa* now dances to and fro in the little room, leaping, casting his legs out to the sides, and spinning. In the meantime, we have purified our *khataks* in the incense smoke and are waiting to ask our questions.

Now what one hopes for from a great seance has taken place: a person has wound himself so deeply in concentration that he has even drawn the onlookers into this vortex of self-oblivion. The tiny room is fairly bursting with tension and expectation. Life has been captured within these four rude walls. I have long since given up my aim of observing carefully. I am too deeply moved by the selfless abandon of this man, the facility with which he follows the ebb and flow of the drum rhythm, entirely loses himself in the waves of sound. This shaman has drawn me to the utmost point into his state of mind; his rocking motions have become for me the flow of being. In this process, the development of trance—which our Western science has been unable to explain, no matter how hard it has tried—has revealed itself in the simplest way.

We ask our questions. But before he answers, there is more dancing and drumming. Then come the answers, poignant and prophetic—and right on the mark. Then finally the healing. Before that, once again, dancing. Another god is entering the oracle, as indicated by a change in the drumming, a different chant, and renewed whistling. Whistling always indicates the departure or arrival of a *lha*, another being. A cloth is laid over the painful spot, and the drum, held upright, is pressed onto it. Now the *lhapa* sucks the sickness out through the drum with his mouth. Then slowly, visibly for everyone, he spits out a black fluid. Next he rinses his mouth out with water. It is healing by sucking, the most archaic approach to healing sickness.

The seance now approaches its end. The *lhapa* kneels down, drums vigorously, and once again the chant reaches a climax. Then he pulls the crown from his head, and abruptly quiet returns. Only the soft whistling of the receding *lha* is still to be heard. Now there is utter silence. Suddenly a belch is heard in the room. The god has left us for good, and the man is there once more. Mischievously he glances at the round of exhausted, empathizing faces; we can still hear the drumming in our ears. (Toward the end of another seance, his daughter had to quickly lean against his back to keep him from falling over when the god left him.) He muttered audibly, stretched, and leaned against the wall, by way of conclusion tossed another handful of rice into the air, and finally came to himself again completely. At once everything was gathered up and stowed back in the shaman's pouch. We began to make small talk.

To get into a trance, this *lhapa* did not use hyperventilation—he breathed completely normally—nor were any particularly violent body movements to be seen, only a slight trembling of the legs. He was old, and perhaps because of long practice, he had less need of drastic triggering techniques than younger shamans. He seemed to have developed his own style and to be completely tuned in to it. Nothing could have perturbed him. His whole consciousness attended to the eternally identical drum rhythm. His nerves had already been trained by many trances, and in the course of time his trance ritual had grown ever shorter. His ceremony made a greater impression on me than that of any other oracle. His chant, now tender, now erupting with great force in concert with his dancing, which lasted well over an hour, put me into the state of mind that all rhythmic repetition brings, the feeling of being on the threshold of trance. . . .

Almost all accounts of oracular seances fail to describe the general state of mind, the onlookers' sense of experiential participation. The whole suggestive-hypnotic framework in which the patients are placed or into which they are drawn is an artfully arranged setup that is perhaps equal in effect to the subtle process of the trance. A session with an oracle is like a short psychotherapeutic treatment, although modern psychology comes nowhere near its power of psychological and emotional impact on the individual. Here, centuries, even millennia, of trial and error in generation after generation have accumulated a clear knowledge of how body and mind, feeling, thought, and action may be consciously altered and influenced.

The hellish din, the wild, unbridled movements of the oracle, the living presence of a god, the unexpressed expectations of the spectators—all this brings about a loss of ego that is further intensified by the general excitement and the tumultuous disorder in one's normal thought flow. In this atmosphere, we find ourselves in another world, which purifies us of our everyday mental pettiness. The tumult of the seance aims at a first level of catharsis. The patients, impressed by the supernatural events, direct their attention entirely toward the arriving god; awe overcomes them.

To begin with, we are dealing with a deluge of stimuli, which then turns in a natural way into stimulus deprivation, a narrowing or focusing of consciousness that is the goal and purpose of the entire drama. Now we are sufficiently prepared to follow the oracle's words with rapt and reverent attention and receive his message in an appropriate manner, for we are inwardly empty.

Helplessly our gaze roves about the extravagant, colorful scene of the drama, always seeming to lag moments behind the action. Everything goes much too fast. Thus compelled by our ineptitude to register everything purely, we are carried away on the current of events. An auditive and visual vortex develops around us that we are incapable of pulling ourselves out of. The high voice of the oracle and the sound of the bell vibrate in our ears. We actually experience the sound waves and feel our own "drumskin" vibrating in sympathy. The collaboration of the drum and bell seem to me to be no accident. The drum in the right hand and the bell in the left complement each other. The low dull sound of the drum and the high-pitched sound of the bell come together. If we really listen and let ourselves be carried along by the rhythm, then we truly enter into the action of the seance, which, if looked at purely in the light of reason, seems to be no more than a jumble of cheap effects. Anyone who does not deliberately fight against the spectacle can for at least a time let himself be drawn into the vortex of this wild symphony. I myself was always carried away again by the breathtaking spectacle, though I would rather have remained a detached observer.

The inner participation of the audience is of great importance, as the oracles also never tire of stressing. Once the ceremony took place under inauspicious circumstances. I had brought a number of other Europeans along, who regarded the goings-on as an insult to their rationality. This not only led to a very short seance, but also provoked the god to unfavorable comments about us. We did not believe in him, and therefore he produced no healing effect for us. The atmosphere was simply no good. As the oracle was constantly interrupted and struck at by the disparaging glances of the European participants, no real trust or mutual attunement could develop. Critical and fault-finding attitudes, lack of understanding and narrow-mindedness had blocked the free impulse to let go of ego.

By contrast, in good seances, I often forgot to keep the watcher in myself alert; I finally gave up my running commentary on events, stopped classifying. And then something developed that I would like to describe as a symphony. I could identify with the dancing shaman, the chanting oracle, and at least from time to time enter into his state of mind, experience in sympathy with him the fragmentation of the ego structure and the external world. I became myself a little bit of a shaman. The urge arose to emulate him. I wanted to jump up and join in his work. His ritual had a contagious effect. As the drama began to draw to a close, I felt a bit crestfallen, disappointed that it was already over. Finally it had been possible to abide in this whirlwind of ego-abandonment, just as a child spins in a circle in order to experience that feeling of giddiness that stands outside our normal ego-defined experience.

Already in the child's game we experience the longing of our kind toward decentralization. Everywhere in the world children have discovered this game, and here lie the true origins of shamanism — in this longing for the happy feeling of ego loss. All of humanity seeks it in its clinging to love, in singing, dancing, dreaming, or spinning in the intoxication of alcohol or drugs. All of these, though diluted, are trance-fostering states or states tending toward trance. Trance is no special or exceptional state. The whole of our emotional life strives toward one point, to attain a pinnacle, the experience of flowing, in which compulsive and rational moments, which always dam the flow, are disabled. Our overall human quest for good humor, for feeling good, present here only as a hint, reaches the point of intense feeling in trance. And the whole atmosphere of the seance is itself in some way only a reduced, diluted reflection of the trance itself, of that state of sympathetic flow, dissolution, emptying out, pure being.

# PART SIX

# Gathering Evidence on a Multifaceted Phenomenon

In recent decades, anthropologists have worked hard to present indigenous conceptions and practices "from the native's point of view," as Clifford Geertz put it. In the best of cases, they have spent years living with people, learning their language, and interviewing them with tape recorders.

Anthropologists wrote many excellent reports on shamans during this period. They paid careful attention to what shamans said and did, and developed a richer understanding. They learned to see shamans as artists, actors, intellectuals, and people with an interest in knowledge.

This new understanding inspired scholars to rethink other fields. For example, classicist Walter Burkert used

Gerardo Reichel-Dolmatoff's studies of Amazonian shamans to reinterpret paleolithic cave activities in Europe.

During this period, observers began to interview shamans and simply publish the transcripts. And shamans, such as Fernando Payaguaje, started publishing their own books.

# 41

# A Washo Shaman's Helpers

DON HANDELMAN

(1967)

*A Washo Indian, born in 1885 in Nevada, on the western frontier of the United States, Henry Rupert was a shaman formed in the two worlds. Sent to a government boarding school in Carson City, the state capital, Rupert was forced to learn English and a trade. He became a typesetter at a daily newspaper. But he could not avoid his calling to heal. So he took the tools that were presented to him and became a new kind of shaman, mixing traditions from an increasingly mixed-up culture. "Henry Rupert exemplifies the shaman as a creative innovator and potential 'cultural broker,'" wrote American anthropologist Don Handelman. In the 1960's, Handelman found Rupert, then in his eighties, living quietly on the small Indian reservation in Carson City and "continuing to cure, meditate, and tend a flourishing orchard in the desert."*

In 1902, at the age of seventeen, Henry experienced his power dream, the event which marked him with certainty as shamanic material and which conferred certain abilities upon him. He described it to me as follows: "I was sleeping in the school dormitory. I had a dream. I saw a buck in the west. It was a horned buck. It looked east. A voice said to me: 'Don't kill my babies any more.' I woke up, and it was raining outside, and I had a nosebleed in bed."

Henry interpreted the dream in the following way. The conjunction of buck and rain suggested that he could control the weather, since the buck was the "boss of the rain." The buck was standing in the west, but looking east. The Washo believed that the souls of the recently dead travel south but that, soon after, the souls of those who have been evil turn east. The buck looking east was interpreted as a warning against developing certain potentialities which could become evil. The voice in the dream was that of a snake warning against the indiscriminate taking of life; previously Henry had killed wildlife, insects, and snakes without much concern. The rain, as he awakened, indicated that his major spirit-power would be water. Awakening with a nose-bleed placed the stamp of legitimacy upon the whole experience, since the Washo believed that this kind of physical reaction is necessary if the dream is to confer power. The fact that his spirit-power was to be water was unusual, since most Washo shamans had animate rather than inanimate objects as their spirit helpers. Thus, while water baby was a fairly common spirit helper, water was not. In addition, weather control was highly unusual among the Washo, being more prevalent among both the Northern Paiute and the Shoshone.

The dream stressed certain potentials, specifically a Washo calling, that of shaman. It also confirmed the validity of Henry's early behavioral models, Welewkushkush and Charley Rube, and their philosophy of living in harmony with the natural world. In so doing, it de-emphasized those aspects of White society and culture which contradicted Washo values and behavioral expectations, but it did not forbid Henry the continuation of his quest for knowledge in the White world. Rather, it suggested that he pick and choose his way in relation to earlier models, thus serving as both a warning and a promise of greatness. That it was a power dream was congruent with Henry's aspirations and expectations concerning himself and his future.

At this transition point in Henry's life, shortly before he left the Stewart School, the dream served as a guidepost which integrated both his childhood years and his years at the school. His indecisions regarding the future were resolved, and his aspirations of becoming a shaman were crystallized. But his ideology of healing remained inchoate, for he had not yet acquired the requisite shamanic techniques.

He felt the need to help his people when they were ill, but he knew not how. Nevertheless, he was aware and insightful, and in learning through what he called the "law of nature" he set the stage for years of thought and introspection, aware also that discoveries came slowly: "One little thing may come every eight or ten years; you can't grab it in one bunch." . . .

In 1907, Welewkushkush suggested that Henry hire another shaman to help him train and control his powers. The Washo believed that when the power, or spirit helper, first comes to a shaman he becomes ill, and that the novice shaman then hires an older experienced shaman to teach him how to extrude and control the intrusive spirit-power. Although Henry had experienced only a nosebleed in 1902 and did not consider this as a "sickness," he followed his uncle's advice and hired the well-known Washo shaman Beleliwe, also known as Monkey Peter. The experienced shaman could also help the novice to renounce his power, if such was the latter's desire. I do not know what the customary period of time was between the power dream and the hiring of another shaman to control the power, but in Henry's case some five years elapsed.

Beleliwe, instead of giving Henry specific advice, told him what he could accomplish with his power. He spoke of the two old women who had first brought the power of healing to the Washo, and he warned that the power of blood is evil. He also described some of the feats which shamans could accomplish, citing the cases of an old woman who had walked up the perpendicular side of a cliff, of Welewkushkush who had walked under the waters of Lake Tahoe without drowning, and of Southern Washo who danced in campfires. Then he told Henry: "All kinds of sickness will look pretty tough, but it will melt; it seems like you can't do anything with it, but it will melt." However, the actual content of the shamanic ritual had to be learned by observing other shamans at work. . . .

Henry performed his first successful cure in 1907. A brother of Frank Rivers had died of alcohol poisoning. His mother was deeply grieved and became very depressed. A White doctor was called in but was unable to calm the woman. A few days later Henry, as he was passing by, heard the old woman crying. He went in, washed her face, and prayed for her. She recovered. It is significant that this first cure was performed on the mother of his best friend—within a milieu where his confidence would be bolstered. It is also significant that Henry's family, with the exception of Welewkushkush, knew nothing of his shamanic power or his achievements with weather control until after this cure. His reticence is an example of the self-doubt that always plagued him—doubt in his abilities and fear that he would not find the answers his curiosity demanded—but which drove him to greater efforts.

In his first cure, Henry used techniques generally similar to those utilized by other Washo shamans. Traditional Washo curing rituals required a shaman to work for three consecutive nights from dusk to midnight, and a fourth night until dawn. In the course of the ritual, repeated every night, Henry used tobacco, water, a rattle, a whistle, and eagle feathers. He began by smoking, praying, washing the patient's face with cold water, and sprinkling all his paraphernalia with cold water. He then blew smoke on the patient and prayed to come in contact with water. A peace offering followed, in which he paid for the health of the patient by scattering grey and yellow seeds mixed with pieces of abalone shell around the body of the patient; the seeds symbolized food, and the shells symbolized money. Next he chanted, prayed, and again blew smoke on the patient and sprinkled his paraphernalia with cold water. Arising, he walked about blowing his whistle, attempting to attract the disease object or germ from the body of the patient and into his own body, whence it might be repulsed and captured by the whistle. Then he sat down again and blew a fine spray of cold water over the body of the patient. This ended the first half of the curing ritual, which was repeated each night.

At some time during the course of the ritual, Henry would receive visions relating both to the cause of the illness and the prognosis. They usually involved either the presence or absence of water. Thus a vision of damp ground suggested that the patient was ill but would live a short while; muddy water suggested that the patient would live but would not recover completely; ice suggested that Henry must break through the ice and find water; burning sagebrush suggested that the patient would die quickly unless Henry could stamp out the fire. Over the four-night period the content of these visions, or occasionally dreams, tended to change. Thus, Henry might see a fire or a burned-over hillside on the first night, damp ground on the second, muddy water on the third, and on the fourth night a stream of clear, cold water or the Pacific Ocean rolling over the Sierra Nevada. The portent of the vision of the fourth night overrode those of the visions seen on the previous nights.

During 1907–08, Henry Rupert acquired his second spirit helper, a young Hindu male. He used, at infrequent intervals, to visit a high school in Carson City which contained the skeleton of a Hindu, and on one of these visits the spirit of the Hindu "got on" Henry. Since the Hindu was a "White power," this precipitated a major conflict in Henry's fantasy world and in the most important area of his life, his healing. As a spirit helper, the Hindu demanded to be used in curing sessions. Henry's problem was how to reconcile the opposing demands of his Indian and Hindu spirit helpers. The confrontation and its resolution came in a dream: "I saw this in a dream. The Hindu's work says: 'You will do great things if you make us the leader in this kind of work.' The two Indian women say no: 'We started this with Henry Rupert; we were the first. He (the Hindu) has no right here; this work belongs to us.' I didn't know what to make of it. I pondered on it for a long time. Finally I decided, and I told them what I decided: 'We all do the same work; let's help each other and be partners.' And that is the way it works today; nobody is the leader. The Hindu wanted to be the leader in this kind of work. The two women said no. I fixed it."

This dream dramatically illustrates the basic conflict between opposing themes in Henry Rupert's life: his desire to expand his potentials for learning and healing by utilizing non-Indian resources and his desire to follow the childhood models he loved and respected. His resolution of this conflict was highly sophisticated; he utilized a more complex level of conceptualization and synthesis in which both op-posing themes were subsumed under a common rubric, that of heal-ing, which applied to both categories of spirit helpers. This rubric was neither Washo nor "White" but constituted an ethic which cross-cut different ethnic and racial categories. I prefer the term "ethic" to "principle" because the synthesis had definite moral connotations of aiding and succouring others, and because to Henry the fact that he had become a healer was more important than either his being born a Washo or his forays into non-Indian knowledge. It was the Hindu who first gave Henry his insights into the components of the "law of nature" and offered him the code of living which he has since fol-lowed: to be honest, discreet, and faithful; to be kind and do no harm. These conceptions often ran counter to the behavior of traditional Washo shamans, but they were consistent with the models of Welew-kushkush, Charley Rube, and Beleliwe. The ethic of healing which Henry developed was an integrated and complete synthesis; he was never troubled again by this kind of acculturative conflict.

After Henry acquired the Hindu spirit helper a number of changes occurred in his curing techniques—the first of his innovations of which I am aware. Before beginning a cure, he would now place a handkerchief on his head to represent the Hindu's turban, and when he blew water on the patient he prayed to the Hindu to come and rid the patient of his illness. He also began to place his hands on the pa-tient's head, chest, and legs in a symbolic attempt to encompass the whole being of the patient with his power. He also began to envision himself differently while curing; while sitting by the side of the patient he saw himself as a skeleton with a turban on its head moving quickly around the body of the patient.

Henry did not perform his second cure until 1909, two years later. It was this cure which established him as a legitimate shaman among the Washo. The patient was a Washo whose family was camping on the Carson River near Minden, Nevada. This man had been treated by both shamans and White doctors without success, although the doctors had diagnosed his case as typhoid fever. Henry, although as a novice shaman he had been consulted as a last resort, was successful in curing the patient. . . .

As Henry's fame as a healer spread he began to receive patients from a wide variety of ethnic groups. Though not common, it was not unknown for Washo shamans to treat Northern Paiute and Shoshone patients, but Henry treated these and Hawaiian, Filipino, Mexican, and White patients as well. In this trans-cultural healing he was successful, doubtless because his ethic of healing gave him increased confidence in dealing with non-Indians. His status as a healer grew continuously, and he became known and respected as a successful shaman from the Shoshone Yomba reservation in central Nevada to Mexican enclaves in Sacramento. His increasing renown attracted non-Indian patients who had exhausted other alternatives. A number of cases will illustrate the diversity of his clientele.

In curing a Protestant minister, who came to him with severe headaches, Henry received the following diagnostic vision. He saw a large auditorium in which were seated on one side a group of Whites and the minister, and on the other a group of Indians representing various tribes. Between the two was a large stage on which dressed steers were falling, forming a large pile of meat ready to eat. Everyone in the auditorium ate of the meat, except for the minister. Henry told the latter that he would lose his headaches, but that he had made one mistake. The minister had been in the habit of serving tea and cake after his sermons, but while his congregation ate, he did not. This, said Henry, was the cause of his headaches, and the minister admitted the correctness of the assessment. The vision was a sophisticated reflection of the interrelationship between Henry's ethic of curing and his restructured cosmology. As he explained to the minister, the latter's abstention, in a congregation of both Whites and Indians who broke bread together, was inconsistent with both Henry's ethic of curing and the minister's status as a servant of God.

Exactly what the social consequences of Henry's personal innovations are likely to be is uncertain. It is clear that the Washo have little knowledge of either the extent or content of these innovations, although they recognize that he does not doctor in the traditional Washo manner. At present there are no budding young shamans among the Washo, and it is unlikely that future shamans would take the traditional path to gaining supernatural power. Although Henry does not proselytize, he offers an alternative, but the regimen and qualities required are either unappealing or rare. Nevertheless, the potentiality exists, and this could open a fascinating new chapter on shamanic healing among the Washo.

# 42.

# Magic Darts, Bewitching
# Shamans, and Curing Shamans

MICHAEL HARNER

(1968)

*This is a finely detailed account of the practices of Jívaro (Shuar)
shamans. Michael Harner focuses in particular on their use of magic
darts, which they call* tsentsak. *Harner also shows that curing
shamans are complementary to bewitching shamans. Intriguingly, the
substance of these darts bears similarities to ectoplasm, the viscous substance that Victorians reported exuded from the bodies of mediums in
trance and which formed the material for the manifestation of spirits.*

The Jívaro Indians of the Ecuadorian Amazon believe that witchcraft
is the cause of the vast majority of illnesses and non-violent deaths.
The normal waking life, for the Jívaro, is simply "a lie," or illusion,
while the true forces that determine daily events are supernatural and
can only be seen and manipulated with the aid of hallucinogenic
drugs. A reality view of this kind creates a particularly strong demand
for specialists who can cross over into the supernatural world at will
to deal with the forces that influence and even determine the events of
the waking life.

These specialists, called "shamans" by anthropologists, are recognized by the Jívaro as being of two types: bewitching shamans or curing shamans. Both kinds take a hallucinogenic drink, whose Jívaro

name is *natema,* in order to enter the supernatural world. This brew, commonly called *yagé,* or *yajé,* in Colombia, *ayahuasca* (Inca "vine of the dead") in Ecuador and Peru, and *caapi* in Brazil, is prepared from segments of a species of the vine *Banisteriopsis,* a genus belonging to the Malpighiaceae. . . .

The use of the hallucinogenic *natema* drink among the Jívaro makes it possible for almost anyone to achieve the trance state essential for the practice of shamanism. Given the presence of the drug and the felt need to contact the "real," or supernatural, world, it is not surprising that approximately one out of every four Jívaro men is a shaman. Any adult, male or female, who desires to become such a practitioner, simply presents a gift to an already practicing shaman, who administers the *Banisteriopsis* drink and gives some of his own supernatural power — in the form of spirit helpers, or *tsentsak* — to the apprentice. These spirit helpers, or "darts," are the main supernatural forces believed to cause illness and death in daily life. To the non-shaman they are normally invisible, and even shamans can perceive them only under the influence of *natema.*

Shamans send these spirit helpers into the victim's bodies to make them ill or to kill them. At other times, they may suck spirits sent by enemy shamans from the bodies of tribesmen suffering from witchcraft-induced illness. The spirit helpers also form shields that protect their shaman masters from attacks. The following account presents the ideology of Jívaro witchcraft from the point of view of the Indians themselves.

To give the novice some *tsentsak,* the practicing shaman regurgitates what appears to be — to those who have taken *natema* — a brilliant substance in which the spirit helpers are contained. He cuts part of it off with a machete and gives it to the novice to swallow. The recipient experiences pain upon taking it into his stomach and stays on his bed for ten days, repeatedly drinking *natema.* The Jívaro believe they can keep magical darts in their stomachs indefinitely and regurgitate them at will. The shaman donating the *tsentsak* periodically blows and rubs all over the body of the novice, apparently to increase the power of the transfer.

The novice must remain inactive and not engage in sexual intercourse for at least three months. If he fails in self-discipline, as some do, he will not become a successful shaman. At the end of the first month, a *tsentsak* emerges from his mouth. With this magical dart at his disposal, the new shaman experiences a tremendous desire to bewitch. If he casts his *tsentsak* to fulfill this desire, this means he will become a bewitching shaman. If, on the other hand, the novice can control his impulse and reswallow this first *tsentsak*, he will become a curing shaman. . . .

The degree of illness produced in a witchcraft victim is a function of both the force with which the *tsentsak* is shot into the body, and also the character of the magical dart itself. If a *tsentsak* is shot all the way through the body of a victim, then "there is nothing for a curing shaman to suck out," and the patient dies. If the magical dart lodges within the body, however, it is theoretically possible to cure the victim by sucking. But in actual practice, the sucking is not always considered successful.

The work of the curing shaman is complementary to that of a bewitcher. When a curing shaman is called in to treat a patient, his first task is to see if the illness is due to witchcraft. The usual diagnosis and treatment begin with the curing shaman drinking *natema*, tobacco water, and *pirípirí* in the late afternoon and early evening. These drugs permit him to see into the body of the patient as though it were glass. If the illness is due to sorcery, the curing shaman will see the intruding object within the patient's body clearly enough to determine whether or not he can cure the sickness.

A shaman sucks magical darts from a patient's body only at night, and in a dark area of the house, for it is only in the dark that he can perceive the drug-induced visions that are the supernatural reality. With the setting of the sun, he alerts his *tsentsak* by whistling the tune of the curing song; after about a quarter of an hour, he starts singing.

When he is ready to suck, the shaman regurgitates two *tsentsak* into the sides of his throat and mouth. These must be identical to the one he has seen in his patient's body. He holds one of these in the front of the mouth and the other in the rear. They are expected to catch the supernatural aspect of the magical dart that the shaman sucks out of the patient's body. The *tsentsak* nearest the shaman's lips is supposed to incorporate the sucked-out *tsentsak* essence within itself. If, however, this supernatural essence should get past it, the second magical dart in the mouth blocks the throat so that the intruder cannot enter the interior of the shaman's body. If the curer's two *tsentsak* were to fail to catch the supernatural essence of the *tsentsak,* it would pass down into the shaman's stomach and kill him. Trapped thus within the mouth, this essence is shortly caught up by, and incorporated into, the material substance of one of the curing shaman's *tsentsak*. He then "vomits" out this object and displays it to the patient and his family, saying, "Now I have sucked it out. Here it is."

The non-shamans think that the material object itself is what has been sucked out, and the shaman does not disillusion them. At the same time, he is not lying, because he knows that the only important thing about a *tsentsak* is its supernatural aspect, or essence, which he sincerely believes he has removed from the patient's body. To explain to the layman that he already had these objects in his mouth would serve no fruitful purpose and would prevent him from displaying such an object as proof that he had effected the cure. Without incontrovertible evidence, he would not be able to convince the patient and his family that he had effected the cure and must be paid.

The ability of the shaman to suck depends upon the quantity and strength of his own *tsentsak*, of which he may have hundreds. His magical darts assume their supernatural aspect as spirit helpers when he is under the influence of *natema,* and he sees them as a variety of zoomorphic forms hovering over him, perching on his shoulders, sticking out of his skin, and helping to suck the patient's body. He must drink tobacco water every few hours to "keep them fed" so that they will not leave him. . . . Shamans constantly drink tobacco juice at all hours of the day and night. Although the tobacco juice is not truly hallucinogenic, it produces a narcotized state, which is believed necessary to keep one's *tsentsak* ready to repel any other magical darts. A shaman does not even dare go for a walk without taking along the green tobacco leaves with which he prepares the juice that keep his spirit helpers alert. Less frequently, but regularly, he must drink *natema* for the same purpose and to keep in touch with the supernatural reality.

While curing under the influence of *natema*, the curing shaman "sees" the shaman who bewitched his patient. Generally, he can recognize the person, unless it is a shaman who lives far away or in another tribe. The patient's family knows this, and demands to be told the identity of the bewitcher, particularly if the sick person dies. At one curing session I attended, the shaman could not identify the person he had seen in his vision. The brother of the dead man then accused the shaman himself of being responsible. Under such pressure, there is a strong tendency for the curing shaman to attribute each case to a particular bewitcher.

# 43.

# "Remarkably Good Theater"

JOHN T. HITCHCOCK

(1973)

*American anthropologist John T. Hitchcock spent four years in Nepal studying shamanism. He provides a detailed and lively report of a shaman's performance, which calls attention to its theatrical nature. Hitchcock found people consulting the shaman as a healer and as an oracle in a barn. He also found magic arrows.*

Sakrante, the shaman, turned and looked at me, and in the dim firelight his eyes were black and staring. Suddenly, still squatting, he began hopping toward me. With each jump the bells on his leather jacket jangled and clattered, and in the gloom behind him, I could hear his assistant beating steadily on the drum. A final noisy hop and he had reached me and had grabbed my shoulders in both hands. Thrusting his face close to mine, he began snuffling along my neck. I felt the feathers from his head-dress on my cheeks. He paused a moment, grunting and breathing loudly; then quickly, with the steely strength of a blacksmith's arms and hands, he twisted my torso to have a look at my back; and after snuffling along it, he twisted me back again, facing him. He was staring intently at my left shoulder. Sweat was running down his cheeks and his charcoal-smeared eyes were opening wider and wider.

"Ho!" he bellowed and lunged at my shoulder with the point of his drumstick. I felt a sharp pain as he jabbed and pressed the point deeply into my shoulder. Holding the stick tight against me he placed the palm of his other hand over the end of the stick, and began sucking with immense effort on the back of his hand. His lips made loud smacking noises and his rapid drawn-in breaths became muffled growls in his throat. The drum pounded on insistently, and gradually Sakrante began sucking in time with its rhythm. Making a final, deeper thrust, he quickly drew away and still squatting, hopped backwards. To avoid the fire pit he lurched sideways and fell to the ground. There was a raucous clatter of bells and tins. "Water! Water!" he yelled as he rose to his knees and the host who sat near the fire handed him a brass vessel. Tilting his head back he poured a stream of water into his mouth. Bulging his cheeks he swished it about and gestured impatiently toward the host's son. The young man held a brass vessel toward him. With a vomiting spasm that ended in a long groan, Sakrante emptied his mouth. The liquid was viscous and bloody. Fearfully the young man covered the vessel with a corner of his blanket. He would bury the contents—an abhorent substance shot into me by an evil spirit's magic arrow—in one of the rocky places his family used as a latrine.

When Sakrante stared at me at the close of his all-night séance I felt a twinge of genuine apprehension. How possible it then seemed that something was in my shoulder and how real its ugliness and danger! And how confidently relaxed I had felt when he finished treating me, for it was easy that night to accept his power to cleanse and to heal.

Both my apprehension and my confidence derived from the skill of an accomplished actor; and were released in me by the same suspension of disbelief that I experience during a good play or dramatic film. Sakrante's acting and his all-night "play" belong to an ancient Himalayan shamanistic tradition, handed down for countless generations, and making a connection so far as I now can tell, between him and shamans who once performed for reindeer-herders on the frigid Siberian tundra. It may well be that this tradition is—in anything like its old Siberian vitality—only to be found today where I experienced it, on the southerly slopes of the immense Dhaulagiri massif.

I do not think it does Sakrante or his shamanistic tradition a disservice to speak of it as remarkably good theater. I know Sakrante thought of himself as a performer, a better performer than other shamans. He paid careful attention to stage effects and he took pride in his costuming and music. He knew that during the course of his evening's work, he would transform himself from the person everyone knew as one of the valley's Untouchable blacksmiths into a Culture Hero who lived during the First Age of the World: Rama himself, the very First Shaman. He also knew (whatever else he may have believed) that by his acting, and his use of traditional props, he would make real—more real than neighboring shamans—the world of spirits whose help he would require and whose powers he would test.

The quick winter darkness had fallen when he began his séance that night. Up and down the valley, as was their custom, people had barred their doors and had gathered around their flickering firepits to chat for a while and have a last pipe before rolling up in their thick wool blankets.

Sakrante's stage was a small section, perhaps fifteen feet by fifteen feet, in the center of a long cattle shed, with walls and roof made of bamboo matting. At one end a row of cattle were tethered, and at the other, a row of buffaloes.

Sakrante had been called by a young man and his wife, members of a trading group, who wished for general protection. They were suffering from no particular ills, were engaged in no specially intense competition or quarrel. Yet they were uneasy, perhaps because nothing lately had gone very wrong. As a precaution they wanted Sakrante to foretell the future, to pry out any witch-evil that might be lurking and discover any malalignment of their stars.

Sakrante and his nephew, a young man who had become his pupil and always carried his heavy wicker basket of gear, had come to the cattle shed just at sundown and had been well fed. One of the rewards of being a shaman was such a meal, a brass tray heaped with rice, a little bowl of heavily spiced chicken and butter, and another little bowl of home-distilled liquor. By the time he and his nephew had finished eating, family members from nearby houses in the small hamlet had begun crowding into the cattle shed. They were squeezed together, wrapped in blankets and formed a semi-circle opposite Sakrante, who had seated himself before a small fire. They bantered and chatted, and drew deeply on hand pipes that were passed back and forth; but all were aware of Sakrante and knew that he was about to begin. To some extent he already had been removed from his everyday self. For after the meal the host had purified the place where he was now sitting by washing it with a mixture of cowdung, mud and water—the usual way of setting a place aside for a special, and often sacred purpose. . . .

In the early portion of the séance the dramatic theme most heavily stressed is danger from the other world—though at the same time that the danger is being made more real, so is Sakrante's power, for he is showing also how he can control it. Drumming and singing and calling out the names of many spirits, as Sakrante does during a séance, is like opening a door to the other world. The first to come is the tutelary deity, followed by other spirits Sakrante calls. But at the same time uncalled spirits may crowd in. Some of them are not associated with any particular place in the vicinity, but others are known to live nearby, in a waterfall, a spring, a rock, or a part of the forest. All are potentially dangerous and can "strike" the shaman, his client, and the audience. One of the methods used for "striking" is a magic arrow that pierces the skin and leaves a festering head like the one Sakrante removed from my shoulder. . . .

Some hostile and uncontrolled spirits are apt to enter the cattle shed, and even more frightening, some person present—a close and apparently friendly neighbor or relative—may be a witch, whose mere glance can cause illness and other misfortunes. To enable himself to see the witch, as well as any spirits who may have wormed their way into the enclosure, Sakrante says a spell over some pieces of charcoal as he crumbles them in his hand. Using the dust he smears his eyelids. In the near darkness this makes his eye sockets seem even deeper set and his dark eyes still more dark and large. By doing this Sakrante now can see, even though his audience can't, any witch that may be present or any lurking spirit. As he carefully scans the shed and the audience, he provides protection for himself by smearing each shoulder and each knee and then rubs a vertical thumbmark of charcoal on his forehead. To protect the audience and his client he gets up and goes about making a similar mark on each forehead, including those of the children. These marks protect but do not give supernormal sight. . . .

His drum has been propped by the fire so as to warm the head and make it taut. He picks it up, together with his drumstick, says a spell over both, bows his head to the drum, bangs it a few times, testing the timbre. Then he holds it before his face and makes a number of respectful bows to each section of the audience. He is ready to begin singing.

His song, to which he drums rhythmically and with constantly varying dynamics, stresses further the theme of protection. For what he sings is a spell to make helpless any fearsome spirits. In the song they are named one by one and by magic means are "tied up"—though the word here means more like what we mean when we say "tie up in knots." The song is long, the names many, and for the audience the recital brings to mind the hosts of dangerous beings that are hovering all about. . . .

To bring his tutelary spirit and other spirits to him and get them to possess him, he begins drumming and singing another spell. During the long spell, spirits begin to appear. Sakrante says they come upside down, with their feet toward the roof. Eventually they swarm onto his body and then enter it, some through his mouth, ears, leg and arm joints—but mostly through his nose, where they give off an odor that he says is slightly excremental. Possession occurs when one of them enters his heart. He sees a flash of fire and feels drunk.

The audience knows what is happening because Sakrante begins to drum more rapidly. Then his drumming gets slower and slower, as if he could only move his hand with a tremendous effort. The drumming stops and now instead of singing he forces air loudly through his lips, shouts unintelligible syllables, and groans. As the possession deepens, he snaps the drum out at arm's length and one hears the jangle of the ring fastenings on the handles and the tinkle of a little bell that is fastened inside. Suddenly Sakrante falls over on the ground, jerking his arms, head and legs spasmodically. A moment later he is up and has begun to dance drunkenly about the fire, using the well-known shaman's dance beat. Still dancing he leans down and in his teeth picks up the iron tripod beside the fire pit and tosses it toward a part of the audience who rapidly pull themselves out of the way. Lurching to his stool, he sits down on it. The drumming ceases. He merely quivers. The only sound is the tense jingling of the drum's bell and handle links.

The audience knows that this possession is for any one of them who wishes to know the future. Covered with his blanket, the son of the host's brother creeps forward and places a folded piece of birch-bark between Sakrante's toes. Sakrante resumes his drumming, more smoothly and steadily now, and then still drumming and using a kind of recitative, he begins chanting the words of the spirit who is possessing him. As he begins uttering the spirit's words, the person addressed, as well as older members of the audience, call out greetings. They address the spirit respectfully using the word "God," but the spirit does not reply in kind. To emphasize the immense superiority of its insight compared to an ordinary human's, it replies, "O you, donkeys, listen well!" And then it begins to foretell the future for the person who has placed the birchbark, but in a very oblique way. Regarding time, for instance, it reports: "In the month of June, or if I am mistaken, in the month of July or August." It is equally imprecise about the nature of the coming event, though it is evil of some kind, may affect humans or animals, and looms from the direction of the young man's in-laws. When Sakrante stops speaking, he gradually lowers the drum, so that it rests between his legs. Although he still is trembling, the initial state of possession is over and he is ready to answer questions about what the spirit has said. . . .

During the subsequent part of the evening, or if necessary during a second and even third all-night session, shamans in this part of Nepal may perform a number of different rituals, all of them involving long story-songs. The most common ritual is performed to remove effects of witch-power. Others change a harmful astrological configuration, bring back a strayed portion of the soul, propitiate the Forest Spirit, or frighten and drive away the troublesome spirit of a dead child. . . .

The last ritual that evening was devoted to extraction of evil substances and Sakrante performed it as I have described, not only for me but for the host and his wife and a number of others who were present. During this final performance, a hint of dawn light could be glimpsed through the crack over the cattle shed door; and when at last he had finished, Sakrante sat exhausted on his stool, his drum finally still.

I remember that even after Sakrante had removed his costume, slowly and carefully putting each item away in the wicker basket, the spell cast by his drumming and singing remained on us all. Not until a section of bamboo matting had been rolled aside and we had filed out to stretch ourselves in the warmth of the rising sun, did the lingering awareness of this man, not as blacksmith but as powerful First Shaman, begin to dissolve and fade. I recall how much the effect was like leaving a city theater, with the same momentary sense of duality—of a clash between the vivid footlight world, like Sakrante's world of unseen spirits, and the newly impinging sidewalk world of street lights and neon. My confusion that morning between the fire light and sun light is perhaps my best tribute to Sakrante's artistry and its dramatic embodiment of a mountain tradition.

# 44

# Two Kinds of Japanese Shamans: The Medium and the Ascetic

## CARMEN BLACKER

## (1975)

*Carmen Blacker, an English lecturer in Japanese at Cambridge University, conducted an in-depth study of shamanic practices in Japan. She shows that they derive from several sources, including Siberia and Polynesia, and that there are two kinds of Japanese shamans.*

Even today, although in intellectual circles in Japan an aggressive secularism tends to be the rule, the belief still persists among many sections of the community that the causes of all calamity in human life lie in the spiritual realm. Sickness, accident, drought or fire are the work either of angry ghosts or of offended numina. To discover the causes of these misfortunes we must therefore look into the other dimension where these beings live and enquire what spirit is responsible and the reason for his anger. . . .

Ordinary men and women are powerless to deal with these perilous and ambivalent forces. Certain special human beings, however, may acquire a power which enables them to transcend the barrier between the two worlds. This power bears no relation to the physical strength or mental agility with which we are ordinarily endowed. It is of a different order altogether, acquired by means which often weaken a man's bodily health and strength, and which appears from time to

time in boys who are virtual halfwits. It is a special power to effect a
rupture of plane, to reach over the bridge and influence the beings on
the other side.

I use the word "shaman" . . . to indicate those people who have acquired this power; who in a state of dissociated trance are capable of
communicating directly with spiritual beings. These people in Japan
appear in two complementary forms. The first, whom I shall call the
medium or the *miko*, is exemplified by the sibyl Teruhi [a character in
a Japanese play]. She can enter a state of trance in which the spiritual
apparition may possess her, penetrate inside her body and use her
voice to name itself and to make its utterance. She is therefore primarily a transmitter, a vessel through whom the spiritual beings, having left their world to enter ours, can make their communications to us
in a comprehensible way.

The second and complementary source of power, whom I call the
ascetic, is exemplified by the Saint of Yokawa [another character in
the same play]. He is primarily a healer, one who is capable of banish-
ing the malevolent spirits responsible for sickness and madness and
transforming them into powers for good. To acquire the powers necessary for this feat he must accomplish a severe regime of ascetic practice, which should properly include, besides fasting, standing under a
waterfall and reciting sacred texts, a journey to the other world.
Whereas with the medium, therefore, it is the spiritual beings who
leave their world and come to ours, with the ascetic the passage is in
the opposite direction. It is he who must leave our world and make his
way through the barrier to visit theirs. This journey he may accomplish in ecstatic, visionary form; his soul alone travels, his body left
behind meanwhile in a state of suspended animation. Or he may accomplish the journey by means of symbolic mimesis; the other world
projected by means of powerful symbolism on to the geography of our
own, he can make the journey through the barrier in body as well as
soul.

Corresponding with each of these figures is a particular kind of
trance. With the medium, infused or possessed by a spiritual being, a

number of physical symptoms are commonly found. These include a violent shaking of the clasped hands, stertorous breathing or roaring, and a peculiar levitation of the body from a seated, cross-legged posture. I have seen both men and women propel themselves some six inches into the air from this position, again and again for several minutes on end. A violent medium is always considered more convincing than a docile one, the non-human character of the voice and behaviour indicating more vividly the displacement of the medium's own personality by the entry of the divinity. This kind of trance, we shall later see, can either be self-induced, or can be stimulated by a second person, usually the ascetic.

The second type of trance is entirely different. It is a deep, comatose state of suspended animation. This is the condition into which the ascetic's body must fall if his soul is to leave it in order to travel to other realms of the cosmos. His body remains behind, an empty husk, while his soul traverses barriers through which it cannot follow. We shall find that today this trance occurs only rarely. The capacity for this kind of dissociation, and for the visionary journey which goes with it, seems to have diminished in recent centuries, and today the magic journey is most commonly accomplished by symbolic action in full waking consciousness.

I have said that both the medium and the ascetic are shamans because each in their particular manner of trance acts as a bridge between one world and another. . . .

[The shaman is] a gifted person of a distinctive kind. He is at once a cosmic traveller, a healer, a master of spirits, a psychopomp, an oracular mouthpiece. These various powers, however, are combined and organised round the central faculty of trance; of so altering his consciousness at will that he can communicate directly with the inhabitants of the supernatural world.

We shall see that the medium and the ascetic in Japan can on this definition justifiably be called shamans. We shall find examples of initiation sickness, of the supernatural call, of the "out of the body" trance in which the soul travels to heaven and hell. We shall find assistant spirits, magic clothes and instruments, and abundant evidence of the interior heat which produces mastery of fire. The cosmos in Japan, it is true, is somewhat differently shaped, with no evidence of the wondrous giant Tree at the centre of the world. It is true too that among the initiatory visions of the medium and the ascetic few have so far come to light which describe the dismemberment of the body, reduction to a skeleton and resuscitation with new flesh on the bones. In place of the Tree, however, we shall find an almost equally splendid Mountain; and in place of the dismemberment and remaking of the body we shall find other symbolism which equally unequivocally points to the initiatory schema of death and rebirth.

. . . It is not meaningful to treat either of these figures in isolation from the other. Complementary though they may at first appear, the medium and the ascetic are closely bound together. Both must undergo the same ascetic practice before their particular kind of power can be acquired. Both must be present at certain rituals in order to achieve the necessary communication with spirits. Sometimes both kinds of power seem to be present, or at any rate overlapping, in the same person. During the feudal period it was common to find marriages between the two kinds of people, an ascetic husband married to a female medium. Clearly we have two mutually dependent functions, which it is convenient to treat under the same nomenclature.

The phenomena of shamanism in Japan are further complicated by the fact that they do not derive from a single homogeneous source: like the Japanese race, language and mythology, shamanism in Japan is of mixed origin. Japanese ethnologists usually relate the instances of shamanism in their country to two broad streams of culture which intermingled in prehistoric times. A northern stream, deriving from Altaic or Tungusic practices on the Asian continent and spreading throughout Korea, Hokkaido and the Ryukyu islands, mingled with another stream deriving from a southerly source, Polynesia or Melanesia. . . .

Both the medium and the ascetic may still be encountered today. The medium, it is true, survives only sparsely and in somewhat dilapidated form in certain districts of the north-east, certain islands off the Izu peninsula and in certain village rituals where her gifts are combined with those of the ascetic. The ascetic however, is still to be found in many districts of Japan. Living alone or in enclaves, such men and women may be met in the Nara district, in the environs of Kyoto, in Shikoku and Kyushu, along the coast of the Japan Sea, in the north-east and even occasionally in Tokyo itself. These people still employ techniques of trance and exorcism which bear the authentic stamp of an ancient origin.

# 45.

# Music Alone Can Alter a Shaman's Consciousness, Which Itself Can Destroy Tape Recorders

DALE A. OLSEN

(1975)

*American ethnomusicologist Dale A. Olsen studied shamanic curing among the Warao Indians of the Orinoco Delta in the Venezuelan tropical forest. In this insightful piece, he points out that certain shamans modify their consciousness with music alone. He also tells an intriguing story about the fate of his tape recorders.*

Is it possible that music alone, without the aid of hallucinogens, is capable of causing the religious leader, the shaman, to reach an altered state of consciousness in which he has contact with the supernatural world? I believe it is, at least within the curing context of Warao shamanism. Although several scholars including Barral (1964) and Wilbert (1972) mention tobacco as a trance-inducing intoxicant among the Warao, there are many examples of apparent trance states without its use. True hallucinogens have not been known in the Orinoco Delta, and even tobacco, which is not a true hallucinogen, was originally absent from Warao culture. . . .

Certainly during initiation rites there is an excessive inhaling and ingesting of tobacco smoke which undoubtedly has a chemical effect on the shaman. During curing, however, so much emphasis is placed upon singing and, in some instances, upon shaking a large rattle with both hands that the excessive use of tobacco does not occur. Cultural conditioning, however, is the important anthropological deep structure within which the magical use of music for curing among the Warao is placed. Music, combined with cultural conditioning, produces, I believe, a "pure" trance, similar to the meditative trance state achieved by Buddhist monks while using music to reach enlightenment. Music is the vehicle, or the shamanic tool, among the Warao that induces this so-called "pure" trance state during the shaman's benevolent curing role and even, perhaps, during his malevolent role as an inflictor of destruction and illness.

The shamanic trance state of the Warao shaman while inflicting illness, destroying material objects, or curing is not a wild affair. There is no yelling, no rolling on the ground, and no loss of physical control as among the narcotic-using Yanomamo Indians of the Venezuelan and Brazilian Amazon, who are culturally, linguistically, and musically related to the Warao. Likewise, the Warao shamans do not become possessed, nor do they lose consciousness as do many other tropical forest Amerindians of South America. The Warao shamanic trance state is, rather, deeply meditative, during which the shaman is experiencing maximum contact with his supernatural helping spirits and the illness-causing spirits over which he, as owner of the spirits, has control. This deep meditative trance state, in which the shaman is completely involved with the supernatural world, is unthinkable and indeed impossible without music. And I would like to emphasize again that such a trance state is possible without the aid of tobacco. . . .

Three types of shamans officiate in Warao cosmology: the *wisiratu*, the priest/shaman and owner of the *hebu* spirits; the *bahanarotu*, the so-called "white" shaman and owner of the *bahana* spirits; and the *hoarotu*, the so-called "black" shaman and owner of the *hoa* spirits. Almost always when the wisiratu cures, and occasionally when the bahanarotu cures, a large gourd rattle called *hebu-mataro* is used. The hoarotu never uses a rattle. Each religious practitioner begins his trance state as soon as he begins to sing, and upon completion of his song or song cycle he returns completely and immediately to his former, pre-trance state. Unlike the narcotic-induced trance states of many other Amerindian cultures which usually require considerable time for the effects of a drug to wear off, the Warao shamans are once again "normal" Warao as soon as they have finished their curing or inflicting task. This, I believe, is an example of "pure" trance as expounded by Eliade. A wisiratu shaman explained to me that while he is singing he is not a person like other Warao; he is a supernatural being. As the wisiratu speaks, through song, to the hebu spirits and the hebus answer through him, he becomes transformed into a hebu himself. In another instance a bahanarotu shaman refers to his transformation into a powerful supernatural being as he sings "I am the hebu." He later explained that his helping spirit, who lives within his chest, is himself speaking in the second half of the song. The hoarotu shaman also experiences a similar transformation into a powerful supernatural being, as noted in the following inflicting song text. In order to record this complete "bewitching" song I had to pay the shaman the equivalent of the price he had paid his teacher. After the proper price was agreed upon the shaman began a song directed at completely destroying UCLA's Nagra III tape recorder and my inexpensive Concord cassette recorder. Toward the end of the lengthy song, he sang the following passage about a great scissors in the spirit world of Hokonamu, in the east where the sun rises, and about his transformation into a being with scissors-like sharp teeth: "Oh great scissors in Hokonamu, you will destroy the machines of the foreigner. . . . With all of the body of the scissors, with the sharp blades and the handle, I am going to destroy the high quality machines of the foreigner. . . . With *my* sharp and filed teeth, *I* will destroy all of the cables and wires of the machines. Inside of you, oh foreign machines with the good voices, I am going to place the Hoa." These few examples of transformation emphasize the following belief in Warao shamanism: the shaman becomes the spirit about which he sings. This contact with the supernatural world and the shaman's ultimate transformation into a powerful being is facilitated and hastened by the ritual music which he sings. The shaman of the last example explained that "this song is so powerful that both tape recorders will be completely destroyed within two weeks." During his ecstatic state the shaman did not smoke, but only sang. He continued to explain that had he desired to destroy the machines immediately, he would have smoked a long cigar, called *wina* in Warao, and at the end of the song glared and growled at the machines, all the time blowing tobacco smoke at them. Fearful, however, that I would be destroyed as well, because of the power of the additional magical arrows and my proximity to the machines, he refrained from doing so.

*[Editors' note: Twenty-four years after this text was published, we asked Dale Olsen if the shaman's song had affected his tape recorders. He reported that several weeks after the event, the batteries contained in the UCLA Nagra III tape recorder leaked acid into the machine's wires and destroyed it. His inexpensive tape recorder fared little better: It began to mangle tapes and broke beyond repair when he attempted to fix it.]*

# 46.

# Shamans Are Intellectuals, Translators, and Shrewd Dealers

GERARDO REICHEL—DOLMATOFF

(1975)

*Austrian-born Colombian anthropologist Gerardo Reichel–Dolmatoff did some of the best fieldwork ever. He dedicated his entire professional life to studying the indigenous people of Colombia. Reichel–Dolmatoff had great respect for shamans, whom he saw as humanists with an interest in knowledge. His reports on shamans are among the most detailed and complete. Here he refers to indigenous shamans in the Vaupes area in the Colombian Amazon.*

Shamanism is well developed among the Indians of the Vaupes, and the shaman (or payé, as he is commonly called in that area), is probably the most important specialist within the native culture. It is he who, representing his local group, establishes contact with the supernatural powers and who, to the mind of his people, has the necessary esoteric knowledge to use this contact for the benefit of society.

The principal spheres of action of a payé are the curing of disease, the obtaining of game animals and fish from their supernatural masters, the presiding over the rituals in the individual life cycle, and defensive or aggressive action against personal enemies. In all these

216

aspects the role of the payé is essentially that of a mediator and moderator between superterrestrial forces and society, and between the need for survival of the individual and the forces bent upon his destruction—sickness, hunger, and the ill will of others. In the course of his activities the shaman (we shall use this term interchangeably with payé) must therefore obtain the assistance of a number of spirit-helpers, contact with whom is established through the use of narcotic drugs. Apart from this, the payé must obtain a series of concrete objects of wood, stone, or other substances that contain the essence of certain power concepts and form his instruments of practice.

The office of payé is not hereditary, but it seems to be fairly common for one of the sons of a well-known shaman to follow his father's calling. More important than family tradition, however, are certain psychological and intellectual qualities that mark a person as a potential payé, and that will be recognized in his youth by those surrounding him. Among these qualities are a deep interest in myth and tribal tradition, a good memory for reciting long sequences of names and events, a good singing voice, and the capacity for enduring hours of incantations during sleepless nights preceded by fasting and sexual abstinence. But these are, perhaps, minor qualities; there are others, more important, that develop only in the course of long training and experience, if not in the course of an entire life. Above all, a payé's soul should "illuminate"; it should shine with a strong inner light rendering visible all that is in darkness, all that is hidden from ordinary knowledge and reasoning. This supernatural luminescence of the payé is said to manifest itself when he speaks or sings, or when he explains his or other's hallucinatory experiences. Of a payé whose explanations remain obscure to the listener, it is said that "his soul is not seen, it does not burn; it does not shine." This powerful emanation is thought to be directly derived from the sun, and to have a marked seminal character. The sun's fertilizing energy is transmitted to the payé in the sense that he himself becomes a carrier of a force that contains procreative and fortifying components. Closely related to this concept is the ability of the payé to interpret mythical passages, genealogical recitals, incan-tory formulas, dreams, or any signs and portents a person may have observed. The payé's interpretations thus "shed light" upon these matters, in the strict sense of the expression. It is of importance, then, that the payé himself be able to have clear and meaningful hallucinations. His vision must not be blurred, his sense of hearing must be acute; that is, he must be able to distinguish clearly the images that appear to his mind while in a state of trance, and to understand the supernatural voices speaking to him. Much of this capacity is, undoubtedly, acquired over the years, the payé developing his own key of interpretation, but some of it is said to be already discernible at an early age. The older people will watch out for any signs a youth may give, and they will discuss them with an experienced payé. . . .

Among the many activities of a Tukano shaman, one of the most important refers to his relationships with *Vaí-mahsë*, the supernatural Master of Animals. This spirit-being can manifest itself in many guises, but is generally imagined, and seen in hallucinations, as a red dwarf, a small person in the attire of a hunter armed with bow and arrow. He is the owner and protector of all animals—fish, game, and all others that dwell in the forest and the rivers—and success in hunting and fishing depends largely upon his good will. . . .

Contact with the Master of Animals is established during hallucinatory trance and through the intermediation of *Vihó-mahsë*, the Master of Snuff. The payé, lying in his hammock, will absorb the narcotic powder and, in his trance, will ascend to the Milky Way, the abode of *Vaí-mahsë*. With the latter's help he then enters the hill where the Master of Animals dwells, and there they begin to bargain for food or medicinal herbs, for vengeance upon enemies or for a successful hunting season. The representatives of the celestial, subterranean, and underwater dimensions thus meet with the payé and, in a trance combined with songs and dances, will now decide the destiny of men. . . .

In his trance, the payé arrives at the hill and approaches the northern entrance, where he knocks three times with his stick rattle. From inside *Vaí-mahsë* voice asks: "What is it you want?" "I want food!" is the payé's reply. Now the door opens before him and he enters the hill.

Inside, along the walls and on the rafters and beams, innumerable animals are crouching as if asleep. In a corner several *boraro*-spirits are sitting, somnolent and with hunched shoulders; jaguars and snakes are lying on the floor, and brightly colored birds sit on the rafters. "Take whatever you need!" says *Vaí-mahsë*. The payé fills two large baskets with certain species of game animals and carries them to the door. There the animals awaken as if from a stupor and scurry away into the forest, always in pairs, a male and a female. The payé returns for more and, with the help of *Vihó-mahsë*, carries two more baskets to the door. But, at the same time, when he is taking the baskets out into the open, some noxious animals, too, will escape from the hill and, always in pairs, will stray into the forest—jaguars, snakes, and maybe a couple of bush spirits. . . .

Many of a payé's activities are concerned with the curing of disease. Tobacco smoke, splashing with water, the sucking out of pathogenic substances, and lengthy incantations are all standard practice and are, in many cases, accompanied by the use of narcotic drugs. It is during his hallucinations that a payé can diagnose a disease, know its cause, discuss its treatment with *Vihó-mahsë*, and learn the correct formulas he has to pronounce over the patient. Sometimes the patient, too, must take a hallucinogenic drug, and he will then describe his visions to the payé, in search of clues to the causes and adequate treatment of the affliction. . . .

The practice of aggressive sorcery aimed at harming or killing personal adversaries occupies all payés. Not all of them, however, are really so inclined, but often they will yield to pressure, and many consider the practice of aggressive magic to be an unavoidable part of their office. . . .

Hallucinatory trances are used as practical and efficient means of experiencing the presence of what, in the native culture, is taken for the metaphysical. However, this supernatural sphere is not the one of divine or godlike beings, but one of morally ambivalent spirits who are sacralized versions of living beings and whose help has to be obtained for very practical ends. As the Tukano see it, there exist supernatural beings—quite apart from the Sun Father—who have absolute knowledge and absolute power. Any illness has a cure, and any social ill can be redressed if only one can find a channel of communication with the forces that "know" the remedies and solutions. Narcotic drugs provide the key to this sphere of absolute knowledge, and the only problem, then, is to understand the language of these spirit-beings. Herein resides the ability of the payé, to interpret their utterings and signs correctly.

Drug-induced ecstasy seems to have two main objectives in Tukano shamanism: to find cures for diseases and ways to punish one's enemies. As illness is not taken to be the natural lot of mankind but is always thought to be caused by the ill will of people or their spirit-helpers, the problem of curing a disease is, in all essence, a process of reestablishing workable relationships with others, even in the event some of these "others" are spirit-beings, who, after all, "are people." The ecstatic emphasis of Tukano shamanism can be seen as a quest for clues and procedures that will allow the user to restore a "dis-ease" produced by tension-fraught interpersonal relationships. Acting as a spokesman and intermediary, the payé is not a mystic, but a practical specialist in communications. . . .

Shamanistic trance provides a mechanism for conflict solution. As has been pointed out already, the payé may discuss the causes of an illness in terms of a social etiology, but he will refrain from making personal judgments or accusations. This pattern, of keeping the solution of social tensions within the bounds of private action, does not diminish the importance of the trance experiences as effective means of settling conflicts arising from social conditions. The aggressive aspects, then, take the character of cathartic rituals of great effectiveness.

In the second place, the concept of spirit-possession seems to be completely lacking in Tukano culture. A payé is always himself; never is he seized or invaded by a spirit; he simply interprets and transmits what this spirit shows him or tells him. He never becomes an instrument of other forces but always remains a translator and interpreter, a shrewd dealer trying to learn as much as possible from the beings that people the world of his visions; he never submits to them as a blind tool of uncontrollable forces. His soul may be wandering, but it is not being replaced by the intrusion of any external agency.

One might ask here: Who are the "enemies" the Tukano make so much of? Revenge is a recurrent theme in Tukano culture, and every man feels constantly threatened by people who wish him ill or by spirits that might be the supernatural helpers of these people. There is endless talk about fighting and killing; about taking violent vengeance on this or that person; about destroying the adversary with illness, lightning, or carefully prepared "accidents" while he is hunting or traveling. And in these matters people bide their time; there is already great satisfaction in long and careful preparations, the learning of spells, and the interpretation of dreams and visions. But, in reality, nothing much ever seems to happen. People hardly ever come to blows, and much less will they readily kill a man or destroy his property; the Tukano are a gentle, friendly people. All aggressiveness, then, is acted out in the hallucinatory dimension, or at least in a state of high excitement induced by the recital of spells and the violent gestures that accompany them. The idea that sorcery has a delayed action is, of course, important because of its essentially realistic aspect. Magical aggression has a good chance of bringing results if given time; thus, it is geared to probability. Given sufficient time, the individual can expect to see his enemy fall ill or die. Obviously, if more immediate effects were expected, the aggressor would often be disappointed.

To act "as if" is a common attitude underlying much of Tukano thought and behavioral patterns. Everyone knows that, in this world, a hill is a hill, and fish are just animals that can be caught and eaten; but everyone also knows that there is "another" world where the hills appear as if they were houses, and fish behave as if they were people. The conditional *as if* is explicit in spells and incantations in which nature is perceived as imbued with human motivations and possibilities of action. The hunter approaches his prey as if it were human; lightning strikes as if it had been cast by someone. . . .

A final word must be said here about the practitioner himself. As

221

far as we were able to judge, there is nothing psychologically abnormal about a payé. Hysteroid or epileptoid symptoms seem to be wholly absent, and anything resembling fits or seizures is simply the consequence of intoxication, not a trait of a psychotic personality. On the contrary, the payés we have known always gave us the impression of being sober, level-headed people, quite normal members of their society.

What distinguishes a payé from others is that he is an intellectual. As such, he is not much given to small talk and the simple pleasures of the home. He often has a tendency to keep apart from others, to be silent, and to abstain from noisy conversation and ribald joking. He may take lonely walks, mumble spells, or sit staring into the dark. But he is immensely curious; he is always interested in animals and plants, the weather, the stars, diseases—anything that to others is unpredictable. He is a humanist, in the sense that he is interested in the "pagan" antiquities of his own cultural tradition: in myths of origin, in archaelogical sites, in long-forgotten place names, and in stories of legendary migrations. And he will enjoy the company of other, like-minded men. When a few friends gather he will talk and sing all night long. He will recall past events, speak of some special "cases" in his practice, and will be a great raconteur.

A Tukano payé does not receive a sudden call to office, in an overwhelming traumatic experience, but develops his personality slowly and steadily, the driving force being a truly intellectual interest in the unknown; and that not so much for the purpose of acquiring power over his fellow men as for the personal satisfaction of "knowing" things which others are unable to grasp.

# 47

# Shamans, Caves, and the Master of Animals

WALTER BURKERT

(1979)

*In this thoughtful piece, Swiss professor of classics Walter Burkert argues that shamanism derives from the symbolic quests that occurred in Paleolithic caves.*

There are two pieces of evidence linking the quest for animals with the Beyond: shamanism used as hunting magic, on the one side, and the cave paintings of the upper Paleolithic on the other. Shamanism has attracted the attention of classical scholars as a phenomenon of ecstasy, it has been discussed as a possible source for the belief in the immortality of the soul—notably by E. R. Dodds—and as a possible source of epic tale. What has not been brought out in these perspectives is the fact that shamanism is intimately bound up with animals, and is used in hunting societies in direct relation to hunting, the basic means of subsistence. The most vivid examples come from the Eskimos of Greenland, who used to live largely on seal hunting. They believe that the seals belong to a mistress of animals, Sedna, the Old Woman "down there." If a tribe fails to find enough seals and is threatened by famine, it must be due to the wrath of Sedna; and this is the situation for the shaman to step in and help by appeasing Sedna. A festival is called, and the shaman, in a trance, sets out to travel to the deep sea; he meets Sedna and asks why she is angry. It is because of human sins, especially those of women, who have broken certain taboos; Sedna herself is covered with filth on account of their uncleanliness. The shaman has to tidy up Sedna, to ask her forgiveness. Of course he succeeds, finally, and comes back from his ecstatic travel bringing with him the animals. The hunters start real hunting immediately, their optimism renewed, and as a result will prove successful. Rasmussen witnessed such a ceremony in 1920. . . .

The Eskimo evidence is most impressive, but is not isolated; it is assumed to be derived from Asia. Similar shamanistic practices, to secure the success of hunting and to gain power over the animals, are attested in the whole of the Arctic region, with Tungus and Yukaghirs, Samoyedes and Dolgans; there is not only a mistress of seals, but a whole set of supernatural owners of game, such as, for example a mother of walruses or a mother of reindeer; there are male owners, even, in certain Eskimo tribes. Shamanism has been observed in many Siberian tribes who are no longer hunters; there shamanism may be confined to the functions of healing and of guiding the dead to their rest; but it is safe to assume that shamanism originated with the oldest, the hunting societies.

Discussion is going on as to how old exactly shamanism is, and how widespread, a problem intertwined with the proper definition of shamanism. There are attempts to limit the concept to a well-defined stage of Siberian or Arctic culture. Yet the phenomenon envisaged, the dealings of a powerful helper of man with a supernatural owner of animals, is definitely not confined to the Arctic Circle. Striking evidence has recently been reported from primitive hunters in the Amazon region. They have a medicine man or shaman, *payé*, whose main obligation is to enter into contact with the masters of animals, the master of game in the mountains at the edge of the woods, and the master of fish in the depth of the river, to make them send animals for hunting and fishing. The *payé* fulfills his role both in a trance provoked by certain drugs, and by actually wandering to those distant cliffs where generations of shamans have left their pictographs. . . .

The other piece of evidence has the advantage that its great age is beyond dispute—though exact chronology is difficult. Its interpretation, however, raises problems which cannot be answered with any certainty. The cave paintings of western Europe, such as those of Altamira or Lascaux, have become world-famous. But what prompted man to this artistic tour de force remains a mystery. Clearly it was not just art for art's sake; some of the caves are terribly difficult of access, and incredible courage and skill were necessary to get there; they never served for habitation. There are some relics of actions performed there, footprints, marks of spear-throwing at clay models, a bear's skull and probably a bear's skin brought into the cave and spread over a bear figure. The dominating subject, at any rate, is game for hunting, wild cattle above all, and wild horses, besides stags and some other species. Here we have, in splendid art, the animals of the Beyond. Connections with hunting practice cannot be denied. And if hunting is a fundamental form of the "quest," then entering such a cave must have meant a difficult journey to another world where one could meet animals. For more detailed interpretation, there are several possibilities of ritual patterns, magic, initiation, shamanism, which have been used to explain these monuments; they may nearly converge on one pattern of ritualized quest.

The "dancing sorcerer," the masked figure in the cave of Trois Frères, has been called a shaman; another scene, in the cave of Lascaux, representing a wounded bison, a man apparently dead, and a bird, has been interpreted as a shamanistic seance. These can hardly be more than possibilities; and there is the notable difference that a true shaman, in his spiritual travel, does not need either caves or artistically perfect pictures. Still rock paintings are produced and used by the Amazonian shamans, and even Siberian shamans currently use animal figurines in their performance. The Yakut shaman wears an "opening of the earth" symbol which is called the "hole of the spirits"; and perforated stones, little caves, as it were, are considered the abode of spirits all over Asia, testifying to the provenance of spiritualism from the cave. Above all there is the uninterrupted evolution from hunting customs to sacrificial ritual which we have traced. The shaman always is a specialist of sacrifice; there is hardly a shamanistic session without an animal appropriately being killed and, in the end, eaten.

Thus in terms of action patterns—which underlie even the tales surveyed—we may hypothetically state the following evolution: The basic program of the "quest," hunting as a way to "get" food, is, when thwarted by failure, transformed into a symbolic "quest," exploring the unexplorable, hoping for the unexpectable, overcoming despair by detour. Thus men penetrated into those dark caves; and as they repeated this symbolic quest, it became an established ritual; to penetrate, by a daring and difficult exploit, into these underground chambers in order to reestablish and bring back the hope of affluence. Elsewhere the quest might just lead to the mountains at the edge of the habitable world. Shamanism is a transformation of this theme, using the special mediumistic talents of certain individuals instead of the outward apparatus of caves and pictures.

# 48.

# "Plant Teachers"

## LUIS EDUARDO LUNA

## (1984)

*Colombian anthropologist Luis Eduardo Luna discusses "plant teachers," a central concept among mestizo shamans in the Peruvian Amazon. Luna shows that much can be learned by listening to people and paying attention to what they say. For once, anthropologists and shamans speak the same mother tongue: Spanish.*

In the city of Iquitos and its vicinity there is even today a rich tradition of folk medicine. Practitioners, some of whom qualify as shamans, make an important contribution to the psychosomatic health of the inhabitants of this area. Among them there are those called *vegetalistas* or plant specialists and who use a series of plants called *doctores* or plant teachers. It is their belief that if they fulfill certain conditions of isolation and follow a prescribed diet, these plants are able to "teach" them how to diagnose and cure illnesses, how to perform other shamanic tasks, usually through magic melodies or *icaros*, and how to use medicinal plants.

Four shamans were questioned about the nature and identity of these magic plants, what are the dietary prescriptions to be followed, how the transmission of shamanic power takes place, the nature of their helping spirits, and the function of the magic melodies or *icaros* given to them by the plant teachers. . . .

Crucial to shamanic practices is the belief that many plants, if not all plants, each have their own "mother" or spirit. It is with the help of the spirits of some of these plants, which I have called "plant teachers," that the shaman is able to acquire his powers.

When the four informants were questioned about the origin of their knowledge they all answered: *La purga misma te enseña* (The purgative itself teaches you), referring to the *ayahuasca* beverage. Other plants, some of which I learned were used as additives to *ayahuasca,* were also mentioned. Suspecting that at least some of them might be psychoactive, I started to make a list and if possible collect all those plants that "teach medicine." I found in the shamans' reports that plants they called *doctores* or *vegetales que enseñan* (plants that teach) either: (1) produce hallucinations if taken alone; (2) modify in some way the effects of the *ayahuasca* beverage; (3) produce dizziness; (4) possess strong emetic and/or cathartic properties; (5) bring on specially vivid dreams. Quite often a plant has all these characteristics, or some of them. I was somewhat perplexed about how to find the right way of questioning my informants about the plant teachers. If I use, for instance, the Spanish verb, *marear* (to make you dizzy), for example: *Don Celso, marea esta planta?* (Don Celso, does this plant, when taking it, make you dizzy?) the answer could be: "Yes, it is a good medicine," or "Yes, in your dreams the spirit of the plants presents itself to you," or "Yes, it makes you throw up everything," or "Yes, it teaches you," or "Yes, it makes you see beautiful things," or finally "Yes, if you combine it with *ayahuasca*." Similar answers were given to me when I put the question differently, like, *Don Emilio, es esta planta doctor?* (Is this a plant teacher?) or *Don Alejandro, tiene madre esta planta?* (Does this plant have its "mother"?). This set of associations is interesting indeed. The association of psychoactive plants with emetics and vermifuges has been pointed out by Rodriguez and Cavin (1982). The association between dreams and hallucinations is a common theme in shamanic literature. As far as I understand, all psychoactive plants are considered potential teachers. I once asked Don Emilio if he had ever taken the mushroom *Psilocybe cubensis,* which grows widely throughout the region on cow dung. He answered positively: *Bonito se ve. Dietandole debe enseñar medicina* (You see beautiful things. If you keep the diet it might teach you medicine).

The four informants I worked with do not agree as to whether all plant teachers produce visions. According to Don Alejandro, all the plants that have "mothers" *marean* (make you dizzy). This implies that there are plants without "mothers," with which Don Celso and Don Emilio do not agree. Don Celso says: "The mother of the plant is its existence, its life." Don Emilio affirms that all plants, even the smallest, have their "mothers." Some of the plant teachers produce visions only when associated with *ayahuasca*. Others produce only *una mareacion ciega* (a blind dizziness), in which you do not see anything. Other plants teach only during the dreams. . . .

All four informants insist that the spirits of the plants taught them what they know. Don Celso never had a shaman as his teacher. On one occasion he made a very significant remark: "That is why some doctors believe that the *vegetalismo* (or science of the plants) is stronger than *la medicina de estudio* (Western medicine), because they learn by reading books. But we just take this liquid (*ayahuasca*), keep the diet, and then we learn." Don Alejandro told me that very soon he learned more than his teacher, an Indian captured by the caucheros (rubber workers), because the spirits of the plants taught him so much. Don José claims that his *murrayas* taught him everything he knows. . . . [H]e identifies them with the spirits of dead shamans. In his ecstatic trance they enter his body and talk to him in Cocama, a Peruvian tribe language. Don José is the only one of the four informants who manifests what could be labelled spirit possession. He sometimes maintains long dialogues with the spirits, who talk through his mouth in a loud voice.

The spirits, who are sometimes called *doctorcitos* (little doctor) or *abuelos* (grandfathers) present themselves during the visions and during the dreams. They show how to diagnose the illness, what plants to use and how, the proper use of tobacco smoke, how to suck out the illness or restore the spirit to a patient, how the shamans defend themselves, what to eat, and, most important, they teach them *icaros*, magic songs or shamanic melodies which are the main tools of shamanic practices.

# 49.

# A Shaman Endures the
# Temptation of Sorcery
# (and Publishes a Book)

FERNANDO PAYAGUAJE
(1990)

> *For three years, three young Secoya Indians interviewed their grandfa-*
> *ther Fernando Payaguaje, a* yagé *(ayahuasca) shaman. They tran-*
> *scribed hundreds of pages in Secoya, then edited them and translated*
> *them to Spanish, and published a small book in his name called* The
> Yagé Drinker. *It is one of the clearest books on ayahuasca shaman-*
> *ism, though as yet not translated into English. The shaman's three*
> *nephews are Alfredo Payaguaje, Marcelino Lucitande, and Jorge*
> *Lucitande.*

To be able to graduate, one needs to drink *yagé* at least fifteen times
over several months. After that, one should be able to cure any kind of
illness. But to get to that stage, one must endure much deprivation and
suffering.

For example, I was married, and could not sleep with my wife; if I
wanted to be the best and most knowledgeable healer, I could not visit
her. I was in another house near her, preparing *yagé* and drinking it
without cease, as my obligation was to perfect myself more and more.
This also happens later on, the healer often suffers from not being able

to look after his family; there are times when he must stay away, because he has to maintain himself in good condition and look after his health. He is not allowed to use a dish used by a pregnant woman, and he must also keep at a distance from her; if he does not respect these requirements, he will have headaches and other pains. The same occurs if the woman is menstruating; in that case, she has to remain hidden and keep apart from her husband until it passes. Then she must wash with hot water, guaba leaves, and other leaves; if she does that she will be able to give her husband food once again. Women should also avoid walking near the *yagé* house during a ceremony, and they should preferably stay inside their house; otherwise the masters of fish and of the forest animals will not respond to the *yagé*'s call. They must also withdraw when the *yagé* is cooking. All of these rules are for women. However, they may drink *yagé* and be healers, and it is good if they can heal bites and other things, when their family is suffering.

While one drinks *yagé*, one keeps a severe food diet. There are few fish that one may eat, and the same is true of meats. One should also avoid ripe hot peppers, and eat only unripe ones, and so on; if one eats just any kind of food, one learns nothing. This is why one must be patient and endure deprivation. Often you have to stay in your house without going visiting, so that no one offers you prohibited foods; what is more, apprentices need a new cooking pot of their own. Their hammock needs to be well guarded: If they leave the house, they tie it up high so that no women or visitors use it. The master warns them of all this. Otherwise, if they return to the house, bathe, and lie down in a badly used hammock, they could suffer pains, and lose the power of visions. That is why they must protect themselves. . . .

Some people drink *yagé* only to the point of reaching the power to practice witchcraft; with these crafts they can kill people. A much greater effort and consumption of *yagé* are required to reach the highest level, where one gains access to the visions and power of healing. To become a sorcerer is easy and fast. I did not aspire to that, but to become the most wise and knowledgeable; my idea was to attain leadership of a big family or clan, some ten or twenty families, and to be able to look after them and heal them all. It was only with this idea in mind that I found the strength to reach the highest level. . . .

One is sitting in the hammock but, at the same time, one is in another world, seeing the truth of all that exists; only the body remains postrate. The angels arrive and they offer you a flute; you play it, as it is not the healer who teaches, but they themselves who make us sing when we are drunk. How fine it is to see the totality of animals, even those who live under water! How could it not be beautiful to distinguish even the people who live inside the earth? One can see everything, that is why it is fascinating to drink *yagé*.

But it is not simple. On drinking thick *yagé*, I managed to see the sun, the rainbow . . . everything; the vision ended and I noted that my heart was hot, like a recently burned pan. I could feel the heat inside, burning me; even without working I sweated all day. Continuous visions assaulted me, I sweated and I bathed myself very often. I felt able to practice witchcraft and to kill others, even though I never did, because my father's advice contained me: "If you use that power now, you could kill someone, but then you would never get over being a sorcerer."

In those days I dedicated myself to *yagé*; I went to visit Cuyabeno and returned home to hear similar warnings: "When you feel a bit drunk, you must rise above the anger that comes over you; do not become violent and do not harm anybody," my father said.

"No, I will know how to contain myself," I said.

For days I put up with that heat; I remember drowning in sweat, that is the dangerous moment for the person who is preparing himself: One should not even look straight at people, but only listen to them.

"Now I will bring another kind of *yagé*," said my father. "The time has come to try it."

We prepared it good and thick, and upon drinking it, he removed those arrows I had inside me; I stopped sweating and became like a child. That is how my father pulled out the violence from me so I would not practice sorcery, but learn to heal instead. At that instant I moved up in grade: Now I could see sorcerers as clearly as the sun; the healers were mirrors. That way, when I settled in the Cuyabeno area, I was able to discover a Siona sorcerer from Río Aguarico; sorcerers do not look at people face to face; they stand as if they were ducking. That is the kind of person who brought about so many fights in the past.

# 50.

# Interview with a Killing Shaman

ASHOK AND PETER SKAFTE

(1992)

*Danish anthropologist Peter Skafte has studied shamanism in Nepal for many years. The following excerpt is based on a recorded interview Skafte conducted with a shaman called Ashok, from West Nepal. Ashok's trajectory shows how difficult it can be to be a shaman in the current world. We enter the interview as Ashok is describing the first sign that he might become a shaman.*

"One evening, as the sun was setting, I got off the fisherman's boat and headed back along the riverbank, toward my house. I was walking with a few people from my village who were also on their way home. Suddenly I heard voices, but when I checked with the other villagers, they said they didn't hear anything. Then I heard the loud blast of a conch shell being blown, and I saw a long line of dark figures moving along the opposite shore. Pointing to the procession, I asked my companions who those people could be. They looked at me as if I were crazy and said that nobody was there. When the procession was directly across from me, I froze with fear. I realized I was looking at a legion of *masaans* [grave-yard spirits]. *Bir Masaan*, the king of all the masaans, was riding on a white horse at the head of the procession. I began trembling, but I did not speak about what I saw. After that event, I often saw the masaans by the river at dusk, but it took several years for me to realize that this spiritual ability was something special and that I was destined to become a shaman."

"How did you come to realize this?" I asked him.

"My village is on the crest of a big spur that extends down from the mountains. Below the village, on one side, there is a huge cliff, and below that cliff is a small temple dedicated to *Bajra* [the thunder god]. One day, when I was sixteen years old, I was herding cattle near that temple. It was a hot afternoon, and I lay down behind the temple and fell asleep. I had a wonderful dream in which Bajra stood before me. He had a long beard streaked with gold, and he wore beautiful clothing. Bajra said, 'It is time for you to learn to become a shaman. I will be your teacher.' When I awoke, I was trembling in the area of my heart, but the trembling stopped as I drove the cattle home. Later that evening, I suddenly went into trance—I began to shake and I could not utter a word. My brother-in-law, who is a shaman, was summoned. He tried to find out which spirit had possessed me, but it would not reveal itself. I remained in trance, without speaking, for a week.

"My parents were beside themselves with worry. They feared that I was suffering from sorcery. As the days passed with no change in my condition, they became terrified that I would never return to normal. Then, one night, Bajra came to me in a dream and taught me a mantra. After I repeated his words, I went to my brother-in-law's altar, took his drum, and began drumming and trembling.

"My brother-in-law shouted to the force who possessed me, 'Who are you? Where are you from?' Bajra answered through me, 'I am Bajra and I come with good intentions. Ashok must become a shaman and you must be his guide. Open his eyes so that he can see to travel the right way to the upper, middle, and lower worlds.' My brother-in-law answered, 'If Ashok will become a virtuous shaman, I will be his guide, and he may use anything on this altar to assist him in his travels.' Then my brother-in-law made me take the oath of fire, and he gave me a drum and other necessary ritual items."

"How long did it take you to become a shaman?" I asked.

"I studied with my brother-in-law for two years, and Bajra taught me many mantras in my dreams, on certain nights when the moon was full. Then my progress toward becoming a shaman was interrupted. In accordance with my parents' wishes, I married at age eighteen and moved to Kathmandu to make a living. The city was overwhelming to me, and I was confused by all the new things I saw. I started to come under the influence of new friends, who ridiculed shamans as backwards and uneducated. They told me that the ancient 'superstitions' were stumbling blocks to progress. Soon I began doubting the worth and power of what I had learned.

"But the worst crisis was yet to come. Three of my new friends persuaded me to go into business with them, importing goods from India for sale in Kathmandu. Although my family needed every penny I earned, I started giving my partners a large portion of my pay each week, and I even borrowed money from relatives. Six months passed, but no goods ever arrived. When I confronted my partners about the situation, they shrugged and said that someone had cheated them in India and that they had lost all of my money. They left me standing alone in the street.

"I had never felt so frustrated and powerless in my life. It is not easy to accept that you have been used as a fool. The more I thought about it, the more angry I became. In the heat of passion, I directed a deadly mantra against my partners. Now, in hindsight, I realize that I not only sought revenge but also wanted to prove to myself the power of my mantras.

"Within a few weeks, one of the men became very ill. He died three days later. Frightened, I tried to undo the spell on the other two, but it was to no avail. One man developed severe dysentery and the other was hit by a car. By the end of the month, both were dead. Because I had vowed to the gods that I would use my power only to serve others, not to hurt them, I lived in terror of being punished for breaking my oath. And my fears came true. My little son and daughter became ill with terrible fevers and died within a month.

"For a long time afterwards, I thought about killing myself. I felt I didn't deserve to live. Then, one night, I had a dream in which I was lost in the twisting back streets of Kathmandu. I turned a corner and came face to face with Bajra. 'Go back to your place of origin,' he said. 'Learn all that you can and take up your rightful work.' I told my wife that we had to return home and that I was going to follow my calling to be a shaman. She replied, 'I am willing to go. My heart has been broken in this cruel city.'"

# 51.

# Invisible Projectiles in Africa

MALIDOMA PATRICE SOMÉ

(1994)

*Malidoma Patrice Somé is a boburo, or a medicine man and diviner from the Dagara culture in Burkina Faso, West Africa. He holds two doctorates from the Sorbonne and Brandeis University. He wrote a book called* Of Water and the Spirit: Ritual, Magic, and Initiation in the Life of an African Shaman. *It contributes to the growing evidence of shamanism in Africa. Here Somé discusses invisible projectiles used by Dagara medicine men who have "gone private," meaning to say who practice their art hidden from view and not for the common good. These projectiles are reminiscent of those discussed by shamans from Australia to the Amazon.*

The most common technique utilized by people who have gone private is the lobir (plural lobie), an invisible projectile known to warriors of the secret societies. A lobir can take any form. The most primitive is an object that is thrown into a person's body. The most advanced is a living thing, ranging from a lobir the size of a worm to one as big as the practitioner can guide.

Funerals provide the ideal context for all sorts of wizard wars. After each funeral celebration a certain number of unfortunate men and women become gravely ill because they have been shot unaware by an enemy or have been hit by a lobir intended for somebody else. Those who attack people with lobie hide themselves and their doings. They may come to the funeral with strange feline-skin bags on their backs containing a secret arsenal invisible to the uninformed eye, or they may mix with the singers unnoticed.

The contents of these bags are kept secret because no one checks the contents of another person's bag. Most males, especially those who are directly related to the deceased, carry animal-skin bags on their backs when they attend funerals. These bags are a kind of Dagara first-aid kit, and contain cowrie shells and medicine objects used for healing. Because funerals are not a closed circle, and since everybody is morally obligated to participate at one time or another, many different kinds of people show up.

Most of the time those who have gone private can harm their chosen victims without being noticed. With a simple movement of their hand, they can fire the invisible projectiles intended for their enemy. Once hit, this unfortunate person feels little pain. In fact, they experience nothing more than the need to scratch. Later, however, the itching will become worse and worse until the person is finally debilitated and forced to leave the funeral circle in search of a healer.

Why would someone who lives within a tribal community want to harm others in this way? Because such actions give pleasure to an evil person. As they say, this person is possessed by bad spirits. For those of you who have begun to construct a romantic picture of indigenous life, let this be a warning. For the indigenous world is not a place where everything flows in harmony, but one in which people must be constantly on the alert to detect and to correct imbalances and illnesses in both communal and individual life.

Like bullets fired from the barrel of a gun, lobie can work against anyone. Just as one must wear a bulletproof vest to ward off bullets, one can have a "lobirproof" vest magically placed over one's body. Unlike the bulletproof vest, which has its limitations, the lobirproof vest is perfect. Once built into your body's energy system, it will be part of you for the rest of your life. Moreover, anyone who shoots at a person thus protected could very well find himself being hit by his own lobir because this "vest" has the power to deflect the hostile projectile back to its sender. This is very dangerous for the evildoer, for as they say in my tribe, you can't defend yourself against your own bullet once it is returned to you.

I remember a story my father once told me about a lobir. He was attending a friend's funeral. In the middle of one of the cathartic communal dances, he was stung on the left hand by something that looked like a bee. This bee, however, tore straight through his skin and disappeared into his arm. My father could feel it moving around under his skin, its wings still whirring.

The pain was so excruciating that he fell onto the dusty ground and passed out. People carried him into the emergency room of the local healer, who looked at the moving lobir and recognized its maker by the speed with which Father's hand was swelling. After stilling the moving lobir, the healer made a tiny incision and chased the "bee" out by plunging an arrow into Father's body. When the bee-lobir flew out, he squashed it before it could escape.

Father was given medicine to restore his strength. Before he was able to return to the funeral, he had to wash himself with a special potion designed to form a shield against such invisible projectiles. Since that day, Father has been extremely cautions about lobie, even with his immunization. I have heard numerous similar reports. And, when I was four years old, I saw my grandfather extract lobie that looked like bones, needles, feathers, and fur from the bodies of victims. A person in my tribe who ignores these warnings because he or she feels invulnerable is exhibiting a dangerous vanity.

During the second day of Grandfather's funeral the *nimwie-dem*, "those who have eyes"—medicine society members, initiated people, and some people who had an exceptional eye for observation—kept tabs on what was happening around them so that they could take appropriate actions. An ordinary person cannot see lobie. To have that ability you either have to know how to use them or be immunized against them. To the average person, lobie might look like something as harmless as the sun's rays, but to trained seers they might, for example, appear as a multitude of tiny shooting stars, traversing space at varying speeds. Some of the "stars" disappear when they hit a human body.

If a person is struck by a lobir, he or she will inevitably scratch where the thing has vanished, alerting the shooter that the lobir has found its mark. But sometimes these minute "stars" land on the ground, endangering anyone who happens to walk on them. The unfortunate victim might leap into the air like a cat who has accidentally stepped on a hot coal, but there will be no further complications beyond a simple skin burn. A lobir cannot hurt you if it is not specifically designed to hurt you. My father once explained that the reasons some projectiles fail to hit their target is because the shooter has an incomplete knowledge of the victim's energy field. The missile becomes confused shortly after being fired. It falls on the ground and sometimes dies quickly thereafter. Those who are able to see them urinate on them when they fall onto the ground (assuming they can do so without infringing on the laws of decency). To urinate on a lobir is to kill it instantly. The thing catches fire and burns to ash.

# PART SEVEN

# Global Knowledge and Indigenous Knowledge Come Together and Remain Apart

In 1901, Franz Boas wrote:

One of the chief aims of anthropology is the study of the mind of man under the varying conditions of race and of environment. The activities of the mind manifest themselves in thoughts and actions, and exhibit an infinite variety of form among the peoples of the world. In order to understand these clearly, the student must endeavor to divest himself entirely of opinions and emotions based upon the peculiar social environment into which he is born. He must adapt his own mind, so far as feasible, to that of the people whom he is studying. The more successful he is freeing himself from the bias based on the group of ideas that constitute the civilization in which he lives, the more successful he will be in interpreting the beliefs and actions of man.

When it came to the study of shamans, it took anthropologists and other researchers close to a century to put Boas's wise advice into practice.

Claude Lévi-Strauss set the stage in 1962 with his book *The Savage Mind*. He showed that magic and science require the same mental operations and complement each other. He made it theoretically acceptable to take shamanism seriously.

It would take researchers two more decades to find common ground between the practices of science and shamanism.

By then, the world had become a more complicated place. A global culture was emerging. Shamanism increasingly appeared in the marketplace. The New Age movement had become fascinated with shamanism. And anthropologists found a "force field" that kept them from understanding shamans. They also found ways of overcoming it.

# 52.

# Science and Magic,
# Two Roads to Knowledge

## CLAUDE LÉVI—STRAUSS

## (1962)

*In his book* The Savage Mind, *Claude Lévi–Strauss, the master of dialectics in anthropology, places magic, which includes shamanism, on the same intellectual footing as science.*

Instead of opposing magic and science, it would be better to compare them as two parallel modes of acquiring knowledge. Their theoretical and practical results differ in value (as science is certainly more successful than magic from this point of view, although magic foreshadows science in that it sometimes also works). But both science and magic require the same sort of mental operations, which differ not so much in kind as in the different types of phenomena to which they are applied.

These relations are a consequence of the objective conditions in which magic and scientific knowledge appeared. The history of the latter is short enough for us to know a good deal about it. But the fact that modern science dates back only a few centuries raises a problem which ethnologists have not sufficiently pondered. The Neolithic Paradox would be a suitable name for it.

It was in neolithic times that humanity mastered the great arts of civilization, which are pottery, weaving, agriculture, and the domestication of animals. No one today would think of attributing these enormous advances to the fortuitous accumulation of a series of chance discoveries or believe them to have been revealed by the passive perception of certain natural phenomena.

Each of these techniques assumes centuries of active and methodical observation, of bold hypotheses tested by means of endlessly repeated experiments. . . .

To transform a weed into a cultivated plant, a wild beast into a domestic animal, to produce, in either of these, nutritious or technologically useful properties which were originally completely absent or could only be guessed at; to make stout, water-tight pottery out of clay which is friable, unstable, or liable to pulverize or crack . . . ; to work out techniques, often long and complex, which permit cultivation without soil or alternatively without water; to change toxic roots or seeds into foodstuffs or again to use their poison for hunting, war, or ritual — all these achievements no doubt required a genuinely scientific attitude, sustained and watchful interest, and a desire for knowledge for its own sake. Only a small proportion of observations and experiments (which must be assumed to have been primarily inspired by a desire for knowledge) could have yielded practical and immediately useful results. There is no need to dwell on the working of bronze and iron and of precious metals or even the simple working of copper ore by hammering which preceded metallurgy by several thousand years, and even at that stage they all demand a very high level of technical proficiency.

Neolithic, or early historical, humans were therefore the heirs of a long scientific tradition. However, had they, and their predecessors, been inspired by exactly the same spirit as that of our own time, it would be impossible to understand how they could have come to a halt and how several thousand years of stagnation have intervened between the neolithic revolution and modern science like a level plain between ascents. There is only one solution to the paradox, namely, that there are two distinct modes of scientific thought. These are certainly not caused by different stages of development of the human mind but rather by strategic levels at which nature is accessible to scientific enquiry: one roughly adapted to that of perception and the imagination, the other at a remove from it. It is as if the necessary connections which are the object of all science, neolithic or modern, could be arrived at by two different routes, one very close to, and the other more remote from, sensible intuition.

# 53.

# Shamans, "Spirits," and Mental Imagery

RICHARD NOLL

(1987)

*American clinical psychologist Richard Noll finds mental imagery on the common ground between shamanism and psychology. Noll tries to define "spirits" and shamanism as mental imagery and the technique of controlling it.*

What, then, are "spirits"? Cross-culturally, "spirits" are subjectively described as those transpersonal forces that we experience as moving in us or through us but are not entirely moved by us. This means that these (usually) personified forces or agencies are autonomous entities with their own agendas. Generally they cannot be contacted and engaged while we are in an ordinary state of waking consciousness, but are more clearly seen when we are in altered states. Dreams are the most common altered state in which they appear. . . .

Spirits are an incontestable part of humankind's "experienced reality," and, regardless of what their "ultimate reality" is, cross-culturally they seem to represent the forces of transformation that can either enhance growth or inflict illness or even death. Therefore, they are by their very nature both good and evil, both guides and deceptors, both healers and destroyers, the creators of life and the servants of death. To seek out these transformative powers willingly, as the shaman does, brings one into intimate contact with the secrets of existence itself. To open one's soul to these double-edged forces is thereby to transform oneself. Thus, "spirits" can be thought of as ego-alien energy currents that step forward from the shadows of the "not-I" to introduce new information to the individual who cannot access this information while in an ordinary state of waking consciousness.

The shaman intentionally induces these altered states called "ecstasies," "trances," or "visions" in order to contact and manipulate spirits for distinct purposes. Shamans are therefore known as both "masters of trance" and "masters of spirits." Spirits are employed to effect changes in the shaman himself or in others (as in healing), or to make changes in or receive information about the outer physical world. This latter function of spirits is a common characteristic of *magic*. A more formal definition of shamanism is an ecstatic healing tradition which at its core is concerned with the techniques for inducing, maintaining, and interpreting the vivid experiences of enhanced mental imagery that occur in the deliberately induced altered states of consciousness in the shaman.

The key to the esoteric training of the novice shaman—and of the novices of many magico-religious traditions worldwide—is the development of enhanced skills in mental imagery. . . . In shamanism, the development of visual imagery seems to be of particular importance, although there is an auditory component developed as well.

Shamanic training in such "vision cultivation" is a two-phase process. First, the neophyte is trained to increase the vividness of his internal visual imagery through various psychological and physiological techniques. Many of them are considered extreme by our culture's standards: pain stimulation, hypoglycemia and dehydration, forced hypermotility such as long periods of dancing, acoustic stimulation (particularly drumming), seclusion and restricted mobility, sleep deprivation, hyperventilation, and the ingestion of hallucinogens. Practicing any of these techniques would induce an alteration in one's state of consciousness. Experimental studies in psychology have shown that mental imagery can become so vivid that it can block out the awareness of normal visual perception. It is as if the vibrant world within becomes so bright that it blocks out the light from the world around one.

Once the novice can experience vivid "life-like" imagery, a second phase of training begins, aimed at increasing control over internal imagery. Shamans engage and interact with the visionary contents and learn to master spirits in this way. . . .

Humankind has traditionally consulted extramundane entities for expanded knowledge and empowerment, for they are traditionally considered "sources of wisdom" that are transpersonal and able to convey crucial information beyond the normal constraints of space and time. Guardian spirits, angels, deceased ancestors, natural deities have all been contacted through the occult rituals of many traditions. The practitioner usually initiates dialogues with spiritual entities by first inducing an altered state of consciousness, which allows these "invisible guests" to be seen and heard. However, in some instances it is *they* who knock first on the doors of imaginal perception. Called or not called, they offer symbolic potential for transformation, whether for oneself, for others, or for desired changes in the physical environment.

Thus, instruction from spirits can facilitate spiritual transformation, and such "guardian spirits" or "spirit guides and teachers" are invoked by the shaman/practitioner, who believes he is tapping into the collective repository of the wisdom of our species. These beings are not imaginary in the sense of being not real, pure fantasy, or artificially made up. They are imaginal, existing in a realm of experience in which they inhabit a reality of their own, a *mundus imaginalis* or "imaginal world," as Henri Corbin deems it, which is co-existent with the mundane experiential world of our ordinary state of waking consciousness. Imaginal beings are part of our experienced reality and have probably been so since the birth of human consciousness.

# 54

# Dark Side of the Shaman

MICHAEL F. BROWN

(1989)

*American anthropologist Michael F. Brown studied the magical practices
of the Jivaro Aguarunas in the Peruvian Amazon. Then he spent a year
in Santa Fe, New Mexico, where he found people who embrace parts of
shamanism, while spurning its dark side, to fit it into their modern lives.*

Shamans, who are found in societies all over the world, are believed
to communicate directly with spirits to heal people struck down by
illness. Anthropologists are fond of reminding their students that
shamanism, not prostitution, is the world's oldest profession. When, in
my role as curious ethnographer, I've asked Santa Feans about their
interest in this exotic form of healing, they have expressed their admi-
ration for the beauty of the shamanistic tradition, the ability of
shamans to "get in touch with their inner healing powers," and the superiority of spiritual treatments over the impersonal medical practice
of our own society. Fifteen years ago, I would have sympathized with
these romantic ideas. Two years of fieldwork in an Amazonian society,
however, taught me that there is peril in the shaman's craft.

A man I shall call Yankush is a prominent shaman among the
Aguaruna, a native people who make their home in the tropical forest
of northeastern Peru. Once feared headhunters, the Aguaruna now
direct their considerable energies to cultivating cash crops and pro-

tecting their lands from encroachment by settlers fleeing the poverty of Peru's highland and coastal regions.

Yankush is a vigorous, middle-aged man known for his nimble wit and ready laugh. Like every other able-bodied man in his village, Yankush works hard to feed his family by hunting, fishing, and helping his wife cultivate their fields. But when his kinfolk or friends fall ill, he takes on the role of *iwishín*—shaman—diagnosing the cause of the affliction and then, if possible, removing the source of the ailment from the patient's body.

In common with most peoples who preserve a lively shamanic heritage, the Aguaruna believe that life-threatening illness is caused by sorcerers. Sorcerers are ordinary people who, driven by spite or envy, secretly introduce spirit darts into the bodies of their victims. If the dart isn't soon removed by a shaman, the victim dies. Often the shaman describes the dart as a piece of bone, a tiny thorn, a spider, or a blade of grass.

The Aguaruna do not regard sorcery as a quaint and colorful bit of traditional lore. It is attempted homicide, plain and simple. That the evidence of sorcery can only be seen by a shaman does not diminish the ordinary person's belief in the reality of the sorcerer's work, any more than our inability to see viruses with the naked eye leads us to question their existence. The Aguaruna insist that sorcerers, when discovered, must be executed for the good of society.

Shaman and sorcerer might seem locked in a simple struggle of good against evil, order against chaos, but things are not so straightforward. Shamans and sorcerers gain their power from the same source, both receiving spirit darts from a trusted instructor. Because the darts attempt to return to their original owner, apprentice shamans and sorcerers must induce them to remain in their bodies by purifying themselves. They spend months in jungle isolation, fasting and practicing sexual abstinence. By wrestling with the terrifying apparitions that come to plague their dreams, they steel themselves for a life of spiritual struggle.

There the paths of sorcerer and shaman divide. The sorcerer works in secret, using spirit darts to inflict suffering on his enemies. The shaman operates in the public eye and uses his own spirit darts to thwart the sorcerer's schemes of pain and untimely death. (I say "he," because to my knowledge all Aguaruna shamans are men. Occasionally, however, a woman is accused of sorcery.) Yet because shamans possess spirit darts, and with them the power to kill, the boundary between sorcerer and shaman is sometimes indistinct.

The ambiguities of the shaman's role were brought home to me during a healing session I attended in Yankush's house. The patients were two women: Yamanuanch, who complained of pains in her stomach and throat, and Chapaik, who suffered discomfort in her back and lower abdomen. Their illnesses did not seem life threatening, but they were persistent enough to raise fears that sorcery was at the root of the women's misery.

As darkness fell upon us, the patients and their kin waited for Yankush to enter into a trance induced by a bitter, hallucinogenic concoction he had taken just before sunset (it is made from a vine known as *ayahuasca*). While the visitors exchanged gossip and small talk, Yankush sat facing the wall of his house, whistling healing songs and waving a bundle of leaves that served as a fan and soft rattle. Abruptly, he told the two women to lie on banana leaves that had been spread on the floor, so that he could use his visionary powers to search their bodies for tiny points of light, the telltale signature of the sorcerer's darts. As Yankush's intoxication increased, his meditative singing gave way to violent retching. Gaining control of himself, he sucked noisily on the patients' bodies in an effort to remove the darts.

Family members of the patients shouted words of concern and support. "Others know you are curing. They can hurt you, be careful!" one of the spectators warned, referring to the sorcerers whose work the shaman hoped to undo. Torn by anxiety, Chapaik's husband addressed those present: "Who has done this bewitching? If my wife dies, I could kill any man out of anger!" In their cries of encouragement to Yankush, the participants expressed their high regard for the difficult work of the shaman, who at this point in the proceedings was frequently doubled over with nausea caused by the drug he had taken.

Suddenly there was a marked change of atmosphere. A woman named Chimi called out excitedly, "If there are any darts there when she gets back home, they may say that Yankush put them there. So take them all out!" Chimi's statement was an unusually blunt rendering of an ambivalence implicit in all relations between Aguaruna shamans and their clients. Because shamans control spirit darts, people fear that a shaman may be tempted to use the cover of healing as an opportunity to bewitch his own clients for personal reasons. The clients therefore remind the shaman that they expect results—and if such results are not forthcoming, the shaman himself may be suspected of, and punished for, sorcery.

Yankush is such a skilled healer that this threat scarcely caused him to miss a step. He sucked noisily on Yamanuanch's neck to cure her sore throat and, after singing about the sorcery darts lodged in her body, announced she would recover. For good measure, he recommended injections of a commercial antibiotic. Yankush also took pains to emphasize the intensity of his intoxication. Willingness to endure the rigors of a large dose of *ayahuasca* is a sign of his good faith as a healer. "Don't say I wasn't intoxicated enough," he reminded the participants.

As Yankush intensified his singing and rhythmic fanning of the leaf-bundle, he began to have visions of events taking place in distant villages. Suddenly he cried out, "In Achu they killed a person. A sorcerer was killed." "Who could it be?" the other participants asked one another, but before they could reflect on this too long, Yankush had moved on to other matters. "I'm concentrating to throw out sickness, like a tireless jaguar," he sang, referring to Chapaik, who complained of abdominal pains. "With my help she will become like the tapir, which doesn't know how to refuse any kind of food."

After two hours of arduous work, Yankush steered the healing session to its conclusion by reassuring the patients that they were well on their way to recovery. "In her body the sickness will end," he sang. "It's all right. She won't die. It's nothing," he added, returning to a normal speaking voice. Before departing, the patients and their kin discussed the particulars of Yankush's dietary recommendations and made plans for a final healing session to take place at a later date. As the sleepy partipants left Yankush's house for their beds in other parts of the village, they expressed their contentment with the results of his efforts.

During the year I lived near Yankush, he conducted healing sessions like this one about twice a month. Eventually, I realized that his active practice was only partly a matter of choice. To allay suspicions and demonstrate his good faith as a healer, he felt compelled to take some cases he might otherwise have declined. Even so, when I traveled to other villages, people sometimes asked me how I could live in a community where a "sorcerer" practiced on a regular basis.

When a respected elder died suddenly of unknown causes in 1976, Yankush came under extraordinary pressure to identify the sorcerer responsible. From the images of his *ayahuasca* vision he drew the name of a young man from a distant region who happened to be visiting a nearby village. The man was put to death in a matter of days. Because Yankush was widely known to have fingered the sorcerer, he became the likely victim of a reprisal raid by members of the murdered man's family. Yankush's willingness to accept this risk in order to protect his community from future acts of sorcery was a source of his social prestige, but it was also a burden. I rarely saw him leave his house without a loaded shotgun.

In calling attention to the violent undercurrents of shamanism, my intention is not to disparage the healing traditions of the Aguaruna or of any other tribal people. I have no doubt that the cathartic drama I witnessed in Yankush's house made the two patients feel better. Medical anthropologists agree that rituals calling forth expressions of community support and concern for sick people often lead to a marked improvement in their sense of well-being. Shamans also serve their communities by administering herbal medications and other remedies and even, as in Yankush's case, helping to integrate traditional healing arts with the use of modern pharmaceuticals. At the same time, however, they help sustain a belief in sorcery that exacts a high price in anxiety and, from time to time, in human life.

In their attempts to understand this negative current, anthropologists have studied how shamanism and accusations of sorcery define local patterns of power and control. Belief in sorcery, for example, may provide a system of rules and punishments in societies that lack a police force, written laws, and a formal judicial system. It helps people assign a cause to their misfortunes. And it sustains religions that link human beings with the spirit world and with the tropical forest itself.

What I find unsettling, rather, is that New Age America seeks to embrace shamanism without any appreciation of its context. For my Santa Fe acquaintances, tribal lore is a supermarket from which they choose some tidbits while spurning others. . . . Yankush's lifetime of discipline is reduced to a set of techniques for personal development, stripped of links to a specific landscape.

New Age enthusiasts are right to admire the shamanistic tradition, but while advancing it as an alternative to our own healing practices, they brush aside its stark truths. For throughout the world, shamans see themselves as warriors in a struggle against the shadows of the human heart. Shamanism affirms life but also spawns violence and death. The beauty of shamanism is matched by its power—and like all forms of power found in society, it inspires its share of discontent.


*(Editors' note: In 1999, ten years after Brown wrote this text, the shaman he calls Yankush was murdered in a sorcery-related vendetta.)*

# 55.

# Shamans Explore the
# Human Mind

ROGER WALSH

(1990)

*American anthropologist and medical doctor Roger Walsh argues that
the existence of spirits as perceived by shamans is a question that cannot
be decided. He also suggests that shamans are pioneers in exploring as
yet poorly understood capacities of the human mind. Walsh tries to
stake out an agnostic position that remains halfway between bringing
scientists and shamans together and keeping them apart.*

If we are to be completely honest, we must acknowledge that even
now we have not disproved the possible existence of spirits (intelligent, non-material entities independent of the channel's mind) or their
role in some channeling. Indeed, it is not at all clear that it is possible
to disprove them.

To put the matter in more precise philosophical language, we seem
to have here a case of what is called "ontological indeterminacy." This
means that the fundamental nature, or ontological status, of the source
of information cannot be decided definitely because the available information or observation can be interpreted in many ways and we
have no absolute method by which to determine which interpreta-
tion(s) may be best.

Practically speaking, this means that people's interpretations of the phenomena will be largely determined by their personal beliefs, philosophy, and "world hypothesis." The world hypothesis consists of the fundamental beliefs about the nature of the world and reality that underlie the life and work of a community. Most people simply take the consensual assumptions of their culture or subculture unquestioningly and interpret the world accordingly.

People's decisions about the nature of spirits and channeling therefore depend in large part on their prior assumptions about the nature of reality. For example, a person who believes in philosophical materialism assumes that everything that exists is either matter or entirely dependent on matter for its existence. Such a person will obviously view "spirits" very differently from the religious practitioner or theologian who believes in a transcendent realm of pure spirit. For the philosophical materialist all sources of inner wisdom, information, advice, or visions—all perceived entities, voices, and images—are simply mental constructions, the expressions of neuronal fireworks, and probably deranged fireworks at that. From this point of view, shamans' experience and spirits are likewise only creations of mind, and all worlds, spirits, and souls are merely mental projections. Therefore, the materialist considers shamans mistaken at best or psychotic at worst.

Things are very different for the believer in panpsychism. This is the view that everything in the universe, including plants and inanimate objects, has some kind of psychological being or awareness. Those who hold such beliefs will find no problem with the idea that at least some of the helpers, voices, and visions encountered during shamanic experiences are indeed spirits.

Of course, it must be admitted that we have no proof whatsoever that all sources of inner wisdom have the same nature. For all we know, some might be merely aspects of mind, and not terribly impressive aspects at that, while others might conceivably be some transcendent source or sources within or beyond us. At the present time we may simply not be able to decide definitively between these interpretations. Consequently, the only intellectually honest position may be an agnostic view of spirits and channels in which we confess their indeterminacy and our ignorance.

This may be honest but it may not be terribly satisfying. Indeed, it may be annoying and irksome. Yet our annoyance may be a reflection of our unwillingness to tolerate ambiguity and our attachment to our own opinions and world hypothesis. Diverse philosophies and spiritual traditions repeatedly urge us to acknowledge that we just don't know—indeed cannot know—the ultimate nature of many things. We are encouraged to recognize the "radical mystery" of existence and, in the language of Zen, to keep "don't know mind."

In light of all this, the fact that we cannot decide once and for all about the existence of spirits, channels, and nonphysical entities is not so surprising. It simply reflects our current ignorance and perhaps even perpetual limitation on our knowing. This may not be terribly satisfying but it may be usefully humbling.

Given the present limitations on our knowledge, what can we conclude about the shaman's spirits and their counterparts in other countries and centuries? To begin with, it is clearly possible for many people to access inner sources of information and wisdom that may be experienced as entities separate from themselves. The information so obtained may often be trivial, nonsensical, and egotistical, but it may occasionally be meaningful, profound, and life-changing. It appears that we may have underestimated the range and depth of information available within us, the number of ways in which it can be accessed, and the frequency and impact of channeling. For channeling, through its effects on individuals, cultures, and religions, has changed the course of history.

While one can interpret the nature of this process in many ways, it clearly points to realms and capacities of the human mind that as yet are little understood. We may have underestimated ourselves and the wisdom, imagination, and creative power that lie latent within us. Shamans appear to have been the first pioneers to begin exploring and mining these resources.

# 56.

# Training to See What
# the Natives See

EDITH TURNER

(1992)

*American anthropologist Edith Turner wrestles with her discipline's incapacity to take reports about spirits seriously. In her view, breaking out of the academic worldview and seeing spirits as her indigenous informants see them allows her to reach a better, and more ethical, understanding of the phenomenon.*

What spirit events took place in my own experience? One of them went like this. In 1985 I was due for a visit to Zambia. Before going I made up my mind to come closer than I had previously done to the Africans' own experience, whatever that was—I did not really know what. But so it eventuated, I did come closer. The research developed into the study of a twice repeated healing ritual that actually culminated during the second one with my sighting a spirit form. In an article entitled "A Visible Spirit Form in Zambia," I describe exactly how this curative ritual reached its climax, including how I myself was involved in it; how the traditional doctor bent down amid the singing and drumming to extract the harmful spirit and how I saw with my own eyes a large gray blob of plasma emerge from the sick woman's back. Then I knew the Africans were right, there is spirit affliction, it isn't a matter of metaphor and symbol, or even psychology. And I began to see how anthropologists have perpetrated an endless series of put-downs in regard to the many spirit events in which they have participated—participated in a kindly pretense. They might have obtained valuable material, but they have been operating with the wrong paradigm, that of the positivists' denial.

To reach a peak experience in a ritual it really is necessary to sink oneself fully in it. Thus for me, "going native" achieved a breakthrough to an altogether different worldview, foreign to academia, by means of which certain material was chronicled that could have been garnered in no other way. . . .

Members of many different societies, even our own, tell us they have had experience of seeing or hearing spirits. Let us look more closely at how anthropology has been dealing with the question in the past. Mainline anthropologists have studiedly ignored the central matter of this kind of information—central in the people's own view—and only used the material as if it were metaphor or symbol, not reality, commenting that such and such "metaphor" is congruent with the function, structure, or psychological mindset of the society. . . .

So one asks, what are the ethics of this kind of analysis, this dissection? May we continue in this age of multi-power as well as multi-cultures to enter a foreign society, however politely, measure it up according to our own standards, then come back home and dissect it in a way entirely estranged from the ethos of the people concerned? . . .

We eventually have to face the issue head on, and ask, "What are spirits?" And I have to ask the thorny question, "What of the great diversity of ideas about them throughout the world? How is a student of the anthropology of consciousness who participates during fieldwork expected to regard all the conflicting spirit systems in different cultures? Is there not a fatal lack of logic inherent in this diversity?" And an old suspicion returns, "Is this kind of subject matter logical anyway?" Then we need to ask, "Have we the right to force it into logical frameworks?"

Moreover there is disagreement about terms. "Spirits" are referred to in most cultures. Some Native Americans refer to "power." "Energy," ki or chi, is known in Japan and China, and has caught on among western healers. "Energy" was not the right word for the blob that came out of the back of the Ndembu woman, it was a miserable object, purely bad, without any energy at all, and much more akin to the miserable ghosts of suicides. One thinks of energy as formless, but when I see internal organs, the organs aren't "energy," they had form and definition; or when I saw the face of my Eskimo friend Tigluk on a mask, as I saw it in a waking dream, and then saw Tigluk himself by luck a few minutes afterwards, the mask face wasn't "energy," laughing there, it was not in the least abstract. The old-fashioned term, spirit manifestation, is much closer. These are deliberate comings of discernable forms with a conscious intent to communicate, to claim importance in our lives. On the other hand I have indeed sensed energy, very like electrical energy, when submitting to the healing passes of Spiritist women adepts in a mass meeting in Brazil. . . .

Again and again spirit rituals are held, and again and again some indigenous exegete tries to explain that the spirits are present, and that their rituals are the central event of their society. And the anthropologist goes and interprets them differently. There seems to be a kind of force field between the anthropologist and her or his subject matter making it impossible for her or him to come close to it, a kind of religious frigidity. We anthropologists need training to see what the natives see.

# 57

# "Twisted Language," A Technique for Knowing

## GRAHAM TOWNSLEY

## (1993)

*Graham Townsley is a British anthropologist who lived among the Yaminahua people of the Peruvian Amazon. He took the language of Yaminahua shamans seriously, as well as their notions about animate essences in nature, and discovered a coherent way of knowing. There are many reports of a "secret language" among shamans. Townsley is the first, to our knowledge, to have made the effort to decode it. He calls the Yaminahua way of knowing "unthinkable" within the western model of cognition; yet he seems to have thought it out in some detail. He managed to overcome the "force field" between his own cognitive framework and the indigenous one. In so doing, he greatly advanced knowledge about shamans.*

Yaminahua shamanism, like shamanism everywhere, claims for itself a host of extraordinary powers to cure and kill. All of these claims, however, rest on a prior one: shamans understand things in a way that other people just do not. They understand them better and more profoundly. They really know *(tapiakoi)*, they see *(ooiki)*. The idea of this paper is to take this claim seriously and, without diving immediately into familiar anthropological discourses of ritual and symbolism, ask what, exactly, this knowledge might be like. . . .

In this paper I want to look more closely at Yaminahua ideas of knowledge and, finally, at the ways in which shamans construct meanings from the actual experience of their ritual. Although it will first be necessary to discuss some of the basic Yaminahua ideas about the constitution of the world which provide the framework for shamanism and attribute particular significances to its experiences, my focus will, in the end, be upon its practice. The central idea of the paper is that Yaminahua shamanism cannot be defined by a clearly constituted discourse of beliefs, symbols or meanings. It is not a system of knowledge or facts known, but rather an ensemble of techniques for knowing. It is not a constituted discourse but a way of constituting one. Chief amongst these ways and techniques of knowledge are those of song.

The central image dominating the whole field of Yaminahua shamanic knowledge is that of *yoshi*—spirit or animate essence. In Yaminahua thought all things in the world are animated and given their particular qualities by *yoshi*. Shamanic knowledge is, above all, knowledge of these entities, which are also the sources of all the powers that shamanism claims for itself.

Everything about the domain of *yoshi* is marked by an extreme ambiguity—not only for the outside observer, but for the Yaminahua themselves. For most Yaminahua they are things associated with the night, the half-seen and dreams. They are called upon to explain a host of events that seem uncanny, strange or coincidental. However, their significance goes far beyond this; they are implicated in all the literally vital questions of human existence: birth, growth, illness and death.

For humans too are animated by *yoshi*, entities just like the essences of other things, which grow with the body through life and finally cause its death by leaving it and travelling to the land of the dead. The relationship of the *yoshi* to the body in life is a tenuous one. It is said to wander and be subject to the influences of other *yoshi*. It is these influences which are used to explain all illness and constitute the field of shamanic activity.

The basic parameters of shamanic knowledge are thus formed around this highly ambiguous relationship of animate essences and bodies. The source of the ambiguity is that while *yoshi* are very much a part of nature and the bodies they animate, they are at the same time quite beyond them, in a realm where even the *yoshi* of trees and insects live intelligent, volitional lives. . . .

In one way, then, a *yoshi* is simply all the empirical characteristics of the thing with which it is associated, hypostatized and raised to the status of some independent being—an essence. This at least accounts for the very high degree of empirical knowing involved in shamanism. To know the *yoshi* of something is to know in detail the appearance, behaviour and characteristics of the thing it animates. This fine-tuned empiricism is evident throughout shamanic practice and in the shamanic songs to be discussed later.

But *yoshi* are much more than this. They also have an intelligent, volitional existence in a supra-sensory realm. It is this fact which, for the Yaminahua, makes them so hard to know. The only established discourse about this realm is that of mythology. The creation myths which tell how, out of the original chaotic flux of the "time of dawnings," the things of this world came to be, are not simply regarded by shamans as tales of some distant past. The powerful flux of the "time of dawnings" is regarded as in some senses still present in the spirit world. It is precisely these mythical, transformational powers with which *yoshi* are charged and that shamans see themselves as tapping. Origin myths are seen as providing "paths" into this spirit world and true accounts of the nature of *yoshi*. This is why shamans will sometimes chant origin myths, transformed into the elliptical language of shamanic song, because these are "the paths which take you to a *yoshi*." The Yaminahua are only too aware of the extreme ambiguities and paradoxes surrounding *yoshi*. All accounts of them stress their mutability and the fundamental difficulty of knowing them. As a shaman, who like all shamans claims to see and deal with them directly, said to me: "You never really know *yoshi*—they are like something you recognize and at the same time they are different—like when I see Jaguar—there is something about him like a jaguar, but perhaps something like a man too—and he changes . . ." For the Yaminahua there is no possible unitary description of a *yoshi*. They are always "like . . . and not like," "the same . . . but different." This profound duality marks not only all accounts of them but is reflected in all shamanic and ritual dealings with them. As I will discuss later in this paper, these are consciously and deliberately constructed in an elliptical and multi-referential fashion so as to mirror the refractory nature of the beings who are their objects. . . .

Given that shamanic knowledge, beyond its empirical and mythic content, is constituted as a set of ideas and techniques related primarily to dreams, controlled hallucinations and all that a European would call the imaginary, it seems important to consider the Yaminahua model of cognition which frames this knowledge and gives it its particular weight. One of the keys to this knowledge and, more widely, the whole question of the so-called "primitive mind" which shamanism has so often been taken to exemplify, seems to me to lie exactly in an image of the person and knowing subject which, paradoxically, has no place for a "mind" and associates "mental" events with animate essences which can drift free from bodies and mingle with the world, participating in it much more intimately than any conventional notion of "mind" would allow. . . .

In their notion of the person, the Yaminahua have a simple tripartite schema: a body; a social, human self associated with reason and language; an animate, perceiving self which is neither so social nor human, mingling easily with the non-human *yoshi* who are beings of the same type. It can be seen, then, how the Yaminahua have no notion of anything that would approach our idea of "mind" as an inner storehouse of meanings, thought and experience quite separate from the world. All that is "mental" is the property of entities which, although closely related to particular bodies, are not permanently attached to them. It is through the relationship between these two entities that the whole arena of Yaminahua thought about the sameness and difference between the human and non-human develops. And as should be clear by now, it is through the idea of *yoshi* that the fundamental sameness of the human and the non-human takes shape, creating the space for the animal transformations of the human and the attribution of mental and human characteristics to all aspects of nature. This, of course, is the arena of shamanism. . . .

What Yaminahua shamans do, above everything else, is sing. Songs are a shaman's most highly prized possessions, the vehicles of his powers and the repositories of his knowledge. They are usually sung under the influence of a hallucinogenic brew *(shori) [ayahuasca]* made from lianas of the *Banisteriopsis* family and a shrub, *Psychotria viridis.* Learning to be a shaman is learning to sing, to intone the powerful chant rhythms, to carefully thread together verbal images couched in the abstruse metaphorical language of shamanic song, and follow them. "A song is a path—you make it straight and clean then you walk along it."

What a shaman actually does when he cures is sing. His singing will be intermittently accompanied by the blowing of tobacco smoke on the patient or a more rapid, vigorous and staccato blowing onto the crown of the patient's head, but the effective healing power is thought to originate in the song. The blowing effects a sort of physical transfer of the meaning and power of the song into the patient. The word *koshuiti* has its roots in an onomatopeia: *kosh—kosh—kosh* as an imitation of that controlled, staccato blowing sound. The association of different types of breathing with shamanic action is a central one. Thus in contrast to *koshuiti* we have *shooiti,* witchcraft songs, also an onomatopeia: *shoo—shoo—shoo* as an imitation of the powerful, prolonged breath which will "blow away" its victim's soul. The "power" of a shaman's breath is seen as the foremost sign of his bodily transformation. One of the reasons dolphins are feared as shamans is that they unmistakably breath in these "powerful" shamanic ways.

Although these songs are usually sung under the influence of *shori,* I was told on a number of occasions that the *koshuiti* of a really good shaman would be effective even without the drug. Nevertheless, *shori* and shamanic song are inextricably bound up together. It is *shori* that is always considered to give primary access to the world of animate essences. Most Yaminahua men take *shori* regularly and they all sing

to the *yoshi* visions which the drug induces. The songs they sing, however, are not *koshuiti*; they are called *rabiai* and have a different form,
language and intention. They are sung in ordinary, everyday speech.
They are intended to stimulate and clarify the visions of the *yoshi* from
which knowledge might be gained but they are not credited with any
magical efficacy.

*Koshuiti* on the other hand are thought to have real efficacy and are
only sung by shamans. As already mentioned, their language is made
up of metaphoric circumlocutions or unusual words for common things
which are either archaic or borrowed from neighbouring languages.
Each song is defined by a core constellation of these metaphors. Songs
do not have fixed and invariant texts although, particularly in the case
of songs constructed from myths, they may have a minimally fixed
narrative sequence of metaphors and images. Beyond this, the actual
performance of a song is dictated by the skill, intentions and particular visionary experience of the shaman who is singing it. Shamans are
certainly aware of this element of individuality in the performance of
songs and, indeed, are proud of it. They also create new songs and in-
vent fresh metaphors, as is obviously the case with those to airplanes,
outboard motors and so forth. Nevertheless, they do not view even
these modern songs as a totally personal creation. In fact, they are
adamant that the songs are not ultimately created or owned by them at
all, but by the *yoshi* themselves, who "show" or "give" their songs, with
their attendant powers, to those shamans good enough to "receive"
them. Thus, for instance, in their portrayal of the process of initiation,
it is the *yoshi* who teach and bestow powers on the initiate; other
shamans only facilitate the process and prepare the initiate, "clean him
out," so as to receive these spirit powers.

The songs are metaphoric in two distinct ways. They make very
little direct reference to the illness or to the real situation which the
song is intended to influence. Instead, they create elaborate analogies
to it. Confronted by an illness, a shaman sings a song to the moon, to
an animal, or perhaps chants a myth. This is the first way in which
these songs are metaphoric; the overall form of the song as a whole is

constituted by an extended analogy to the real context of the song's performance. . . .

However, at least in the Yaminahua case, the idea that this use of analogy has its rationale in the intent to change the patient's consciousness runs counter to the whole rationale of shamanic practice which, as we shall see, is intended to construct a particular type of visionary experience in the shaman himself and a communication, not with other humans, but with the non-human *yoshi* who populate that visionary experience. The clue to this is given by the fact that most Yaminahua can barely understand the songs. Many shamanic songs are almost totally incomprehensible to all but other shamans. The reason for this is the extensive use of the other mode of metaphorization mentioned. The actual language of the song, used to build up the overall analogy, is itself densely metaphoric. Almost nothing in these songs is referred to by its normal name. The abstrusest metaphoric circumlocutions are used instead. For example, night becomes "swift tapirs," the forest becomes "cultivated peanuts," fish are "peccaries," jaguars are "baskets," anacondas are "hammocks" and so forth. Most Yaminahua are at a loss to understand the senses of these esoteric metaphors. . . .

Whatever it is that other actors understand, it is not such texts, facts or truths, which would all be communicated much better if patients and others could follow the imagery of the songs clearly. They can seldom do this. In the course of trying to understand a number of the songs I had recorded, I could often find *no* non-shaman, even among apprentice shamans, who could make the slightest sense of them.

The important thing, emphasized by all shamans, is that none of the things referred to in the song should be referred to by their proper names. One might assume that these circumlocutions were not consciously metaphoric usages at all, but culturally fixed equivalents which were learnt and employed automatically with no awareness of their metaphoric content. This is certainly not so. In every instance the metaphoric logic of these song-words could be explained with no hesitation. In every case the basic sense of these usages was carried by finely observed perceptual resemblances between the song-word and its referent. Thus fish become "white-collared peccaries" because of the resemblance of a fish's gill to the white dashes on this type of peccary's neck; jaguars become "baskets" because the fibers of this particular type of loose-woven basket *(wonati)* form a pattern precisely similar to a jaguar's markings, rain becomes "big cold lean-to" because the slanting sheets of rain in a downpour resemble the slanting roofs of the lean-tos which the Yaminahua build for shelter when they are away from the village.

Shamans are clearly aware of the underlying sense of their *koshuiti* metaphors and refer to them as *tsai yoshtoyoshto*—"twisted language" (literally: language twisting-twisting). But why do they use them? All explanations clearly indicated that these were associated with the clarity of visionary experience which the songs were intended to create. "With my *koshuiti* I want to see—singing, I carefully examine things— twisted language brings me close but not too close—with normal words I would crash into things—with twisted ones I circle around them—I can see them clearly."

There is a complex representation of the use of metaphor and its capacity to create immediate and precise images, contained within these simple words. Everything said about shamanic songs points to the fact that as they are sung the shaman actively visualizes the images referred to by the external analogy of the song, but that he does this through a carefully controlled "seeing as" the different things actually named by the internal metaphors of his song. This "seeing as" in some way creates a space in which powerful visionary experience can occur. It is in this visionary experience that the magical efficacy of the song is thought to lie. The song is the path which he both makes and follows. It sustains and directs his vision. Whether or not the patient can understand the song is irrelevant to its efficacity as far as he is concerned. . . .

It is, of course, this ability to create and reflect images of great complexity, in the direct and immediate fashion of a creative insight, that has given metaphor its central place in, for instance, European poetic traditions, as Ricoeur and many others have pointed out. It is thus not hard to see how, by only using words which draw attention to the minute similarities between dissimilars, the shaman tries to sharpen his images at the same time as creating a space in which his visions can develop. His statement that normal words would make him "crash into things" conveys the idea well enough.

However, the whole context of thought surrounding this metaphorizing is obviously radically different from that of the poetic metaphor, both in the degree of reality attributed to the things imaged and in their capacity to affect the world. *Yoshi* are real beings who are both "like and not like" the things they animate. They have no stable or unitary nature and thus, paradoxically, the "seeing as" of "twisted language" is the only way of adequately describing them. Metaphor here is not improper naming but the only proper naming possible. The whole strategy of the song is precisely to drag these refractory meanings and images of the *yoshi* world out into this one and embed them unambiguously in a real body. It is interesting in this context that the only thing named by direct, as opposed to "twisted" language, is the woman's body itself at the moment in which, precisely, the images of the song are intended to physically "crash" into it, effecting the real cure.

This conversion of the meaningful into the material is, of course, unthinkable from the standpoint of a model of cognition which places all meaning operations in a "mind," something interior to the person which leaves the material world unaffected. From this standpoint, not even the often mentioned idea of "illocutionary force," or of any speech act or narrative which changes the world by redefining it or changing people's perception of it, could possibly encompass the sheer physicality of the transformations claimed by shamanism. As mentioned before, from the very different standpoint of the Yaminahua model of cognition, the idea that experiences and meanings can be embedded in the non-human world is a less problematic one. It is the concept of a type of perceiving animate essence shared by the human and the non-human alike, creating for them a shared space of interaction, which opens up this "magical" arena of shamanism.

# 58.

# Magic Darts as Viruses

JEAN-PIERRE CHAUMEIL

(1993)

*In lowland Amazonia, shamans attack one another's communities by sending illnesses and other misfortunes in the form of darts, which are invisible to non-shamans. French anthropologist Jean-Pierre Chaumeil finds close correspondences between these shamanic darts and viruses. In his view, Amazonian societies understand how viruses work. The difference between their medical practice and western medicine lies in their respective belief systems.*

Generally speaking, these invisible projectiles are owned by shamans, who keep them inside their own bodies (in the stomach, chest, or arm), and "nourish" them, either directly with their own blood, or with tobacco smoke or juice, which they consume throughout their career; this enables the darts to grow and even to reproduce inside the body. It is generally accepted that these darts come from the supernatural world, mainly from invisible entities or forest spirits with which shamans enter into contact during their initiation. These darts are most often associated with viscous masses or "phlegms," which envelop them delicately (according to the Yagua), or in which they bathe (according to the Jivaro), and which somehow constitute their embryonic or matrix form. The Yagua also say that the phlegm stops the projectiles from sticking together through mutual attraction. They assimilate the phlegm to a lubrifying substance that covers the internal walls of the main organs and facilitates the darts' circulation. According to this definition, the magical projectiles are either a phlegm digest or concentrate, or an embryo conserved in a kind of amniotic liquid. However, the magic-dart concept cannot be reduced to this sole definition. In several indigenous languages, the word for *dart* also means spirit, force, supernatural power, energy, or knowledge (in Quechua, the word for *dart* is *yachay,* from *yacha*: "to know"). It would be difficult to define either of these concepts separately. The notion of power, for instance, inasmuch as it allows itself to be apprehended as such, designates or implies in most societies a force (vital, magic, warlike, or shamanic), the mastery of visions or substances (magic, fragrant, tasty, etc.) or knowledge (ritual, spiritual, esoteric). According to this view, magic darts are as much principles of knowlege, or a body of knowledge, as they are a pathogenic or therapeutic power.

Far from constituting inert objects, the darts are perceived as living entities, which can grow, reproduce, and move around at great speed over very long distances. In this respect, one compares them at times to luminous beams, and that is how they often appear to apprentice shamans. They are also said to be charged with "electricity," like a lightning bolt, or capable of a great force of attraction, like a magnet. However, these "electrical" entities are endowed with very relative autonomy. They do not move around freely in nature but are controlled by forest spirits. Some groups like the Achuar actually have generic spirits for each category of dart. The shamans get pathogenic (or therapeutic) substances from supernatural instances which are themselves sources of illness, given that they possess the darts. The indigenous people therefore seem to be quite familiar with the notion of pathogenic agents in the natural state, but they see them as "controlled" rather than freely moving. . . .

In most cases, contact with the spirits that own the darts requires the ingestion of hallucinogenic beverages, which are prepared, among others, from the *Banisteriopsis caapi* vine, known regionally as *ayahuasca* or *yagé*. To constitute the most diversified stock of darts as possible, shamans must contact as many spirits as they can and increase the number of hallucinogenic doses they absorb in consequence. As a general rule, shamans keep exact accounts of the number of darts they own. To stay competitive, they must keep a constant supply of darts, by feeding them or by getting new ones from the source.

The darts are exteriorized with the help of tobacco smoke or juice, which has the power to make the projectiles "climb back up" toward the mouth or the extremity of a member, depending on the case. . . .

Projected into space, the darts remain in contact with their owner by sound messages, chants, or invisible filaments, and they occasionally communicate among each other by diverse acoustic means (whistling, rustling, etc.). Among the Shuar, the auxiliary spirits called *pasuk* are the ones that mediate relations with the darts, as they are the only ones who speak the darts' "languages." . . .

Each kind of dart is often associated with a type of illness that it is supposed to inoculate and sometimes heal. . . .

The ways of extracting pathogenic darts from the body of victims are quite similar across the western Amazon. They consist of massages, puffs of tobacco smoke, and suctions. However, in some cases, extraction is only possible if the healer has homologous darts, i.e., belonging to the same category as those in the patient's body. The latter will then be "seduced" or "attracted" as if by magnetization and will not be able to resist the desire to join their homologues, thereby ensuring the patient's recovery. Here, the potentially pathogenic and therapeutic character of the darts is evident. Once the pathogenic projectiles are captured, they can be destroyed (by burning, among other techniques) or sent back to the presumed aggressor or to a member of his or her family. They can also be incorporated into the healer's stock of darts. Finally, we should emphasize that most of these notions are widespread in the regional mestizo society. . . .

Not only does the shaman accumulate pathogenic agents in his organism, but he "cultivates" them, and "produces" new ones by feeding them tobacco juice or smoke (or other ingredients). The darts will then reproduce themselves in his body like freshly planted cuttings. Besides, the shaman's body undergoes a feminization during initiation. According to Harner, the transfer of Jivaro darts is very explicitly compared to childbirth, accompanied by a *couvade*. The shaman's body becomes a kind of virological complex, which not only carries viruses but also produces them (as well as counterviruses). . . .

The darts also have a therapeutic value, as a suction force or remedy; like magnets, they "suck up" darts that are generally of the same type and that are lodged in the body. According to the Jivaro, the latter are seduced by their homologues and can then merge into the shaman's corresponding phlegm. Although this is not an absolute rule, it is often necessary to have the same kind of dart as the incriminated object, in order to heal. Sometimes it is necessary to sing the same song as the one recognized as having provoked the illness. Everything happens as if one were dealing with a healing system based on similarities, "virus against virus," that inevitably makes one think of the homeopathic principle of the countervirus.

The darts also form an armor (breastplate, belt, or protection shield) all around the shaman's body (and even around houses). This armor's very tight mesh is reputed to stop all enemy projectiles. This concept of the dart-armor is very widespread in the upper Amazon, among indigenous people as well as among mestizos, who call it *arkana* (from the Quechua *arkay:* "to stop, block, close"). This protection system seems to constitute a form of autoimmune defense acquired by the shaman, who would then appear to be a partially immunized, or vaccinated, body. We have previously described the gradual process of habituation to the pathogenic agent to which the novice must submit, by swallowing pathogenic substances transmitted "mouth to mouth" by a practicing shaman. Likewise, during cures, shamans often stick several darts in their throats, to capture, immobilize, or neutralize the extracted projectile, which they then "vomit" out, or incorporate in their dart stock. They may also do this simply to avoid being affected by the syndromes of their patient and to stop the incriminated dart from insinuating itself into their own organism. . . .

To sum up, whether one considers the darts as agents of illness, therapy, or immunity, everything occurs as if one were dealing with a vast "ethnovirological" complex. Its particularity is the "produced" and "controlled" character of the pathogenic and therapeutic agents that constitute it. One could conclude that, if we produce vaccines and not viruses, indigenous Amazonians seem to have the opposite tendency and "produce" viruses and not vaccines—with the exception, of course, of the "virus producers" themselves, namely, the shamans. In other words the Amazonian societies do not seem to have waited for the arrival of western medicine to understand the functioning principles of a virological system. Examining one aspect of their medical practice shows that they are familiar with its broad lines, the difference lying essentially in the associated belief systems. It is for this reason, no doubt, that the two medicines have always had, until now and with very few exceptions, the greatest difficulties in understanding each other.

# 59.

# Bubble, Bubble, Toil and Trouble: Tourists and Pseudo-Shamans

## MARLENE DOBKIN DE RIOS

## (1994)

*American anthropologist and psychotherapist Marlene Dobkin de Rios has studied the uses of hallucinogenic plants in Amazonian towns for three decades. In the 1990's she found numerous tourists seeking ayahuasca shamans, and finding hucksters. Here, two worlds come together while remaining apart.*

In Peru and Brazil, in Amazonian cities and large towns, there are Mestizo men who become instant traditional healers or ayahuasqueros without undergoing any apprenticeship period, without having any teachers, and without control. They provide American and European tourists mixtures of ten or more different hallucinogenic plants to help them become embedded in the universe and to provide mystical experiences for them. The hallucinogenic plants in question have never been used traditionally in the way that the self-styled healers use them, and there are numerous psychological casualties. The so-called healers fight among themselves, and they have their champions abroad who function as travel agents and tour guides. . . .

A Peruvian lawyer I know described to me a drug session in Iquitos, Peru, that he attended three years ago. There were about 14 people who were taken from the Amazon Lodge where they were staying to a jungle clearing. Two of the people were diplomats from the Russian Embassy in Lima. There were also four Japanese professionals, a business manager from Lima, four Germans and two Australians—all very well-educated and prosperous-looking. The tour lasted four days, and the ayahuasca session took place on the second night. The lawyer laughed when he told me about this session because the Russians vomited violently and with each upheaval, the ayahuasca maestro kept saying, "Go on, vomit up Stalin! Go on, vomit up Lenin!"

Travel literature includes terms like "advanced shamanic training," which is coupled with descriptions of healer so-and-so who has explored inner space, or other such terminology to cue the tourist as to the real meaning. Expensive brochures which cost thousands of dollars to produce in color-separated glory, tell us that we can go on "a spirited journey to . . . the Amazon to study the healing and spiritual transformation techniques of the jungle medicine men. . . . We take part in a night-long ritual led by shaman X to heal ourselves and take the next step in our spiritual development. The next leg of our journey takes us to the headwaters of the Amazon River where amid fresh water dolphins, monkeys and parrots we take part in a three day vision quest led by jungle shamans X and Y." . . .

The "shamans" are hardly tribal natives. Rather, they are middle-class men (generally no women are involved) who have previously hawked goods or services of one kind or another. They see in these Western tourists a source of income; they recognize the tourists' thirst for the exotic. . . . These enterprising middle-class men make money, seduce women, and obtain personal power and control over others from their activities with drugs. Their agents abroad often earn as much as eight to ten thousand dollars from a three-week trip to exotic regions. . . .

The authentic ayahuasca healer has esoteric knowledge not widely shared in his own society. Personal power—access to the world of spirit forces—is important to him, and the healers use their presumed power to treat illness, to bewitch others, and to manage situations in their favor. Ayahuasca healers spend a good deal of time involved in issues of personal aggrandizement. The spiritual quest of New Age upscale tourists are about as foreign to them as belief in animal spirits is to the average American. . . .

There is an evil, exploitive aspect in this touristic enterprise that is impossible to ignore. These "native healers" are common drug dealers, dressed for deception. They provide the exotic setting and prep the tourist to have an "authentic personal experience." Theater is based on illusion and facade. This Amazon drug tourism does not dismantle the illusion or destroy the sense of the exotic. It does, on occasion, leave psychotic depression and confusion in its wake. As a licensed psychotherapist, I have personally interviewed one woman for several hours who was exhibiting psychotic symptoms as the result of her multiple drug experiences and romantic entanglement with one "healer" in Pucallpa, Peru. Another woman, suffering a chronic liver ailment, continues to seek out ayahuasca experiences in Brazil despite the danger to her health.

We may learn a lesson from a quotation from Laura Huxley, writing about her husband Aldous. She was asked if he ever administered LSD to a person other than herself or acted as a guide for someone. She replied, "A guide becomes a person of great power, like a warlock, a witch or a shaman. We always thought that being a guide required a very high ethical sense, because of the ways one could take advantage of people."

# 60.

# Shamans and Ethics in a Global World

ELEANOR OTT

(1995)

*Shamans require a grounded cosmology and the support and criticism of their community to deal with their shadow selves and the dark side of power. American anthropologist Eleanor Ott has a keen eye for good questions. She asks: How can people, who call themselves shamans and operate as individuals outside such a context, act ethically? And in a world where tightly knit communities are giving way to globally interconnected individuals, can there still be "shamans"?*

Until recently the shaman was the heartbeat of a tightly knit indigenous or traditional community that integrated the social and spiritual, material and mythic realms. The shaman, as keeper of generations of accumulated knowledge and experience, entered ecstatic flight not for personal gain or to foster inner growth, but to maintain a reciprocal relationship between the human and the other-than-human worlds, talk with the spirits and return with wisdom and healing. Today many who dub themselves shamans no longer belong to a culture or community embedded in such a shamanic perspective, but rather come from the present generation of those primarily searching to find themselves. Thus, many of the new shamans are ill-equipped to engage in their practice of working with clients who come to them with a variety of physical, psychic, and spiritual ailments. The traditional indigenous shaman has the accumulated cultural experience and wisdom of generations of healers connected to a cosmology that gives meaning to both the illnesses and the shaman's processes of curing them. By contrast, many of the new shamans have but limited knowledge of any cosmology that could inform them and surround them with a sense of rootedness and ultimate meaning. Many of them receive but limited training, some only from second- or third-hand sources, such as anthropologists who once came in contact with shamanism during their field work, or from persons who have had no direct or primary personal experience of the shamanic craft. Perhaps worst of all, some new shamans believe such information and experience can be gleaned from books, without any human teacher whatsoever. . . . All of this results in the new shamans being isolated from a conceptual and contextual community that has an integrated world view and mythos that is incomplete without the role of the shaman.

This isolation from the checks and balances that a supportive and also critical community provides places these new shamans in the ethically questionable situation of doing certain traditional shamanic practices, such as attempting to heal illnesses of the body, mind, or spirit, outside of the bonds that informed and tied the earlier shaman to a cultural community. They are, in fact, outside of any long-standing tradition altogether. This same isolation is the cause of many problems that face the new shamans. Especially this is true in issues of ethics, which depend on a cultural context for their resolution. . . .

Even though no less a scholar than Mircea Eliade applies the term shaman more or less across the board to any one who undertakes "magical flight," who "specializes in a trance during which his soul is believed to leave his body and ascend to the sky or descent to the underworld," Eliade does add this essential qualifier which we would do well to remember: "As for the shamanic techniques of ecstasy, they do not exhaust all the varieties of ecstatic experience documented in the history of religions and religious ethnology. Hence any ecstatic cannot be considered a shaman."

Does this leave us with a clear picture of who the shaman is or of what the shaman does with regard to trance or magical flight? No, and this is the point. The picture is not one but many, because of the incredible richness and diversity of cultural experiences throughout the world. This makes it both hard and easy to use the term shaman. Hard because it is not always readily apparent who among the various practitioners in a society are the shamans, or healers, dreamers, witches and wizards, priestesses and priests, etc. The lines between these categories and others are not the same among the many peoples of the world. Easy because the word shaman can thus be readily slipped on, like a second-hand sweater, even when there may be no justification for it.

Despite the restraint of scholars, the situation today is that the word shaman has been usurped by the popular imagination and the popular marketplace, and is now superimposed on all manner of persons who bear little or no resemblance to a traditional shaman in any culture. Without a community that recognizes the new shamans as an integral part of the culture, what makes these people in fact shamans at all except that they so call themselves? Attendant on this is the issue of what techniques and practices the new shaman is competent to carry out, and how the new shaman avoids the problems of ego inflation, lust for power, greed, and other psychological issues that can arise to test the new shaman's integrity. . . .

Those who seek to manipulate the day to day ordinary world by reaching their hands into the other world of the spirits to bring back other worldly powers open themselves to the possibility of encountering spirits that harm as well as spirits that heal. Dare we doubt that this can be so? Frank Speck told us that among the Penobscot, the *mede'olinas.kwe* was "accredited with the power to kill or injure creatures by pointing a finger at them." The power to do such malevolent work comes from the dark side of the spirit world which one can also encounter in trance, and which one can call to oneself if one is taken over by the motive to seize power for harm. The shaman can be possessed by the greed for power over others, the power that injures, just as much as the shaman can be motivated to work with spirits who provide power on behalf of others, the power that heals.

Let us look at this carefully. Power is directed by the shaman's own inner will for evil or for good. In this sense, power itself is neutral and available to the shaman who shapes power by his own, by her own intention, desire, motive, drive, and will. Especially for the new shaman isolated from a watchful community, it is more difficult to remain pure in heart with regard to issues of power. The fact that the petitioner receives information or direction from the spirit world to act in a certain way or to do a certain thing does not in and of itself justify that action or guarantee that that action will be benevolent. All manner of spirits are there to lead those who turn to the spirit world. But *which* spirits come to the petitioner depends totally on the integrity and intention of the one who is seeking them. When the shaman holds clearly the map of the community's mythos, then the shaman is able to discern among the spirits and to perceive the meaning or truth of the messages the spirits deliver.

The person who talks with spirits must be able to tell what is good information from what is not good information. Here the purpose, the reason for seeking spirit aid means everything. The shaman, according to Eliade, is able "to communicate" with spirits in the other world "without thereby becoming their instrument." We must also add to this, that the shaman is able first to identify who the spirits are who respond to the drumming call, and then, second, not to be seduced by these spirits or possessed by them. Possession by spirits in trance does occur, even among shamans, but the main distinguishing mark of the shaman is that he, that she is able to be in two worlds at once, in this world and in the other world simultaneously.

The issue of what kind of spirits choose to speak to the practitioner does not arise when the person is disciplined, aware of the dangers, is being clear with her- or himself about her or his own underlying motives, and is paying attention to *who* the spirits are who are speaking in reply.

The problem is more likely to happen when the practitioner forgets or ignores the discipline, and allows their vigilance to wander or waver. Under these circumstances, such a person may well be unaware of how difficult it is to recognize or acknowledge that the spirit who visits them may be a projection of their own mind and not a genuine vision visited on their trance mind from the spirit world. Either consciously or unconsciously, each of us can be facile in duping ourselves into thinking or believing whatever serves our ends.

Without a map of the cultural, contextual mythos to which the practitioner belongs, how can such a person possibly evaluate what comes through from the so-called spirit world? How can such a person discriminate between wishful thinking, wish fulfillment and the genuine thing? Only with vigilance and the constant discipline of honestly examining one's own motives, of bringing one's deepest urges for power and control to light, can one get beyond one's own shadow self.

Today where is the community that is consciously wakeful to what the magician, the shaman is doing and so is able and ready to hold up the mirror of critique or censure? . . .

Perhaps the new shamans should consider whether it is important or appropriate in any way to call themselves shamans in order to practice whatever techniques they have mastered for the benefit of others. For some few perhaps who are willing and able to make the lifetime commitment to the discipline that is required, it is appropriate. But for most others, the mantle of the shaman is only a veneer, an outer covering, which they put on and take off as convenient. Better, and more honest, to think of themselves, and call themselves by some other name than by the name that carries with it the weight and responsibility of shaman. However, by whatever title one assumes, the ethical issues remain. As soon as one presumes to be in contact with spirits and powers in the other world, in the world one can contact through trance, then one takes on at the very least the responsibility to act with ethical clarity. . . .

The many roles of the ancient shaman will never totally be acted out again, the world is too much altered and changed. Yet there are aspects of the ancient work that are still valid today because all people share basic human needs for the nourishment and well-being of the body, mind, and spirit. So long as these aspects of life remain ephemeral and uncertain, there will always be a place for the person who can provide relief from the illnesses, pains, and insecurities that humans suffer. The challenge for the new shaman today, if indeed there must be new shamans, is to maintain a strong personal ethical balance, free of self-delusion. This requires wisdom and knowledge and a lifetime commitment to this awesome responsibility. For some few this may be possible. For most, it is better to use their abilities in more contained but equally effective ways, as doctors, psychotherapists, teachers, artists, writers, priests, and others for whom having a relationship with the spirit world is essential for the fulfilment of what they do. For this kind of life, the title shaman is both misleading and unnecessary. . . .

In the past, the shaman was the center of a small tightly knit community that saw itself as the people, and who believed their home place was the center of the world. Today no people can afford such luxury. Every people is inter-connected with every other people around the globe. The shaman today, if there are to be shamans today, must break free of the limited, restricted, ethnocentric view of the past, and must regard the whole world as the home place. They must go beyond all national, cultural, and ethnic barriers. The term "shaman" may no longer be able to carry the additional meaning of the person whose community is the world, and whose duty it is to engage in helping to heal the world.

# 61.

# Shamans as Botanical Researchers

## WADE DAVIS
## (1995)

*Canadian Wade Davis is an ethnobotanist trained in anthropology and biology. He has spent years conducting research in different countries, and has lived among fifteen indigenous societies in the Amazon and the Andes. He considers shamans to be researchers and intellectual peers, and favors a dialogue between shamans and scientists to counter the destruction of tropical forests.*

Possibly the greatest economic potential of ethnobotany lies in the area of folk medicine. Annual worldwide sales of plant-derived pharmaceuticals currently total over $20 billion, and a great many of these drugs were first discovered by traditional healers in folk contexts. The gifts of the shaman and the sorcerer, the herbalist and the witch, include such critical drugs as pilocarpine, digitoxin, vincristine, emetine, physostigmine, atropine, morphine, and reserpine. The forests of tropical America have yielded scopolamine, cocaine, quinine, and d-tubocurarine. An impressive 70 percent of all plants known to have antitumor properties have been found in tropical forests.

This wealth of vital drugs has come from but a minor segment of the tropical flora. In the Amazon approximately 1 percent of the plants have been studied chemically and an astonishing 90 percent have not yet been subjected to even a superficial chemical analysis. Any practical strategy for expanding our knowledge of this living "pharmaceutical factory" must include ethnobotanical research. To attempt to assay the entire flora without consulting Amazonian Indians would be logistically impossible and intellectually foolish.

Yet if ethnobotanists are to seize upon traditional knowledge as a means of rationalizing the preservation of threatened rain forests, they must do far more than search for new wealth. The tropical forest, with its thousand themes and the infinitude of form, shape, and texture, appears at times to mock the terminology of the Western scientist. Millennia ago men and women entered that forest, and through adaptation, cultures emerged, hundreds of them, the complexities of which rivaled even those of the dense vegetation out of which they were born. To stay alive, these men and women invented a way of life and, lacking the technology to transform the forest, they chose instead to understand it.

The intellectual achievements of Amazonian Indians suggest that the ultimate challenge of ethnobotany will lie not merely in the identification and extraction of natural products, but rather in the discovery and elaboration of a profoundly different way of living with the forest. Consider the Waorani of eastern Ecuador. Like many Amazonian groups, the Waorani identify both psychologically and cosmologically with the rain forest. Since they depend on that environment for a large part of their diet, it is not surprising that they are exceptionally skilled naturalists. It is the sophistication of their interpretation of biological relationships that is astounding. Not only do they recognize such conceptually complex phenomena as pollination and fruit dispersal, they understand and accurately predict animal behavior. They anticipate flowering and fruiting cycles of all edible forest plants, know the preferred foods of most forest animals, and may even explain where any particular animal prefers to pass the night. Waorani hunters can detect the scent of animal urine at forty paces in the forest and can accurately identify the species of animal from which it came.

Confronted by this awesome sensitivity to the surrounding forest one cannot help but reflect on whether the ethnobotanical community has really paused to consider the implications of such awareness. Ethnobotanists recognize the shaman as an intellectual peer and properly delineate the experimental nature of shamanistic practice. Yet when we attempt to account for these discoveries, the phrase that is inevitably employed is "trial and error." It is a reasonable term and may well account for certain processes and transformations, but at another level it is a euphemism disguising our ignorance of how Amazonian Indians come up with their insights. Consider, for example, two well-known Amazonian preparations—the arrow or dart poison curare and the hallucinogen ayahuasca. The former is derived principally from a number of species in several genera of lianas (e.g., species of *Chondrodendron, Abuta,* and *Curarea*), and the latter is also a liana (*Banisteriopsis* species). In both instances the active principles are found in the bark.

What is fascinating about these preparations from an epistemological point of view is their elaboration, which involves a number of procedures that are either exceedingly complex or that yield a product the use of which would not have been inherently obvious to the inventor. In the case of curare, the bark is rasped and placed in a funnel-shaped leaf compress suspended between two hunting spears. Cold water is then percolated through and the drippings collected in a ceramic pot. This dark-colored liquid is slowly heated over a fire and brought to a frothy boil numerous times until the fluid thickens. It is then cooled and later reheated until a thick layer of viscous scum gradually forms on the surface. This scum is removed, the dart tips are spun in the viscid fluid, and the darts are then carefully dried by the fire. The procedure itself is mundane. The realization, however, that this orally inactive substance, derived from but a handful of the hundreds of forest lianas, could kill when administered intramuscularly is profound.

In the case of ayahuasca it is the sophistication of the actual preparation that is impressive. The drug may be prepared in various ways but usually the fresh bark is scraped from the stem and boiled for several hours until a thick, bitter liquid is produced. The active compounds are the B-carbolines harmine and harmaline, the subjective effects of which are suggested by the fact that when first isolated they were known as telepathine.

Significantly, the psychoactive effects of ayahuasca are enhanced dramatically by the addition of a number of subsidiary plants. This is an important feature of many folk preparations and it is due in part to the fact that different chemical compounds in relatively small concentrations may effectively potentiate each other. In the case of ayahuasca, the usual admixtures are the leaves of two shrubs (*Psychotria viridis* and *P. carthaginensis*) and a scandent liana (*Diplopterys cabrerana*). All three of these plants contain tryptamines that are orally inactive, unless monoamine oxidase inhibitors are present. The B-carbolines found in *Banisteriopsis caapi* are inhibitors of precisely this kind, and thus they potentiate the tryptamines. The result is a powerful synergistic effect, a biochemical version of the whole being greater than the sum of the parts.

The experimental process that originally led to the manipulation and combination of these morphologically dissimilar plants, and the discovery of their unique chemical properties, is far more profound that the phrase "trial and error" suggests. The patterns that any researcher—and the shaman most certainly has earned that title—observes in nature depend on cognitive constructs and an intellectual synthesis, and reflect, in turn, culturally patterned thoughts and values. Sensitivity to nature is not an innate attribute of South American Indians. It is a consequence of adaptive choices that have resulted in the development of highly specialized perceptual skills. Those choices, in turn, spring from a comprehensive view of nature and the universe in which humans are perceived as but an element inextricably linked to the whole.

It is this unique cosmological perspective that has enabled the shaman to comprehend implicitly the intricate balance that is the Amazon forest. Another worldview altogether, one in which the human race stands apart, now threatens the forest with devastation. Perhaps the most important contribution of the new synthesis in ethnobotany will be its ability to promote actively a dialogue between these two worldviews such that folk wisdom may temper and guide the inevitable development processes that today ride roughshod over much of the earth.

# 62.

# Shamanism and the Rigged Marketplace

PIERS VITEBSKY

(1995)

*British anthropologist Piers Vitebsky has done fieldwork over two decades with the Sora people in India and the Sakha people in Siberia. Whereas Sora shamanism is waning, Sakha shamanism is enjoying a revival; meanwhile, neo-shamanic movements are appearing around the world in global culture. Vitebsky sees shamanism as "chameleon-like" and "elusive," but also as too challenging for the industrial world to accommodate. Like other forms of indigenous knowledge, it disguises itself to survive.*

Using examples from my own experience of the Sora of tribal India and the Sakha of Siberia (pronounced Sakha, formerly known by the Russian term Yakut), I shall explore how it is that shamanic ideas can be considered knowledge in one setting and not in another, wisdom in one setting and foolishness in another—in effect true in one and false in another. How can Sora shamanism become enlightening for western psychotherapists at the very moment when it is becoming inappropriate for the youngest generation of Sora themselves? In what sense has shamanism suddenly become true again for Sakha nationalists after two generations of being false for these same people when they were Soviet communists?

... It is no longer possible to make a watertight distinction between "traditional" shamanistic societies (a mainstay of the old ethnographic literature and of comparative religion), and the new wave of neo-shamanist movements (still barely studied in depth). For shamanism, as with any other kind of local knowledge, the essence of globality today is that it belongs both in the past of remote tribes, and in the present of industrial subcultures. But there are further twists: the shamanic revival is now reappearing in the *present* of some of these remote tribes—only now these are neither remote nor tribal.

Thus, globalization (or modernization) may lead either to the downgrading and abandonment of indigenous knowledge, or on the contrary to its reassertion and transformation. The Sora and the Sakha demonstrate respectively a fall and a rise in the indigenous valuation of their respective forms of shamanism. Both space and time are involved: these processes are going on in various parts of the same globe, at the same time—as is the New Age movement, with which the Sakha have much in common and the Sora virtually nothing.

There is no agreed cross-cultural definition of "shamanism." Indeed, it is characterized by a chameleon-like elusiveness. Shamanic thinking is fluid rather than doctrinal, so that it is questionable whether the practices surrounding shamans should be seen as an "ism" at all. However, I shall not put a great weight on definitional criteria, since much of my argument will apply by extension to the much wider realm of "indigenous knowledge" as this filters in all its diversity through to the New Age. There is, nonetheless, a certain combination of key characteristics which it is reasonable to see as distinctively shamanic. These include a layered cosmology, with the flight of the shaman's soul to other levels of this cosmos, and the power to use this journey to fight, command and control spirits which inhabit these realms and affect human destiny. Thus shamanism is both an epistemology, that is a system of contemplative thought with an implicit set of propositions, and a blueprint for action, as in the location of game animals or the retrieval of kidnapped souls. Shamanic thinking has certain implications for the appropriation of shamanism by global culture today:

- It is *local*, in that cosmic space merges experientially into the space of everyday living through the features, such as graves and sacred sites, of a specific landscape.
- At the same time, it is *holistic*, in that (even allowing for the existence of other tribes, white men, etc.) the cosmos and the local landscape between them give a total rendering of the universe.
- This holism does not imply a steady state: shamanism is also *eristic*, in that the shamanic world-view openly acknowledges the role of battle and risk. The shaman is a hero who makes a bold and necessary intervention into cosmic processes. The power to act is precarious and this human action is fraught with danger.
- Finally, shamans are often politically *dissident* or anti-centrist. In Soraland, Siberia and elsewhere, they are contrasted to non-ecstatic priests or elders who perform more sober, routine cults. . . .

The Sora have shamans, but are not aware of having anything called shamanism. By contrast the Sakha, who have their own Republic in north-eastern Siberia, have almost no shamans but a rapidly growing ideology called shamanism. At the most, there are said to be no more than about eight "real" shamans left among a Sakha population of 350,000 who occupy an area nearly the size of India (now increasingly dominating a guest population of 700,000 Russians and other whites).

The city of Yakutsk contains flourishing societies for the revival of shamanism, and their members are largely doctors, teachers, anthropologists, historians, vets, physicists, biologists, writers and film directors. These people explore shamanism as the ancient wisdom of their own people, from the points of view of healing, self-realization, psychotherapy, telepathy, bioenergetic fields, their own ethnic origins, oral epic tradition and modern theatre.

The Soviet regime (in which the Sakha intelligentsia were themselves implicated) never managed to cope fully with the combination of religiosity and nationalism implicit in Sakha shamanic thinking.

Sakha writers like Oyunsky (a pen name from the Sakha word for "shaman") and Kulakovsky tried to reconcile shamanist and communist themes in the 1920s, but were killed off in the less compromising 1930s. From then until the mid-1980s, shamans were ridiculed or exiled, and at times (especially from the 1930s to 1950s) shot or dropped out of helicopters and challenged to fly.

Until recently, the local knowledge associated with shamanism was cordoned off, studied academically and patronized. . . .

But shamanism is not so much an institution—indeed, when it is not adopted by a revivalist movement it is hardly an "ism" at all—as a part of a wider complex of ideas (and a somewhat variable one). The shamanic world-view was very diffuse throughout everyday life and did not depend solely on one particular kind of performer, even the shaman. Everyone still partakes of this world-view every time they toss a glass of vodka into the fire to feed the hearth spirit, or check the flight of birds to see if they will have a good day. Some practices, such as feeding the fire, are carried out constantly and unselfconsciously by most town-dwellers and even party officials. Meanwhile, the rural population still lives by hunting, cattle and horse herding and a range of corresponding elements and motifs, involving animals, ghosts and features of the landscape, have proved very resilient. So the young intellectuals of the city can turn to their own rural grandparents for authentic "ethnic wisdom," as well as to books on anthropology and folklore, which are very popular reading matter. This wisdom is the local knowledge contained in traditional ideas about man and nature: about seasons, the weather, the behavior of animals, medicinal herbs, health and illness. The village informants, who used to be listed at the back of ethnographies only by way of scholastic documentation, are now becoming public figures. . . .

The Sora and the Sakha represent two contrasting ways in which a local sense of place becomes more global, though less cosmic. In one, locality comes to mean less, in the other, it means more.

Local knowledge is the basis for action by the intellect on the environment and gives to its knowers the conviction of commanding a certain area of experience. This remains "knowledge" for as long as it continues to satisfy that conviction. Under certain circumstances, experience itself can move away from the certainty of knowledge, defy it, slip out of its grasp. An entire system of knowledge, or parts of it, become ineffectual in the face of reality. Here, the Sora present what may be called a standard old-fashioned modernization scenario. They are ceasing to practice shamanism under a complex set of conditions which are dominated by a growing sense of ethnic inferiority. It would be hard to imagine a revival of Sora shamans unless this were part of an ethnic reassertion against the state, brahminism or some other dominant outside force. But since christianization is already a way of asserting oneself against these, a revival seems doubly unlikely. . . .

There is at least a third kind of situation in which shamanic ideas function in the modern world. The Sora and Sakha represent largely "tribal" areas with an indigenous tradition, which is either being abandoned or revived after a recent abandonment. In the western New Age movement, however, shamanism has never been indigenous. These neo-shamanists are practising shamanism for the first time, in a cosmopolitan way but sometimes with the additional claim that it is somehow a revival of ancient wisdom. These movements are inchoate and barely studied, so that any generalization can be no more than tentative. But it seems to me that one can sketch certain prominent overall tendencies.

As in Yakutia, such movements turn to a place or time, real or imagined, which is other than here and now. This is necessary because they state or imply a radical critique of that same here and now. Unlike the Yakuts, the proponents of these movements cannot plausibly claim to be basing themselves on a recent indigenous tradition (unless one invokes druids, etc., and strains the argument to extremes). So in addition, such movements are therefore generally not nationalistic but cosmopolitan and universalist in tone. They cannot be otherwise since the inspiration and legitimation of such syncretistic wisdom is provided by cultures which are avowedly foreign. This knowledge has a local flavor, but it is local elsewhere in time or space: it comes from

Native American shamans, Tibetan lamas, ancient Egyptian priests —
it might even come from the Sakha if their ideas were widely available
in English. As it is adopted into a wider world, this kind of wisdom is
stripped of certain specific elements (such as clan cults and ancestor
worship) which are so local that they do not travel well. But this new
re-localization also takes place on a global scale and with global
claims. Indeed, this is what gives a millennial tone to much New Age
rhetoric: it is both community-based and a new sort of world religion.

Yet, because it is largely middle class and urban, this approach
raises severe problems about where people stand between degrees of
literal belief and of literary conceit, as with the gods and fauns of pas-
toral poetry. The Sakha intelligentsia still lie further back along this
continuum. Most of my friends in this class retain great faith in traditional dream interpretation, read omens, fear ghosts and are in awe of
the power in shamanic objects in their own museum, going so far as to
claim that these still emanate the distinctive smell which surrounds the
shaman's person. . . .

Overall, I suggest that shamanism cannot avoid sharing the fate of
any other kind of indigenous knowledge in the industrial world: its full
implications are too challenging even for radicals to accommodate.

At the global level of decision making, it is the impetus towards action which drags indigenous knowledge into being a commodity
rather than a way of doing and ensures that it could never take deep
root in a new context. Action also pulls it towards current concerns
which may not be local. This is clearest when we see indigenous
peoples themselves bringing their "indigenous knowledge" to what is
now called the "marketplace." Teachers take their students to visit traditional healers and tell them that this is the indigenous knowledge
which we must "collect" and "preserve"; a man from the Sakha Min-
istry of Education gives a deadpan lecture in which he points with a
stick at a diagram of the cosmos and announces which spirits reside at
each level (this is not a lecture for scholars of religious history but instruction for schoolchildren, for whom "Consciousness-Soul" is now a
compulsory subject on the curriculum!).

This is not a true marketplace, but a rigged one in which your product will sell only if you pretend that it is something else, far less distinctive and valuable, but also far less trouble to come to terms with, than what it really is. Jungle herbalists fight pharmaceutical multinationals through the legal quagmire of intellectual property rights, but in a debate which is already set in these companies' terms: plants amount to no more than molecule factories. Indigenous knowledge must be controlled to the point at which it cannot subvert hegemonic knowledge. Indigenous wisdom must be packaged into the format of a database: the butterfly must be killed in order to take its rightful place in the glass case. . . .

Indigenous knowledge, when transplanted and commoditized, comes to take on the fragmentary nature of the society by which it is appropriated. This is surely why indigenous or local knowledge must always remain epistemologically marginal to global knowledge. The one thing global culture cannot recapture is the holistic nature of indigenous knowledge. Even where the epistemology is admired, there is a lack of appropriate context for belief and application.

Even as astronomy sees ever further into space, the arena of human consciousness has shrunk from the cosmos to a mere globe. So ironically, the more global things become, the less holistic they are since they pertain only to this globe. Meanwhile, the coercive nature of interaction between the components of this globe requires, not the homogenization of the Coca-Cola model, but the perpetuation of some kinds of difference. These differences are ones of relative power and involve a sort of class structure of epistemologies in which global knowledge can rest assured of its superiority only if it can point to other, inferior knowledges. Perhaps this is the true consequence of globality: that the coercive nature of the interaction between the different components leads the weaker parties to surrender or to adopt ever more cunning disguises.

# 63.

# An Ethnobotanist Dreams
# of Scientists and
# Shamans Collaborating

GLENN H. SHEPARD

(1998)

*American ethnobotanist Glenn H. Shepard has spent years working
with Matsigenka shamans in the Peruvian Amazon and studying their
knowledge about plants. Here, he describes a dream he had under the influence of a tobacco paste prepared by a shaman.*

It was a brilliant September afternoon at the end of the dry season in
the Peruvian Amazon, when strong breezes and gathering clouds an-
nounce the coming of the long season of rains. I had walked an hour
along a well-used path through the forest to the residence and gardens
of Mariano and his family at Potsitakigia. Mariano, one of my key informants during many months of ethnographic and ethnobotanical research, was sitting in a rustic, open-sided construction thatched with
palm leaves that was the unfinished kitchen area of his new house. We
talked for a few minutes, and then he got a mischievous look in his eye,
and said, "I've got something for you." He reached between the panels
of palm thatch on the underside of the low roof and removed a short
bamboo tube plugged with corn husks. He uncapped the tube and dug
in with a pointed stick, extracting a few wads of a sticky black sub-

stance. "What is that?" I asked. *"Opatsa seri,"* he replied. He put a pinch into his mouth and chewed, grimacing at the taste.

I was surprised. I had heard about *opatsa seri,* "tobacco paste," during some 12 prior months of fieldwork among the Matsigenka. Mariano and other storytellers had described this magical substance in legends about ancient times. *Opatsa seri,* a highly concentrated paste made of tobacco and *Banisteriopsis,* was the substance that first gave "Blowing Spirit," *Tasorintsi,* the transformative powers needed to create the world and all its creatures. It was also used by ancient shamans to change themselves into animals or fly to distant realms. But until that afternoon, none had hinted to me that this mythical substance was still manufactured and consumed. *Opatsa seri* was the philosopher's stone, the stuff of legend.

"Open your mouth," said Mariano. He removed the masticated black quid—about the size of a pencil eraser—from his own tongue and placed it on mine. "Chew."

The little piece of *opatsa seri* was perhaps the most bitter thing I had ever put in my mouth, tasting like a mixture of unsweetened coffee powder, coal tar and Vegemite. A dry, burning sensation slid down the back of my throat. "Is it bitter?" Marianno asked. "Very," I shook my head and winced. "Swallow," he said. I hiccuped a few times as the bitter quid descended, settling uneasily in my stomach.

Mariano explained the use of *opatsa seri* to me in this way. "You take *opatsa seri* in the afternoon. Not too late, or you won't be able to sleep, but like now, when the sun is over there [about 4 p.m.]. It makes you dream. Only good things. People, lots of people. Come back tomorrow and tell me if what I say is not true."

For the rest of the afternoon, I felt a mild and slightly queasy sense of stimulation, like drinking black coffee on an empty stomach. That night, my dreams were nothing short of fantastic. I had returned a decade in the future, and found the village transformed. Matsigenka ethnobotany had become the focus of international medical research. Doctors, chemists and botanists from around the world came and went from vast research facilities, fashioned as neo-Mayan pyramids of gleaming white stone. All the foreign visitors wore beautiful Matsigenka tunics decorated with geometric designs. Matsigenka had become a required language in medical schools around the world. I felt a sharp pang of jealousy when I met a team of Yankee doctors who spoke Matsigenka better than I, notwithstanding their distinct New York accent. I was given a tour of a labyrinthine museum of exquisite pre-Columbian artifacts and Matsigenka *objets d'art*. Then I was taken through endless rows of greenhouses and orchards, where hundreds of medicinal plants were being cultivated for cutting-edge medical research: aromatic herbs, fantastic fruit trees, beautiful flowers, succulent vines. Young Matsigenka botanists, fluent in English, explained the names and uses of different plants and showed me laboratories and clinics where researchers tested new drugs on human and animal subjects. The images were lucid and vivid, in full color, with clear sounds and smells. The dream seemed to last for many hours, and when I woke up it was dark. I wondered whether I had slept an entire day. But when I checked my watch, it was still very early in the morning: only a few hours had passed since I had fallen asleep. I took notes on the dream, amused by the more absurd parts but nonetheless intrigued by the powerful images, apparently induced by Mariano's "dream tobacco."

I went excitedly to Mariano's the next morning to tell him of my extraordinary dreams. He laughed, not surprised, and responded: "I told you so. Tobacco paste is *kepigari*, 'intoxicating.' It is very strong. It was calling to you, it wanted you. It took you to visit the *Saangariite*, the guardian spirits. They are very wise and good, like doctors and teachers. They can show you many things."

# 64.

# Shamans and Scientists

JEREMY NARBY

(2000)

*In 1999 three molecular biologists traveled to the Peruvian Amazon to
see whether they could obtain biomolecular information in sessions or-
chestrated by an indigenous shaman. Canadian anthropologist Jeremy
Narby reports.*

The molecular biologists had no previous experience of ayahuasca
shamanism or of the Amazon, though they did have an interest in alternative healing traditions and shamanism. Their ages ranged from
the late-30s to mid-60s. One worked as a scientist in an American ge-
nomics company. Another was a professor at a French University and
a member of the National Center for Scientific Research (CNRS).
The third taught in a Swiss University and was a director of a research
laboratory.

None of the scientists spoke Spanish and the indigenous ayahuasquero did not speak English or French, so I translated for them. The
first thing to report is that the scientists and the shaman had many
long conversations. The shaman had been studying plants, as an
ayahuasquero, for 37 years. He spent several days answering the biologists' questions.

He also conducted night-time ayahuasca sessions, in which the biologists took part. They saw many things in their visions, including
DNA molecules and chromosomes.

The American biologist, who normally worked on deciphering the human genome, said she saw a chromosome from the perspective of a protein flying above a long strand of DNA. She saw DNA sequences known as "CpG islands," which she had been puzzling over at work, and which are found upstream of about sixty percent of all human genes. She saw they were structurally distinct from the surrounding DNA and that this structural difference allowed them to be easily accessed and therefore to serve as "landing pads" for transcription proteins, which dock on to the DNA molecule and make copies of precise genetic sequences. She said the idea that CpG island structure enables them to function as landing pads had not crossed her mind previously, and that genomic research would soon be able to verify this hypothesis.

The French professor had been studying the sperm duct of animals for many years, first in lizards, then in mice. When a sperm cell comes out of the testes and enters the sperm duct, it is incapable of fertilizing an egg. It only becomes fertile once it has travelled through the duct, where about fifty different kinds of proteins work on it. The professor and his team had spent years trying to understand which protein makes the sperm cell fertile. Understanding this could have implications for the development of a male contraceptive. He brought three questions to one of the ayahuasca sessions. First, was there a key protein that makes sperm cells fertile? Second, why had it not been possible to find the answer to that question after years of research? And, third, was the mouse the appropriate model for studying fertility in men? He received answers from a voice that spoke in his visions. In reply to the first question, the voice said: "No, it is not a key protein. In this organ, there are no key proteins, just many different ones which have to act together for fertility to be achieved." To the second question, it said: "I already answered that with your first question." To the third question, it said: "This question is not important enough for me to answer. The answer can be found without ayahuasca. Try to work in another direction."

The Swiss scientist wanted to consult the shamanic sphere about the ethics of modifying plant genomes. She wanted to know if it was appropriate to add genes to plants to make them resistant to diseases. It so happens that tobacco is an important plant for both genetic engineers and Amazonian shamans. Shamans from many indigenous societies say they speak in their visions with the "mother of tobacco," or the essence of the plant. The biologist reported that she spoke during an ayahuasca-influenced meditation with an entity that the shaman subsequently identified as the mother of tobacco. This entity informed her that tobacco's fundamental role was to serve all living beings. It also informed her that manipulating tobacco's genome was not a problem in itself, so long as the plant could play its fundamental role in an adequate environment, and so long as it was in keeping with that environment. The biologist reported visualizing a resplendent plant growing in a desert thanks to an extra gene which allowed it to resist drought. She came away from this experience with the understanding that genetic manipulations were best gauged case by case, in a way that takes into consideration the scientist's intention as well as the way in which the modified plants will be used by society.

In interviews conducted in their respective laboratories four months after the Amazonian experience, the three biologists agreed on a number of points. All three said the experience of ayahuasca shamanism changed their way of looking at themselves and at the world, as well as their appreciation of the capacities of the human mind. They all expressed great respect for the shaman's skill and knowledge. They all received information and advice about their own paths of research. The two women reported contact with "plant teachers," which they experienced as independent entities; they both said that contacting a plant teacher had shifted their way of understanding reality. The man said that all the things he saw and learned in his visions were somehow already in his mind, but that ayahuasca had helped him see into his mind and put them together. He did not think he had experienced contact with an independent intelligence, but he did think ayahuasca was a powerful tool for exploring the mind.

The scientific information and imagery accessed in ayahuasca visions by the three biologists were certainly related to the information and images already in their minds. They did not have any big revelations. "Ayahuasca is not a shortcut to the Nobel prize," the French professor remarked. They all said that ayahuasca shamanism was a harder path to knowledge than science, and as scientists, they found specific difficulties with it. For example, getting knowledge from an ayahuasca experience involves a highly emotional, subjective experience that is not reproducible. One cannot have the same ayahuasca experience twice, nor can somebody else have the same ayahuasca experience as oneself. This makes it almost contrary to the central method of experimental science, which consists of designing objective experiments that can be repeated by anyone, anywhere, anytime.

The scientists said that more research was needed; and that this would require preparing questions carefully and working with qualified shamans in well-defined conditions. They are all planning to return to the Amazon at some point to continue working on this.

They conducted this preliminary experiment over two weeks. Afterward they visited a school in the Peruvian Amazon for bilingual, intercultural education, where young women and men from fourteen indigenous societies are learning to teach indigenous knowledge and science, in their mother tongue and in Spanish. They are Aguaruna, Shipibo, Huitoto, Ashaninca and so on. The school's goal is to train indigenous primary school teachers. Each people has elected an old "indigenous specialist" to work at the school as the keeper and teacher of its knowledge, language and lore.

The scientists met with the school's director and with the old indigenous specialists. They spoke positively about their recent experience with an indigenous shaman. But several of the specialists warned them about the abuses that can occur with ayahuasca. They said that sorcerers worked with ayahuasca and shot darts into people to cause disease. They said ayahuasca was double-edged. "The plant can show you things that will harm you," said one. They emphasized that using ayahuasca required the presence of a well-trained and talented ayahuasquero.

The specialists asked the scientists about science: What was its nature? Where did its center lie? One of the scientists replied that science was fragmented into many disciplines and was practiced in many countries. He went on to say that he thought it was very important that young indigenous people learned about science, because it was currently the dominant form of knowledge around the world. In reply, one specialist said he thought this was true, but he also thought that the scientists might consider sending their own children to the Amazon to learn about indigenous knowledge. That way, he said, they too would benefit from a complete education.

Once everybody had spoken, the Aguaruna director of the school thanked us for our visit and said: "Here in the Amazon, our knowledge has been taken many times by others, but we have never received any benefits from it. Now we would like to see some returns." He said that an agreement regarding the compensation of indigenous knowledge should be established before any further research was conducted.

This experiment seemed to show that scientists can learn a good deal by working with indigenous Amazonian shamans.

Some observers have suggested that shamanism, as classically defined, is reaching its end. But bringing shamans and scientists together seems more like a beginning.

# Envoi

*"Rahangri then put his question: 'What is the difference between dream and reality? And in dream I include all forms of waking vision.' The poet was surprised, but the inquiry was much to his taste. He replied: 'There is no ultimate difference, for they intermingle, reflect each other, are dependent on each other, cannot exist singly, derive from the same source; each is both illusory and real, and neither is real without the other.'"*

MAURICE COLLIS
*THE MYSTERY OF DEAD LOVERS* (1951)

*"Those who do not expect will not find out the unexpected, for it is trackless and unexplored."*

HERACLITUS

# References and Permissions

The titles of all excerpts were chosen by the editors.

PART ONE

"Devil Worship: Consuming Tobacco to Receive Messages from Nature," by Gonzalo Fernández de Oviedo. From the first volume of his book *Historia General y Natural de las Indias, Islas y Tierra Firme de la Mar Océano* (Madrid: José Amador de los Rios, 1851, 4 vols., orig. 1535). Translated by the editors.

"Ministers of the Devil Who Learn About the Secrets of Nature," by André Thévet. From his book *Les Singularités de la France Antarctique* (Paris: Editions Chandeigne, 1997, first published in 1557). Copyright © Editions Chandeigne. Reprinted by permission. Translated by the editors.

"Evoking the Devil: Fasting with Tobacco to Learn How to Cure," by Antoine Biet. From his book *Voyage de la France Equinoxiale en l'Isle de Cayenne* (Paris: François Clouzier, 1664). Translated by the editors.

"The Shaman: 'A Villain of a Magician Who Calls Demons,'" by Avvakum Petrovich. From his book *La Vie de l'Archiprêtre Avvakum, Ecrite par Lui-Même* (Paris: Gallimard, 1938, translated into French from Russian by Pierre Pascal, first published in Russian 1672). Translated from French to English by the editors.

PART TWO

"The Savages Esteem Their Jugglers," by Joseph François Lafitau. From his book *Moeurs des Sauvages Amériquains Comparées aux Moeurs des Premiers Temps* (Paris: Saugrain et Charles-Etienne Hocherfau, 1724). Translated, adapted, and condensed by the editors.

"Shamans Deserve Perpetual Labor for Their Hocus-Pocus," by Johann

REFERENCES AND PERMISSIONS

Georg Gmelin. From his book *Reise durch Siberien von dem Jahr 1733 bis 1744* (Göttingen, 1751–1752, 4 vols.). Translated by the editors.

"Blinded by Superstition," by Stepan Petrovich Krasheninnikov. From his book *Explorations of Kamchatka, North Pacific Scimitar* (translated by E. A. P. Crownhart-Vaughan. Portland, Oregon: Oregon Historical Society, 1972, first published in Russian in 1755). Copyright © by the Oregon Historical Society. Reprinted by permission.

"Shamans Are Impostors Who Claim They Consult the Devil—and Who Are Sometimes Close to the Mark," by Denis Diderot and colleagues. From their book *Encyclopédie, ou Dictionnaire Raisonné des Sciences, des Arts, et des Métiers* (Paris, 1751–1765, 17 vols.). Translated by the editors.

"Misled Impostors and the Power of Imagination," by Johann Gottfried Herder. From his book *Herder's Sämmtliche Werke* (Berlin: Weissmanniche Buchhandlung, 1877–1913, 33 vols.). The text is from Vol. 13, and was first published in 1785. Translated by the editors.

PART THREE

"Animism Is the Belief in Spiritual Beings," by Edward B. Tylor. From his book *Primitive Culture: Researches into the Development of Mythology, Philosophy, Religion, Language, Art, and Custom* (London: John Murray, 1871, 2 vols.).

"A White Man Goes to a *Peaiman*," by Everard F. Im Thurn. From his book *Among the Indians of Guiana, Being Sketches, Chiefly Anthropological, from the Interior of British Guiana* (London: Kegan Paul, Trench, & Co., 1883).

"The *Angakoq* Uses a Peculiar Language and Defines Taboos," by Franz Boas. From his essay "A Year Among the Eskimo" (*Journal of the American Geographical Society*, 1887, Vol. 19, pp. 383–402).

"The-Man-Who-Fell-from-Heaven Shamanizes Despite Persecution," by Wenceslas Sieroshevski. From his essay "The Yakuts" (*The Journal of the Anthropological Institute of Great Britain and Ireland*, 1901, Vol. XXXI, pp. 65–110, translated from the Russian by W. G. Sumner, originally published in Russian in 1896).

"*Shamanism* Is a Dangerously Vague Word," by Arnold Van Gennep. From his essay "De l'Emploi du Mot 'Chamanisme'" (*Revue de l'Histoire des Religions*, 1903, Vol. XLVII, No. 1, pp. 51–57). Translated by the editors.

PART FOUR

REFERENCES AND PERMISSIONS

"The Shaman's Assistant," by Sergei M. Shirokogoroff. From his book *Psychomental Complex of the Tungus* (London: Kegan Paul, Trench, Trubner & Co., Ltd., 1935). Reprinted by permission.

"Shamans Charm Game," by Willard Z. Park. From his book *Shamanism in Western North America: A Study in Cultural Relationships* (Evanston and Chicago: Northwestern University Studies in the Social Sciences 2, 1938). All rights reserved.

"Climbing the Twisted Ladder to Initiation," by Alfred Métraux. From his essay "Le Shamanisme Chez les Indiens de l'Amérique du Sud Tropicale" (*Acta Americana*, Vol. II, Mexico, 1944, I, pp. 197–219 and II, pp. 320–341). A reworked version of this article was published as "Le Chaman Dans les Civilisations Indigènes des Guyanes et de l'Amazonie" in Métraux's posthumous book *Religions et Magies Indiennes d'Amérique du Sud* (Paris: Gallimard, 1967). Copyright © Gallimard, 1967. Reprinted by permission. Translated by the editors.

"Aboriginal Doctors Are Outstanding People," by Adolphus Peter Elkin. From his book *Aboriginal Men of High Degree* (Sydney: Australasian Publishing Co., 1945). Published by Inner Traditions, Rochester, VT 05767. Copyright © 1977, 1944 by University of Queensland Press. Reprinted by permission.

"Shamans as Psychoanalysts," by Claude Lévi-Strauss. From his essay "L'Efficacité Symbolique" (*Revue de l'histoire des religions*, 1949, Vol. 135, No. 1, pp. 5–27). Published in English as "The Effectiveness of Symbols" in Lévi-Strauss's book *Structural Anthropology, Volume I* (New York: Basic Books, 1963, translated by Claire Jacobson and Brooke Grundfest Schoepf). English translation copyright © 1963 by Basic Books, Inc. Reprinted by permission of Basic Books, a member of Perseus Books, L.L.C.

"Using Invisible Substances for Good and Evil," by Alfred Métraux. From his essay "Religion and Shamanism" in *Handbook of South American Indians*, Julian H. Steward, ed., Vol. 5, pp. 559–599. (Washington: United States Printing Office, 1949). This book was published as part of the Smithsonian's Bureau of American Ethnology bulletins. Reprinted by permission.

"The Shamanin Performs a Public Service with Grace and Energy," by Verrier Elwin. From his book *The Religion of an Indian Tribe* (Oxford: Oxford University Press, 1955). Reproduced by permission of Oxford University Press, New Delhi, India.

310

PART FIVE

by Malidoma Patrice Somé. Used by permission of Jeremy P. Tarcher, a division of Penguin Putnam Inc.

PART SEVEN

"Science and Magic, Two Roads to Knowledge," by Claude Lévi-Strauss. From his book *La Pensée Sauvage* (Paris: Plon, 1962). (Translated into English as *The Savage Mind*, and published in London by Oxford University Press. The editors of this anthology were not satisfied with this translation, and translated anew the original French text, with the approval of the author.) Reprinted by permission of Oxford University Press.

"Shamans, 'Spirits' and Mental Imagery," by Richard Noll. From his essay "The Presence of Spirits in Magic and Madness" (in *Shamanism: An Expanded View of Reality*, compiled by Shirley Nicholson, Wheaton, IL: The Theosophical Publishing House, 1987, pp. 47–61). Copyright © 1987 by The Theosophical Publishing House. Reprinted by permission.

"Dark Side of the Shaman," by Michael F. Brown. From his essay "Dark Side of the Shaman" (*Natural History*, no. 11, pp. 8–10, 1989). Reprinted with permission from *Natural History*. Copyright © 1989 the American Museum of Natural History.

"Shamans Explore the Human Mind," by Roger Walsh. From his book *The Spirit of Shamanism* (New York: Jeremy P. Tarcher/Putnam, 1990). Copyright © 1990 by Roger Walsh. Reprinted with the author's kind permission.

"Training to See What the Natives See," by Edith Turner. From her essay "The Reality of Spirits: A Tabooed or Permitted Field of Study?" (*ReVision*, vol. 15, no. 1, pp. 28–32, 1992; also published in *The Anthropology of Consciousness*, vol. 4, no. 1, pp. 9–12, 1993). Copyright © by the American Anthropological Association. Reprinted with permission.

"'Twisted Language,' a Technique for Knowing," by Graham Townsley. From the author's essay "Song Paths: The Ways and Means of Yaminahua Shamanic Knowledge" (*L'Homme*, 126–128, vol. XXXIII, nos. 2–4, pp. 449–468, 1993). Copyright © by Graham Townsley. Reprinted with the author's kind permission.

"Magic Darts as Viruses," by Jean-Pierre Chaumeil. From his essay "Del proyectil al Virus: El Complejo de Dardos-Mágicos en el Chamanismo del Oeste Amazónico" (in *Cultura y Salud en la Construcción de las Américas*, C. Pinzón et al., eds., pp. 263–277. Bogotá: Instituto Colombiano de Antropolo-

# Notes on the Editors' Commentaries and Further Reading

The quote from Immanuel Kant in the introduction comes from Roger Shattuck's *Forbidden Knowledge: From Prometheus to Pornography* (New York: Harcourt Brace & Company, 1996).

The Mircea Eliade quote in the introduction comes from his book *Shamanism: Archaic Techniques of Ecstasy* (New York: Pantheon, 1964, p. 4).

Regarding critics of Castaneda, see in particular Richard de Mille's book *The Don Juan Papers: Further Castaneda Controversies* (Santa Barbara: Ross-Erikson Publishers, 1980). This book has been reissued by Backinprint.com.

The Jeffrey B. Russell quote in the introduction to Part One comes from his book *A History of Witchcraft: Sorcerers, Heretics and Pagans* (London: Thames and Hudson, 1980, p. 35).

The Gloria Flaherty quote in the introduction to Part One comes from her book *Shamanism and the Eighteenth Century* (Princeton: Princeton University Press, 1992, p. 7).

The quotes on possession from Mircea Eliade's book *Shamanism: Archaic Techniques of Ecstasy* (New York: Pantheon, 1964) are on p. 506 and p. 499.

See Ioan M. Lewis's *Ecstatic Religion: An Anthropological Study of Possession and Shamanism* (London: Penguin Books, 1971), for a discussion of shamanism and possession cults. On the same subject, see Gilbert Rouget's *Music and Trance: A Theory of the Relations Between Music and Possession* (Chicago: University of Chicago Press, 1985). See also Ioan M. Lewis's *Religion in Context: Cults and Charisma* (Cambridge: Cambridge University Press, 1986).

The article by Siegfried Nadel referred to in the introduction to Part Four is "A Study of Shamanism in the Nuba Mountains" (*Journal of the Royal An-*

*thropological Institute of Great Britain and Ireland,* Vol. LXXVI, Part 1, pp. 25–40, 1946).

For further reading on Haitian vodoun, see Alfred Métraux's *Voodoo in Haiti* (New York: Schocken, 1972), Francis Huxley's *The Invisibles: Voodoo Gods in Haiti* (New York: McGraw-Hill, 1966), and Wade Davis's *The Serpent and the Rainbow* (New York: Touchstone, 1997, first published in 1985).

The quote on "narcotics" from Mircea Eliade's book *Shamanism: Archaic Techniques of Ecstasy* (New York: Pantheon, 1964) is on p. 401. See Michael Ripinsky-Naxon's critique of Eliade's position in his book *The Nature of Shamanism: Substance and Function of a Religious Metaphor* (Albany: State University of New York Press, 1993). On Eliade's change of mind late in life, see Peter Furst's "Introduction: An Overview of Shamanism" (in *Ancient Traditions: Shamanism in Central Asia and the Americas*, Gary Seaman and Jane S. Day, eds., pp. 1–28. Niwot, CO: University Press of Colorado, 1994). Peter Furst also co-edited an excellent book with Stacy B. Schaeffer called *People of the Peyote: Huichol Indian History, Religion, and Survival* (Albuquerque: University of New Mexico Press, 1996).

The Clifford Geertz quote in the introduction to Part Six comes from his essay "'From the Native's Point of View': On the Nature of Anthropological Understanding" (in his book *Local Knowledge: Further Essays in Interpretive Anthropology,* New York: Basic Books, 1983).

The Franz Boas quote in the introduction to Part Seven comes from his essay "The Mind of Primitive Man" (*Journal of American Folklore,* vol. XIV, no. LII, pp. 1–11, 1901).

# Topical Index

SHAMANIC VOCATION

inherited, or not    53–57, 65–66, 115, 217
initiation into    16–17, 53–57, 64–68, 70, 99–102, 115–17, 121–24, 169–77, 187–94, 217–18, 222, 230–33, 234–37
psychological aspects of    66, 72–73, 98–99, 103–107, 108–11, 119–20, 181–83, 222
taboos, asceticism, and diet    14, 16–17, 33–34, 36, 48, 53–57, 61, 67–68, 80, 81–83, 99–102, 104–105, 197, 207–11, 227–29, 230–33, 249, 283–84


VARIETIES OF SHAMAN

diviners    12, 14–15, 18, 23–26, 30, 59–62, 102
healers    *passim*
jugglers, tricksters, and magicians    23–26, 27–28, 30, 36–37, 43–46, 57, 58–63, 81–82, 139
killers    102, 112–14, 139–40, 195–99, 234–37, 248, 251–56, 282
mediums    69–70, 76–77, 207–11
neo-shamans    256, 280–85, 291–97
sorcerers    23–26, 102, 104, 219, 230–33, 252–56
transvestites    65
women    55, 65, 98, 115–18, 166–68, 253, 278


THE SHAMANIC THEATER

ascent and descent
  bird    99–100
  ladder    99, 101
  mountain    210
  tree    156, 210
assistant    90–93, 179, 200–202

dance    17, 69, 100–101, 131–34, 179, 205
drama    200–206, 255
drums, rattles, and bells    26, 27, 30, 50, 54–56, 59–63, 70, 86–87, 90–91, 100, 129, 178–83, 200–206, 213
fans    43–46, 117, 254
fire, mastery of    113, 210
heaven and hell    209
music    95, 212–15
participation of audience    76–78, 93, 133–34, 182
payment    34, 60–61, 89, 189, 202, 214
sleight of hand    30, 33, 62, 70
sucking    35, 70, 103, 117, 139, 196–98, 201, 219, 229, 253, 274–75


THE SHAMAN'S VOICE

singing    28, 34–35, 56, 59, 61–63, 70, 128–30, 133, 137–39, 145–46, 179, 203–204, 214–15, 227–29, 263–71
ventriloquism    33, 44–45, 57, 58–63, 146
whistling    179, 190, 253


THE SHAMAN'S GAZE

eye    49–50, 59, 105, 200, 203


THE SHAMANIC LANGUAGE

metaphors, poetics of    265–71
secret tongue of shamans    33, 47, 81


THE SHAMANIC STATE

fits, convulsions, coma    12, 25, 32–33, 45–46, 66, 72, 132, 209, 222, 235, 249
enthusiasm, inspiration    53–57, 72
imagination    37, 259
dream and vision    31, 101, 105, 144–46, 209, 218–22, 249, 264, 268–71, 298–300
knowledge    12, 15, 81, 104–107, 148–53, 245–47, 263–71, 273, 280, 287–89, 291–97, 301–305
power    *passim*

# TOPICAL INDEX

## PERILS OF SHAMANIC PRACTICE

temptations of power    113–14, 140, 152–53, 197, 230–33, 282–84
sorcery and vendetta    195–99, 219–21, 230–33, 236–37, 238–41, 251–56


## SPIRITS

spirits    *passim*
helpers    33–34, 47, 56, 59–61, 67–68, 113, 187–94, 196–99, 204–205, 213–15, 217–20, 274
marriage to    115–16
Master of Animals    218–19, 223–26
Mother of seabeasts    80, 81–83, 223–24
ontological status of    248–50, 257–59, 260–62, 264–71
plant teachers    227–29, 300


## MAGIC SUBSTANCES

arrows    101, 113, 203
cords    121–27
crystals    106, 113, 123
darts    113, 195–99, 238–41, 252–54, 272–76, 304
ectoplasm    195, 260–62
virus and DNA    173, 272–76, 302


## PLANTS

knowledge of    23, 34–35, 84–86, 227–29, 300, 301–305
ayahuasca, natema, yagé    169–77, 195–99, 227–29, 230–33, 252–55, 267, 273, 288–89, 301–305
curare    288
fly agaric    62
peyote    154–57
psilocybe    141–47, 166–68, 228–29
tobacco    11–12, 16–17, 43, 45, 68, 99–101, 112, 137–40, 197–99, 272–74, 298–300, 303

CREATURES

anaconda   269
ant   16–17, 102, 269
antelope   94–96
bird   99–100
caterpillar   46
crocodile   171
deer   45, 48, 187–88
jaguar   101, 219, 254, 265, 269
seal   48, 223
snake/serpent   34, 45, 106, 124–26, 176, 188, 219
walrus   48, 79–80
worm   127


SCIENTISTS

ethnobotanists   286–90, 298–300
molecular biologists   301–305


PSYCHOANALYSIS AND PSYCHOPATHOLOGY

psychoanalysis and psychopathology   72–73, 99, 103–107, 108–11, 119–20

# Acknowledgments

Thanks to Jon Christensen for his advice and editorial skills throughout this project, Marie-Claire Chappuis for her relentless and reliable library work and research assistance, Yves Duc for his help with the German translations, François Gendre for his help with the typing, Mark Waldman for his fine editing, and Jeremy P. Tarcher for being the godfather of this book.

# About the Editors

JEREMY NARBY grew up in Canada and Switzerland, studied history at the University of Canterbury, and received a doctorate in anthropology from Stanford University. He is the author of *The Cosmic Serpent: DNA and the Origins of Knowledge*.

FRANCIS HUXLEY was born of an English father and a Swiss mother. He took his degree in anthropology at Oxford University. His books include *Affable Savages: An Anthropologist Among the Urubú Indians of Brazil*; *The Invisibles: Voodoo Gods in Haiti*; *The Way of the Sacred*; *The Dragon: Nature of Spirit, Spirit of Nature*; and *The Eye: The Seer and the Seen*.

The photo montage is by Swiss visual artist René Walker.